Blessing

We walk so that no living being should die

because of lack of food on a physical level.

We offer this Bhagavad Gita so that no living being

should starve on a spiritual level.

Truth is beyond expression for it is the song of silence

and within this book in these precious writings,

is the expression of the inexpressible.

We offer it to the world and pray that everyone

who casts even a glance upon its sacred text

will be filled with the love of the Divine.

May Krishna's smile open your eyes

May his flute enchant your mind

May his love always fill your heart

and

May we ever become closer to one another.

Chris Barrington

To Roger & Sue.

May you find in these words
a freedom that brings light
to your life.

Walking with the Bhagavad Gita

Bangor July '98

To Dearest Roger and Sue
To find delight in these pages is the
first step - but yours is to share
with many. Thank you for taking
the 2nd step. With gratitude Savitri

Walking with The Bhagavad Gita

Freedom from grief & despair

Volume One

lfp

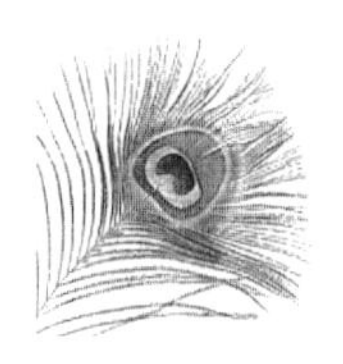

First published in the United Kingdom in 1998 by
Life Foundation Publications, Maristowe House
Dover Street, Bilston
West Midlands, WV14 6AL

ISBN 1 873606 133

Printed by Heanor Gate Printing Ltd,
Delves Road, Heanor Gate Industrial Estate, Heanor, Derbyshire, DE75 7SJ.

Dedication

To Mahatma Gandhi - an ordinary man
who achieved the extraordinary
through living
The Bhagavad Gita

Why walk with the Bhagavad Gita?

We have been walking with the Gita for many years now with rucksacks on our backs carrying only the barest essentials. The Gita has been our spiritual compass - guiding our hearts and minds to know what to do when confronted by all the different situations we encounter on our *Eurowalk 2000* tours.

Our schedule has been intense over the years and has involved meeting literally thousands of people in all different walks of life, from refugees in Bosnia to politicians involved in the peace process in Northern Ireland. It is not always easy to know what to do when confronted by a suffering humanity. How do you comfort a widowed grandmother in Bosnia who is holding onto your arm and begging for help? What can you say to a child that has been orphaned by war? Or an Auschwitz survivor whose face is etched with the deep pain of the past?

One thing we do know is that without the wisdom and guidance of the Gita behind us, we would have missed many opportunities to do the right thing at the right time in the right way. Mother Gita has led us into many adventures over the years and has clearly demonstrated the power of truth to overcome adversity. So many times we found ourselves faced with overwhelming odds and the Gita has reassured us over and over again that *every moment of effort* is never wasted and is completely worthwhile.

Many people have asked us to share the inspiration and motivation behind our walking journeys. For this reason, we have combined our love for, and experience of, this extraordinary manual for living, in the hope that everyone can come to know and understand the promise of freedom that lies at the heart of the *Srimad Bhagavad Gita.*

We invite you to take up this spiritual compass and to put it into your own rucksack together with the most important essentials: *willingness, trust* and *determination.* May you discover, as we have, that the Gita is a clear and precise map of the uncharted territory we call life. It offers each one of us detailed instructions on how to reach home.

Good luck on your journey!

Mansukh, Savitri and John

Eurowalk 2000
Walking with the Bhagavad Gita
1994 - Walk for Rwanda
1995 - Auschwitz
1995 - Ireland - North and South
1996 - Bosnia
1997 - United Kingdom
1998 - Russia
Glasgow
Edinburgh
SCOTLAND
Belfast
NORTHERN IRELAND
Dublin
EIRE
Cork
Bangor
Birmingham
WALES
ENGLAND
London
Amsterdam
NETHERLANDS
Dortmund
Eindhoven
GERMANY
Ghent
Brussels
BELGIUM
Frankfurt
Paris
Munic
FRANCE
Berne
SWITZERLAND
Bordeaux
ITALY
Marseilles

St Petersburg
Moscow
ESTONIA
RUSSIA
LATVIA
LITHUANIA
Minsk
RUSSIA
BELARUS
Warsaw
POLAND
Kiev
Auschwitz
UKRAINE
Ostrava
Olomouc
SLOVAK REPUBLIC
MOLDOVA
Budapest
Chisinau
HUNGARY
ROMANIA
Zagreb
CROATIA
Bucharest
Belgrade
BOSNIA HERTZEGOVINIA
Sarajevo
YUGOSLAVIA
BULGARIA
Split
Sofia
Tirane
ALBANIA

Contents

Contents - Part One

The Glory of the Gita
Dr Mansukh Patel

Page No.

— Part One —

The Glory of the Gita

Dr Mansukh Patel

The Bhagavad Gita has been a part of my life and a part of me for as long as I can remember. My mother even recited the Gita to me as I drank milk from her breast. Although she could not read or write herself, she had memorised stories, songs and Sanskrit verses which washed through me, flooding the cells of my body and mind as well as invigorating my spirit. At night, during our prayer times, my father would always light a little diva*, pick up the Gita which lay on the family shrine, and unwrap it ceremoniously with great reverence. We all sat around together, carefully listening as he recited the verses, absorbing their sound and texture almost as if they were food.

Krishna has never been a fantasy figure to me, or part of a legend or myth. He is real, just like the trees and the birds are real, and the lions and panthers that stalk the great plains of the Rift Valley where I lived as a child. I can remember falling asleep at night to the sound of my mother's voice singing songs of Lord Krishna's mischievous life. The little blue cowherd boy who enchanted the milk maids of Gokul with his winning smile and ethereal flute music. The mischief-maker of Vrindavan whose favourite pastime, when not enchanting the gopis and gopals, was to destroy the demons that threatened to overrule 'dharma' in the land.

**home-made candle*

And so it was that images of Lord Krishna came with me into my sleep, where we met and came to know each other intimately. Perhaps this is why I have always loved him with intensity, for he was my perfect role model and epitomised all that is good and magical in life. Together we went on adventures both at night in my dreams and during the day in my imagination, as I played amongst the long grass of the plains amidst herds of elephants, zebras and gazelles. Everywhere I went, I was always acutely aware of his presence, and as we grew up together, we became bonded to one another in a way that has grown stronger with every passing day.

Perhaps that is why, whenever I open the Gita, I always feel I am with my dearest friend. You know how you love to be with your best friend and to listen to their thoughts and feelings? That's how it feels to me. I always thrill to read Lord Krishna's words as he speaks to his favourite devotee Arjuna because as a child I always imagined I *was* him. When my first son was born I knew that I had to call him after this great spiritual warrior and my second son is called Krishna. They constantly remind me of the two people that have dominated my life in heart and mind for over forty years and every time I call their names I am reminded of the Gita. So it is that she lives with me and within me, her eternal message always singing in my veins, her energy firing my spirit and setting me free inside.

The Bhagavad Gita teaches us the art of living in freedom and how to *design* our life. One of the greatest freedom fighters of all time, and another great hero of mine, Mahatma Gandhi, allowed himself to be guided by it every day of his life. Not only did he read and study the Gita on a daily basis, he had the wisdom and the skill to be able to *apply* the Gita to his daily life. He said on many occasions that it was the very source of his power, as well as being the most practical book he had ever come across.

'When disappointment stares me in the face and all alone I see not one ray of light, I go back to the Bhagavad Gita. I find a verse here and a verse there, and I immediately begin to smile in the midst of overwhelming tragedies - and if they have left no visible scar on me, I owe it all to the teachings of the Bhagavad Gita.'

- Mahatma Gandhi

The Gita teaches us to use our disappointments in a way that is a benefit to us and to our growth. Gandhi's life and achievements are really a testimony to his reverence for the Gita and its application, for he allowed her to permeate his every waking thought, word and deed. This is what helped him to become a guiding light to millions. The only difference between Gandhi and those who just see the Gita as a spiritual text is that he *put it into practice.*

I often try to imagine how Gandhi thought and felt as he entered into his life each day. I love the simplicity with which he lived and his undivided singleness of mind, as well as the tremendous courage he exhibited on so many occasions when faced with overwhelming odds. Like Gandhi, I always turn to the Gita for guidance and strength and have never once found it has let me down.

My own understanding of the relationship between Sri Krishna and Arjuna, and its significance for each one of us, is a deeply personal one. Everything I have learned about the Gita has come from my parents who were two simple, indigenous people, whose understanding was neither intellectual or scholarly. It was a *living* experience that just seemed to come quite naturally to them. In this way, they transferred their great love for Mother Gita to me, and my deepest wish is that I will be able to transmit that same love to you in these next few pages.

Mansukh

The Bhagavad Gita

Background and Characters

The scene is set as the two armies of the great warring factions of the *Pandavas* and the *Kauravas* assemble on the field of *Kurukshetra* preparing to face each other in mortal battle. They are actually two parts of the same family, as their fathers were brothers. The Pandavas' father, *King Pandu*, died very young, leaving his five children under the care of *Bhishma*, his grandfather. Because Pandu's brother, *Dhritarashtra*, was born blind, he could never be crowned King and so Bhishma was forced to rule over the kingdom of Bharat until such time as *Yudhishthira*, Pandu's eldest son, became old enough to rule.

Pandu and Dhritarashtra's sons grew up together, Bhishma treating them all equally as his own, guiding them to maturity through his great wisdom and love. Dhritarashtra had one hundred sons, the eldest of whom was *Duryodhana*, an angry, headstrong young man who was hungry for power and desperate to become King in Yudhishthira's place. He was intensely jealous of the Pandavas and hated their prowess and excellence as they grew up together under the skilled direction of *Dronacharya*, their teacher. Dronacharya was the greatest archer and swordsman of their time and favoured *Arjuna*, Pandu's third son, as his best student.

The two families, constantly at odds, were thus always torn by jealousy and rivalry and when Yudhishthira became old enough to become King, Duryodhana's jealousy reached its zenith. He started plotting against the Pandava's lives and made two abortive attempts to murder them all. He invited them to stay in a palace he had built out of wax, which he set fire to in the middle of the night and when this failed he tried to poison them all. Frustrated by both efforts, he then used trickery and deceit to rob them of their entire kingdom, sending them into exile for thirteen years.

When they eventually returned from exile Duryodhana refused point blank to honour his promise to return their land or even as much land a could be placed on the head of a pin. This meant that Yudhishthira, although a peace-loving man who would do anything to avoid conflict, found himself faced with war as the inevitable means to prevent Duryodhana from overpowering the entire Kingdom of Bharat and therefore righteousness itself. *Arjuna,* Yudhishthira's brother, renowned for his courage as a fighter, was to lead them against Duryodhana's armies. His friend is *Krishna,* Prince of Dwarka, said to be the most adored representation of the Divine and the Supreme Lord.

Arjuna and Duryodhana went to Krishna to ask for assistance and He gave them each a choice. One could have Him on His own for his charioteer but He would not take part in the battle, and the other could have all His armies. Arjuna chose Krishna without hesitation and Duryodhana was thrilled to have Krishna's great armies at his disposal, convinced that he could not possibly lose.

Before we enter onto the field of Kurukshetra where the two armies are preparing to meet, let us first become more acquainted with all these characters and what they really represent for us...

The Pandavas

the great virtues within us

Also known as Dharma Raj, the King of Dharma, Yudhishthira is righteous, noble and completely unable to tell an untruth. He therefore represents the very highest truth and dharma within us.

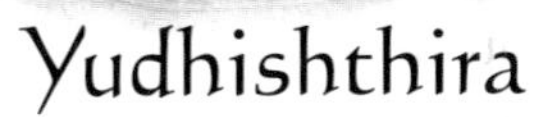
Yudhishthira

A formidable warrior, blessed with miraculous skill and indomitable courage, Arjuna is very open, straightforward and willing to learn. He represents you and I as we stand on the battlefield of life facing all the different parts of ourselves that prevent us from realising our true nature.

Arjuna

Another great and powerful warrior, Bhima is best known for his great strength and sense of humour. He is representative of our deep indestructable power.

Bhima

A skilled horseman, who knows the art of breeding and training horses for battle as no one else does, Nakula represents grace and divine beauty.

Nakula

Wise and learned, he knows the past, present and future and has the wisdom of the three worlds, although he will not reveal anything unless asked. He represents our knowledge and wisdom.

Sahadev

Married to the five Pandavas, Draupadi is known for her eternal, unending joy and is the strength behind the Pandavas - our virtues.

Draupadi

Mother of the Pandavas, Kunti has such devotion for the Lord that whenever she puts her hands together in prayer, He comes running immediately. She therefore represents the part of us that is irresistible to the Lord.

Kunti

Krishna is Arjuna's dearest friend, companion and teacher. He is said to be an incarnation of the Creator Himself and represents the very highest aspect of ourselves and the part we long to identify with. The Self.

Krishna

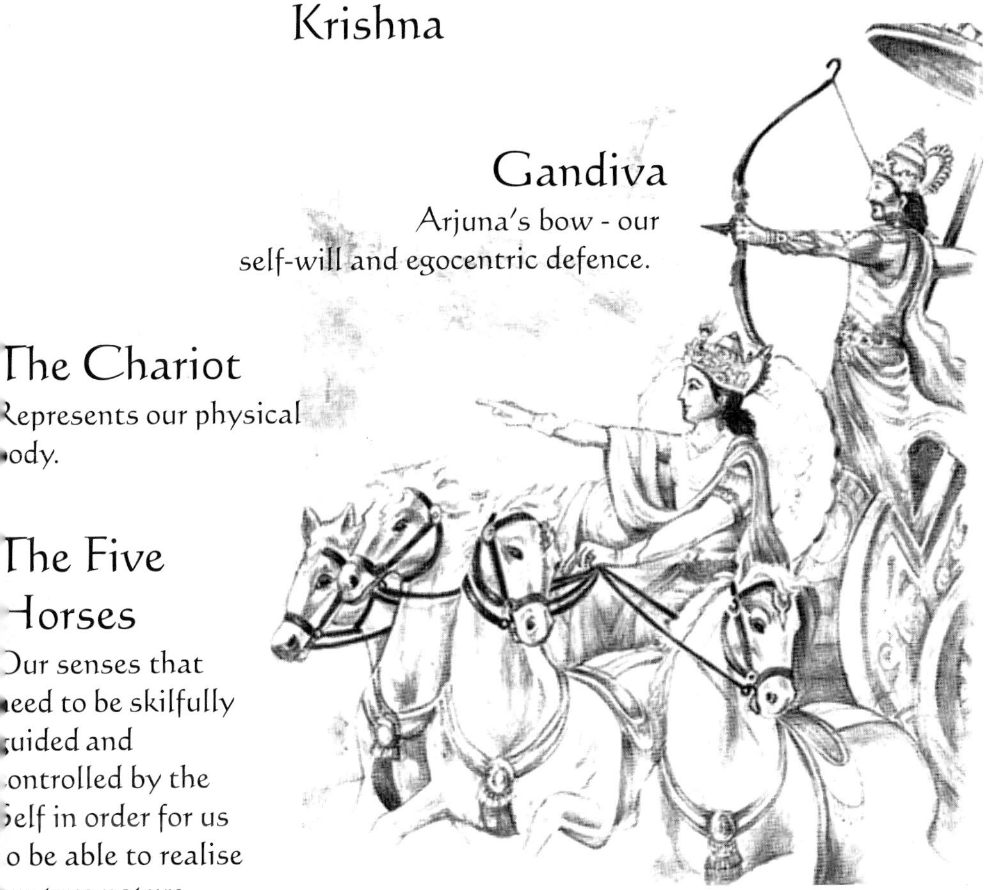

Gandiva

Arjuna's bow - our self-will and egocentric defence.

The Chariot

Represents our physical
ody.

The Five Horses

Our senses that
eed to be skilfully
guided and
ontrolled by the
Self in order for us
o be able to realise
ur true nature.

The Kauravas

the many negative qualities within us

King Dhritarashtra

Born blind he is unable to rule his kingdom. He represents our blind mind which is ignorant of our true nature and is married to.....

Gandhari

the loyal and faithful Queen who blindfolds herself to support her husband. She represents the intell that chooses not to see.

Gandhari gave birth to one hundred sons. When the mind and intellect remain blind, they give birth to hundreds of blind desires that torment and destroy ou life.

A strong, very powerful warrior who together with his brothers represents our egocentric nature. Because they are born out of ignorance, they contain hundreds of qualities which are opposed to dharma such as fear, anger, guilt, arrogance, doubt and pride.

Duryodhana

A brahmin priest in the court of King Dhritarashtra and the King's faithful servant. Sanjaya is a great seer, gifted with divine sight by Veda Vyasa, who acts as the King's eyes. He represents our intuition.

Sanjaya

Bhishma

he noble and indestructible warrior/ rotector and grandfather to both the andavas and the Kauravas. As strict in ersonal and public life as he was terrible in battle, Bhishma set the standard for the Kshatriya conduct. His allegiance to Dhritarashtra forces him to fight against the Pandavas.

Bhishma and Drona represent the positive qualities within us that we dearly love, but that are ultimately a hindrence to the soul's purpose

Dronacharya is the greatest expert in the art of archery, the beloved teacher of both the Pandavas and the Kauravas. He directed all the military operations which upheld the Kuru dynasty.

Dronacharya

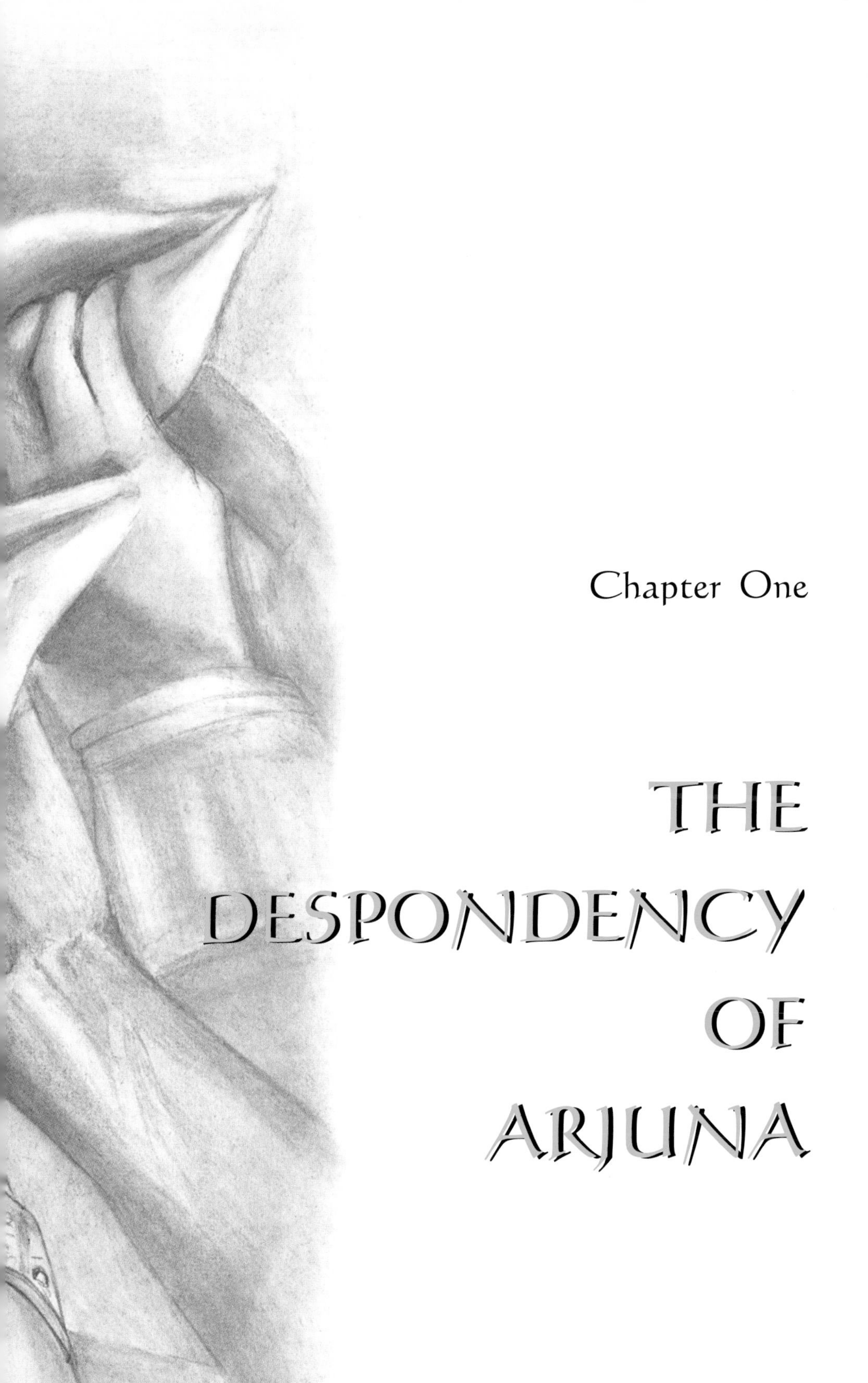

Chapter One

THE DESPONDENCY OF ARJUNA

y chariot, Krishna!' Arjuna's voice shouted above the din to his charioteer. 'Take it between the two armies so that I can clearly see who I have to fight!'

The noise was deafening. Kettledrums, cow horns, tabors and trumpets ripped through the stillness of the soft morning air, resounding their fierce battle cry. Warriors lined up in chariots blew their conch shells, filling the earth and heavens with a roar that tore at the hearts of those assembled on the vast plains of Kurukshetra, which were covered in tents, wagons, weapons and machines, chariots, horses and elephants. On one side stood the vast army of the Kauravas headed by Duryodhana and on the other Arjuna, the greatest of all warriors, born to conquer, led the mighty army of the Pandavas. He stood nobly in his magnificent golden chariot yoked by brilliant white horses, flying the standard of the monkey-god Hanuman, the Lord of the Wind.

As the armies gathered round in a seething mass, two men sat together watching the great display of warriors from a distance.

One was Sanjaya, the great seer, who had been given the gift of divine sight which enabled him to see inside himself everything that was happening on the battlefield. And the other Dhritarashtra, the blind King, his master, to whom he was able to recount everything he was witnessing.

'What do you see, Sanjaya?'

The tremor in the King's voice betrayed his inner turmoil as he grappled with the situation. Although he had tried to stop the war happening, he knew in his heart that he had not tried very hard. His thoughts were drifting back to the day Krishna had come to see him at court.

'A great disaster threatens the house of the Kurus,' Krishna had said to him. 'And I see clouds of destruction gathering in the heavens. If you want to save several of the great heroes of the world from certain death and indeed, all of your children, there is still time to stop your son, Duryodhana.'

'The Pandavas rise up like the jaws of death, Master.' Sanjaya's voice cut through his thoughts.

Both men's eyes were staring into space as one gazed at the images flashing before him and the other looked blankly into darkness.

The King shuddered.

'They appear mighty and invincible,' Sanjaya continued. 'But Duryodhana is regarding them with contempt as a lion would despise a herd of elephants.

At the sound of his favourite son's name, Dhritarashtra's spirits rose. 'What is he doing?' he said anxiously.

'He is boasting to Dronacharya how great his army is, spread out like the sea,' he replied, 'and listing the great heroes and mighty archers fighting on his side.'

'Our army is organised like a fortress, Drona,' Duryodhana is saying proudly 'And marshalled by Bhishma, the most courageous fighter on the battlefield the Pandava's army seems insignificant to me.'

As the King listened he was remembering how terrified he had been by Krishna's words, and how he had called on Gandhari, his Queen, knowing how wise she was and the influence she had over their son. Perhaps together he had thought, they could find a way to persuade Duryodhana to call it off

But the Queen was not happy. 'You are the one who has let your son go too far!' she accused him. 'In spite of all my protests you have let him have control of the entire kingdom and allowed him to mercilessly mistrea Pandu's sons. Now, suddenly, you expect him to obey you. It's impossible!

But she had tried her best, calling Duryodhana to her softly, like a child. ' am your mother,' she said, curling her arms around him. 'Sit by my side and listen patiently to my words. You know how much I love you, and want to protect you, my first born son,' she cooed.

But no amount of begging or cajoling could dissuade Duryodhana from his plans. He was absolutely resolute.

'But you are threatening to bring destruction to the entire House of Kurus! she implored him.

The memories swirled round and round inside Dhritarashtra's brain.

'You cannot win, don't you see?' she cried. 'Krishna and Arjuna are divine beings. They have dharma on their side - and you do not! Duryodhana, they will be the cause of your death, for God's sake!' Her voice was rising to a near shriek.

But her words just made him angry and even more determined to achieve his goal. He stormed out of the palace, seething with rage. Dhritarashtra sighed at the memory as Sanjaya's voice brought him back once again to the present.

'Dronacharya has ordered the troops to arrange themselves in their respective detachments,' he was saying excitedly, thrilled by the scene.

Drona surveyed the incomparable array of skilled warriors that moved before them. His smile was one of supreme satisfaction. It was indeed a sight to stir the heart of any seasoned warrior. There were so many great men present, many of them Kings themselves who had rallied to support Duryodhana, each one a famous warrior and leader in his own right.

'But regardless of their individual or combined greatness and magnitude,' Drona thought, 'there is no army that can defeat Krishna. Duryodhana must know that we simply cannot win this battle.' He knew that despite his bravado and false pride, secretly Duryodhana was very frightened. Suddenly his keen eyes caught sight of Arjuna's chariot speeding rapidly towards them.

'What is he doing?' he asked himself under his breath, instantly fascinated by the tactics of his favourite student.

Krishna had drawn the chariot into the middle of the battlefield and placed it between the two armies. They were surrounded on every side by hundreds and thousands of men, chariots and animals that stretched way out across the horizon and beyond for miles. Arjuna drew in his breath at the awesome sight as his consciousness slowly began to take in and absorb the enormity of the situation.

'They are awaiting your command, Arjuna!' said Krishna. Arjuna suddenl
became aware, almost as though he were waking up from a deep sleep, of
sea of faces that he knew and loved. Arrayed in front of his eyes he sa
fathers and grandfathers, teachers, uncles, brothers, sons and grandsons.

He saw Dronacharya, his teacher, who had taught him all the skills that h
was now about to use to attack him. He saw Bhishma, his grandfathe
who had also been a father to him and had nurtured him all his life
Everywhere he looked the images of friends, relatives and loved ones mad
his head swim and reel. He turned towards his friend.

Krishna,' he said, his voice breaking with emotion. 'These men I see in ront of me are my kinsmen. Looking at their faces, so eager for battle makes ny body shake and I feel weak at the knees. I can hardly stand up and my nind is whirling.'

The bow that he had so proudly upheld only moments before, slipped from is hand as he spoke and he had to lean heavily against the chariot for upport.

What good can there be in killing my own people? What is the point, for God's sake? Just for a kingdom?' he appealed to his friend.

As Arjuna grappled with his conscience, Krishna remained calm and letached, quietly observing his friend's demise into a state of weakness nd dejection. It all seemed very reasonable, but it was also very clear to Krishna that Arjuna's only real problem lay in attachment. He said nothing, owever.

What pleasure can we possibly get from killing Dhritarashtra's sons?' Arjuna continued, his mind spinning in all directions. 'It will only bring nore trouble, for how can we ever be happy again with the blood of our elatives on our hands?'

As they waited for the signal, the two armies on either side of them were rying to understand why Arjuna was taking so long. None of them, owever, could ever have suspected what the most courageous warrior of all ime was actually going through. Not even Bhishma, his grandfather, who new him so well.

Krishna, meanwhile, was thinking how strange it was that Arjuna seemed o have completely forgotten that the Kauravas were all murderers and would appily exterminate their entire family without any trace of remorse in order o achieve their own greedy ambitions.

What's got into him?' He thought. 'These are the people who deprived his rother of his entire kingdom and have continually plotted against his life nd the lives of his family. They have tried to poison and even burn them to leath!'

In fact, there was no monstrosity that the Kauravas were not guilty of and yet Arjuna, blinded by emotion, could no longer see that in the nam of all that was right and good, they simply had to be destroyed.

Krishna looked at Arjuna who was now completely overwhelmed by sorrow downcast and miserable, his eyes full of tears of self pity.

'I have got to shake him out of this,' He thought to himself. 'What do yo think you are doing, Arjuna?' He said fiercely, with no trace of sympath in his voice. Arjuna was momentarily taken aback by the harshness of hi question and just stared at him blankly.

'This despair and confusion does not become you,' Krishna continued 'These kinds of emotions have no place in the heart of a warrior. Do no give in to weakness. You must get up, rise to your full greatness wit courage and pride and fight!'

'How can you be so heartless, Krishna?' Arjuna was quick to reply. 'Yo are asking me to kill my kinsmen and friends. I have every reason to fee upset. Look!' he said, pointing across the field. 'There is Drona, my teache He has given me more instruction that he gave to his own son!

'And Bhishma. He took my father's place when he died and has alway loved and protected me through thick and thin. This is the man who use to gather me in his great, mighty arms and hold me close to his chest in loving embrace. These are the people I should worship - not kill! I woul rather die myself first,' he shouted at Krishna, his eyes filling with tears o pain.

Arjuna searched Krishna's face for a trace of understanding an reassurance. He found none.

'Krishna!' he pleaded. 'I am paralysed by sadness and grief. You must hel me. Please!' He looked at Krishna and seeing him resolute, threw dow his bow in utter despair.

'I will not fight,' he said.

'Arjuna is on his knees and has thrown down his bow, refusing to fight, my Lord!' Sanjaya told King Dhritarashtra excitedly.

For once the old man's face lit up. 'Refusing to fight?' he said jubilantly. 'Has he given up because he can see our armies are far superior to his?'

'Krishna is reasoning with him,' Sanjaya explained, 'and trying to convince him that he must stand up and fight.'

'What?' shouted the King. 'Has the cowherd gone mad? Tell me what He is saying, Sanjaya!'

Chapter Two

THE YOGA OF KNOWLEDGE

The early morning sun spread its red and orange glow througho the sky, glinting softly on the helmets and breastplates of th assembled warriors. Uncertainty rippled through the armies lil a wave, as they questioned the extraordinary encounter they we witnessing in the middle of the field of Kurukshetra.

Duryodhana, heading the Kaurava army, was full of impatience.

'What's he doing? Has he lost his nerve?' he asked his grandfather Bhishm

'No,' said Bhishma wisely, 'just be patient awhile and let us see wh happens.'

He wasn't quite sure himself what was really going on, but he was n willing to disempower Arjuna. He could sense and feel a great power i the atmosphere surrounding them and even though he was much too f away to hear their conversation, he leaned forward in his chariot, as subconsciously hoping to.

Krishna looked at Arjuna and seemed to smile.

Arjuna had exhausted his arguments by now, which meant he could reas with him at last.

'You know Arjuna,' He said calmly, 'although your words sound wis they are not actually based in Truth. In fact, it is pure ignorance that cause you to believe in this way.'

Arjuna simply stared at his teacher with wide, unblinking eyes, his fac marred by confusion as he grappled with Krishna's meaning.

'You really should not be grieving for these people you know,' He continue 'because those who are truly wise do not grieve for anyone - either living dead.

'The truth is that there never was a time when you or I, or all the warrio gathered here today, did not exist and there never will be a time when w cease to exist.'

Those who are truly wise
do not grieve for anyone -
either living or dead.

As Krishna spoke, a mighty hush settled over the plains. Even the restle: horses became still as if to hear His words more clearly. Golden-feather birds circled in the air above them, echoing the silence of the moment as timeless wisdom seemed to settle around Arjuna's heart as he listen despite his bewilderment and confusion. What did Krishna mean? Ho could this be true when he had seen death so many times? What was H really saying to him?

'Don't you know,' said Krishna, 'that we are all immortal and simply cann die?'

Even the monkey-god Hanuman, so proudly flying the great banner abo the chariot, sank down to rest upon the flag pole to listen. The air w charged with expectancy, almost as though the whole world were waitir for an explanation and even the golden chariot beneath them seemed quiver in anticipation.

'Would you get upset if I threw away an old coat?' Krishna asked. Arjur shook his head in response. 'And our body is no different. It is an out covering that contains who we really are. When it is worn out, we just ca it aside like a piece of clothing, but the real Self inside remains untouche indestructible and immortal.

'Weapons cannot touch it. Fire cannot burn it. Water cannot wet it, neith can it be dried by the wind. This vast universe is indestructible and no-o can destroy what is everlasting and imperishable.'

The flickering colours of the rising sun danced across Krishna's face, flashir sparks of light against His crown, creating an almost unearthly glow arour His face.

Arjuna squinted against the light, dazzled by the image.

'The concept that things can be born or die is an illusory one,' He sai 'When the surface of water is agitated by the wind, waves appear, but wh can say what is born or from where?

'And when the wind dies and the water becomes calm again, what is that has died?'

Weapons cannot touch it.
This vast universe
is indestructible
and no-one can destroy
what is everlasting
and imperishable.

Krishna could see that Arjuna was intrigued by His words.

'Take a substance like water,' He continued to explain. 'You could say it destroyed when it is boiled and becomes steam, but in reality it has onl changed its form. It still exists.

'In the same way, people are only afraid of death because they don' understand what it means.

'In fact, the quality of fear is probably the most predominant one that peopl have in their lives. Fear of things that they know about and things tha they don't know about. Fear of leaving their loved ones behind, and losin everything they have accomplished in their lives, as well as fear of th unknown that death presents.'

Krishna was aware that Arjuna, although concentrating intently, was no really grasping what He was saying. He deftly delivered another aspect

'You cannot yet perceive this truth, 'He said, 'because you are entangle in the duality of life. You say, 'this is good and this is bad' or 'this is pleasur and this is pain'.

'But you will have to go beyond this state of perception if you want t really understand what I am telling you.

'Not only is your view of the Real Self misguided, but even if you look at i from the standpoint of duty - you have no choice but to maintain dharm and balance in society.

'Remember, you have been born a Kshatriya, Arjuna - a warrior, and yo have to do your duty. Not for your own sake, but for the good of the whole Don't you know that there is nothing higher for a Kshatriya than to figh for the good of all? And if you run away from your duty, you are deliberatel allowing evil to prevail.

'When a warrior is confronted by such an opportunity as this, he should b overjoyed to uphold dharma and the rights of all living things. It opens th gates of heaven to him. But if you do not fight, you violate your dharma your duty and more importantly your honour. Your enemies will laugh a ou and what could hurt you more than that?'

3ut... ' Arjuna tried to speak, but Krishna wouldn't let him interrupt ecause He needed to really emphasise His point.

Who do you think you are anyway Arjun?' He said quickly. ' And who do ou think is responsible for this whole thing? You? Did you create this vhole universe and all the men here? Don't play this game of self-ighteousness with me,' He shouted.

Arjuna was so stunned by His words that he couldn't even reply.

So get up, Arjuna!' Krishna's voice was firm and authoritative. 'Resolve o face your conflict! You should not consider thoughts of the future and vhether you will win or lose. Do not delight in happiness or be cast down y pain. Just perform your duty and whatever comes, endure it bravely vith a steady mind.

Get involved, Arjuna, and fight with confidence!'

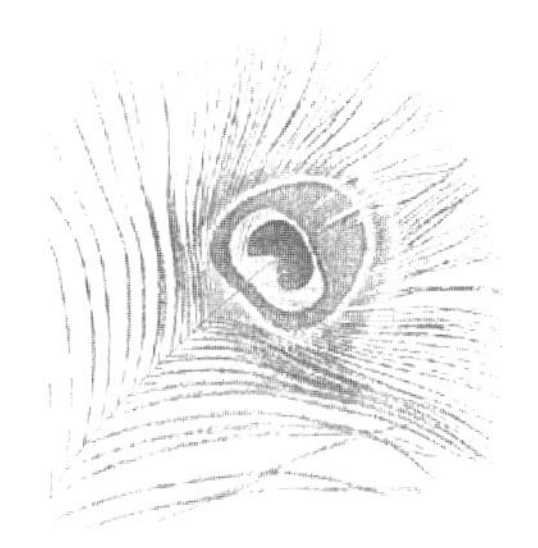

The air between them trembled with an awesome power as Krishna' words enveloped the proud warrior. Surer than any arrow, each on left Arjuna defenceless; he had no armour against such ancient Trut What choice did he have but to face this great challenge?

'But how, Krishna?' he appealed to his teacher. 'How can I realise thi immortal wisdom?'

A sudden cry from a bird high above them pierced the silence, echoing acros the plains, alerting everyone's attention back to the moment. Arjuna' grandfather, Bhishma, standing motionless in his great silver chariot o the far side of the battlefield, watched intently the figures of the two peopl who meant so much to him.

He knew and could sense that Krishna, the great Lord, was imparting wisdom to Arjuna that even the Gods themselves longed to hear. He sighe deeply, knowing there was nothing he could do but to watch, wait and fe the power of it. He put his hands together in prayer, bowing his head i reverence to this great event, and no-one but the passing breeze could se the tears on his cheeks.

Meanwhile, Duryodhana got down from his chariot and stalke impatiently back and forth, inwardly fuming.

'What on earth are they doing?' he shouted at Bhishma.

'You are my general. Do something! Make them get on with it!' His eye darted wildly from side to side as he spoke and Bhishma, in quiet contras stood erect and noble, his eyes as still and calm as a deep lake.

'You have a lot to learn, Duryodhana,' he said quietly. 'We are probabl witnessing one of the greatest events in the history of mankind.

'Why don't you curb your impatience and be still?'

His voice was charged with an irresistible authority, but his words simpl made the young King even more angry. He stabbed at the air with his fis before turning on his heel and storming back to his chariot.

'You have to learn the wisdom of skill-in-action, Arjuna,' Krishna said i
response to Arjuna's question.

'By this I mean perfect balance, unshakeable equanimity, poise and peac
of mind.

'You will have to establish an ever-present awareness of the core of you
real, immortal Self first, without which you cannot be effective in the fiel
of action.'

As the wind began to pick up again, Lord Hanuman's banner ruffled gentl
against the pole. Arjuna looked at Krishna with an almost childlik
fascination. 'How can I achieve this?' he said breathlessly.

Krishna's gaze was direct and piercing. 'The mind has many facets an
aspects that need to be brought under control,' He said, 'so that you ca
use the great power of the mind instead of allowing it to use you. You mus
make it your friend and not your enemy, for then it can become a powerfu
servant.

'If, however, you allow the mind to become your master, it can destroy you
Make your mind so focused and disciplined that you cannot be swayed b
raging emotions. With sincerity and constant practice, the wisdom I an
imparting to you will enable you to accomplish this.'

'But where do I begin?' Arjuna looked bewildered, still caught in a self
made net of confusion.

He gestured wildly with his hands, as if searching for the answers in th
air, whilst far across the plains, Bhishma's eyes were firmly fixed o
Krishna, as he almost willed the words to come to his ears.

'First and foremost you must do your duty, but without any thought fo
the result,' Krishna replied.

'What?' Arjuna couldn't believe his ears. 'That's impossible!' he saic
impatiently.

To fight is your duty at this moment,' Krishna said, ignoring his remark, ut defeat or victory is not your concern and you have no control over it.

f you think that you do, you are like a dog that walks under a cart and hinks it is responsible for its movement and not the bullocks.

Defeat and victory, heat and cold, pleasure and pain - these all come to us nd we must put up with them. Devoting oneself to action without thought or the result or attachment to it, is real skill in action. The success lies in erforming the act, not the result.'

Arjuna looked puzzled and said, 'This course of action seems beyond me. Not to worry about defeat or victory, not to think about the result at all - ow can one achieve this supreme balance of mind? I have no idea how omeone with these qualities would act and behave. How would I recognise uch a person?'

Krishna looked straight ahead of Him, across the vast plains, as if earching for someone who possessed the
visdom He was describing. His eyes were
till and unblinking, firmly fixed upon
ome unseen horizon.

He was looking at Bhishma.

The yellow silk of Krishna's robe rippled gently against His body whic
stood majestic and straight, His dark skin glistening in the sunlight. Th
peacock feather in His crown bowed softly in the wind as He turned t
reply to Arjuna, His compassionate eyes ablaze with light.

'He would have to renounce all cravings which torment the heart,' H
said, 'and instead derive his contentment from within himself alone.

'A wise person does not identify with selfish desires or personal satisfactior
Arjuna. Those who are established in this wisdom are not concerned wit
gratification of the senses which only pull us away from our true Self.

'Pleasures entangle us in the world of the senses. They constantly distrac
us from our spirit and make the mind confused and scattered, which i
fatal to the spiritual warrior.

'As a tortoise withdraws its limbs, the wise withdraw the senses and contro
them. By following the senses without control, strength of will and unit
of purpose are lost. Rampant desires are dictating your actions.'

As he spoke the horses became agitated, as if troubled by some unsee
presence. They began to pull and strain in different directions, causing th
chariot to lurch and sway from side to side and forcing the wheels deepe
into the earth. Krishna pulled the reins tighter to bring them back unde
control.

'Do you see these horses Arjuna?' He said. 'They will scatter in al
directions and upturn our chariot if I don't take a firm hold of them.

'But if I hold them still, I become their master and the chariot remain
firm, just like the mind which has controlled the senses.

'Imagine that this chariot is your body with the wheels as your four limbs
the five horses the senses, and the mind the reins that need to be firml
held in control by your Higher Mind - the highest and most divine part o
yourself.

'Guided by your intuition,' He said, pointing to Lord Hanuman's flag a
it flew proudly above them, 'you will become the master of these ver

As a tortoise withdraws its limbs,
the wise withdraw the senses
and control them.
By following the senses without control,
strength of will
and unity of purpose are lost.

powerful, almost wild senses. Otherwise,' he continued, with a more serious and cautionary edge to His voice, 'they will destroy you, Arjuna.'

His eyes flashed a power that hit Arjuna as forcefully as any arrow. The words of his teacher entered him almost physically, settling deep in his heart, giving birth to new understanding and wisdom.

Arjuna's brothers, the Pandavas, were watching from the other side of the field. The eldest one, Yudhishthira, serene and dignified, waited patiently, but Bhima, his younger brother, was extremely restless and impatient.

'What is Arjuna doing?' he asked Yudhishthira. 'He must know that this is no time to show weakness. In front of the enemy!' His eyes were burning with humiliation as he spoke. 'Why is he doing this now? He is shaming us in front of Duryodhana and all the Kauravas.'

'Hush, Bhima.' Yudhishthira's voice was soothing and calm as he put his hand on Bhima's shoulder. 'Trust your brother. He is a great warrior and he must know what he is doing.'

'But he is disempowering us in front of our enemies!' Bhima's voice was angry. 'His whole honour is at stake here - how can it be right?'

On the surface, Yudhishthira could not disagree with this simply because he was right. It wasn't the right time or place for an emotional breakdown, and to allow the enemy to see his weakness was not a wise thing to do, but still he couldn't afford to doubt Arjuna. He had to uphold him, no matter what happened.

'What if he has lost his nerve?' Bhima was voicing everyone's fear, for all their hopes for victory rested on Arjuna's tenacity, courage and skill as a warrior. Yudhishthira turned to Sahadev, his wise younger brother for his advice. Sahadev, who never spoke unless asked a question, had silently been following the conversation, withholding all comment.

'What is your advice, Sahadev?' he asked him. Sahadev looked ahead, with still, unblinking eyes. 'Leave it to Krishna,' he replied without hesitation or any trace of emotion.

Bhima shrugged his shoulders in exasperation, his usually jovial face contorted by frustration. How could he argue with that? He could see that he had no choice but to trust the situation and somehow to quell his frustration and eagerness to fight.

Krishna and Arjuna, meanwhile, were locked into a timeless space wher
nothing else existed but their mutual quest for truth. Arjuna's mind wa
beginning to wander. He could hear Krishna's words and knew they wer
sound and valuable, but somehow he couldn't quite grasp their meaning.

'You talk about controlling the senses,' he said, 'but I don't quite understan
how they can destroy you.'

Krishna's eyes were full of patience and compassion. No agitation o
irritation ruffled His composure. Although acutely aware of the expectatio
of the two armies either side of them, He remained inwardly very still an
unaffected. In His wisdom, Krishna knew that Arjuna's struggle was no
just his own. Although His words may have been just for His friend'
ears, Krishna instinctively knew that Arjuna was not just searching fo
answers for himself alone, but for the whole of humanity.

He turned to look at Arjuna once again.

'Pleasure and pain are felt through the five senses, aren't they?' He asked
patiently. Arjuna nodded. 'If the mind is always focused on sense objects,
you will find that you become very attached to the pleasure you feel.

'Attachment is a breeding ground for desire, a powerful, compelling force
that motivates all your actions.' He looked at Arjuna. 'Do you understand
me?' He asked.

Arjuna looked confused. 'But desire is part of our inherent nature,' he replied.

'Which nature, Arjuna?' Krishna's words were gentle, not accusing. 'Is it
not your lower nature that craves pleasure? If you aspire towards freedom
and identification with your real Self, you must redirect desire towards the
right focus.'

Arjuna fell silent. 'Even desire for victory, Arjuna.' Krishna's voice pierced
through his thoughts.

'Why?' Arjuna was amazed. 'How can you be motivated without desire
for victory?' he said.

'Desire that is unfulfilled will create anger.' Krishna's words were charged with power. 'And anger carries away our discrimination just like a strong wind pulls a boat off its charted course. You then cannot discriminate between what is wise and unwise and can no longer learn from past mistakes.'

Arjuna could not deny the truth of Krishna's words. Many times he had found the power of anger robbing him of his ability to think and see clearly what to do. All his great skill as a warrior seemed to diminish and become inaccessible to him amidst the mental turmoil that anger created.

Arjuna's mind was beginning to clear a little as the truth filtered through. 'So it is desire that creates anger?' He was surprised.

'And attachment,' Krishna added quietly.

'So you see, Arjuna, you must not allow yourself to be carried away by your mind and senses. You must gradually train them so that you can become their master and use all your power to free the senses from attachment and aversion alike.

'Once they come under your control, your wisdom will become steady and the mind calm. Without a one-pointed mind however, there is no peace and without peace... how can you find true happiness?'

Arjuna nodded. He was beginning to understand.

'Looking outside for peace just disturbs the mind even more.

'You will find that true happiness springs from a tranquil mind. And you can never experience this peace when you are full of personal wants and desires; but when they all merge, like different rivers flowing into the vastness of the ocean, then peace comes easily. Once the restless rivers get to the sea, they become as calm as the ocean.'

As Krishna spoke these words, Arjuna could feel a deep longing rising up within him. An ancient feeling of ... what was it?

It's like waking up to light
in the depths of the night;
for what the world calls daylight
is the dark night of ignorance
to the wise man.

'It's like waking up to light in the depths of night; for what the world calls daylight is the dark night of ignorance to the wise man.'

Krishna's voice seemed to echo through his mind as he struggled to identify what he was feeling. It was as if something very deep was beginning to stir inside him -

'waking up to light in the depths of night...'

'When you abandon selfish desire you become free from the bondage of selfishness and pride and find a place of deep joy and everlasting peace... your true nature,' Krishna continued.

'This, Arjuna, is the real, inner battle.'

Arjuna sighed deeply as he bowed his head. 'A place of everlasting peace...'

Chapter Three

THE YOGA OF ACTION

Arjuna pulled himself together quickly, his mind suddenly flooc with doubt. He was still looking for a way out.

'O Krishna!' he said, 'You seem to be saying that the path wisdom is greater than action. You praise this great knowledge, wh indicates I need to give up action altogether and just sit and medita so why do you ask me to act in this terrible way? Surely the two incompatible? Shouldn't I just focus on spiritual wisdom and forget abc my duty? Why act at all?'

Arjuna was thinking how strange Krishna's ways were and how confus he now felt, like a blind man who has been set out on the wrong road.

'Krishna!' he said impatiently, 'why are you treating me like this?'

The horses reared slightly as Arjuna raised his voice. Krishna was surpris by his words because to Him, everything was very clear. Crystal clear, fact, and for a moment He had to adjust His perception once again Arjuna's confusion and almost climb down into his reality in order to h him to understand and see that action is the means to this great wisdo

'Listen to the deeper meaning in what I have said, Arjun,' He replied gen without any trace of impatience.

'You need to realise that I have spoken about the two paths in this wo that have existed since the beginning of time. The path of knowled followed by the great sages, and the path of action.

'Two rivers may flow in different directions and appear to be separate, b eventually they will meet in the ocean. In the same way, although th teachings appear diverse, they have the same goal and both will lead self-realisation.

'Don't you think it would be foolish to imagine that a person can becon free from his duty simply by not doing it?' He looked keenly at Arju 'Wouldn't it be ridiculous?' He asked him again.

'It would be like trying to cross a river by getting rid of the boat!'

Two rivers may flow
in different directions
and appear to be separate,
but eventually they will meet
in the ocean.

'Think about this carefully, Arjun,' Krishna continued. 'It is impossible fo
anyone in a physical body to avoid action because every living thing i
born to act.' His words were very clear and strong. 'And you simply cannc
avoid your obligations.

'If you look at anything in nature, no matter how small it is, there is constar
movement as that life form acts out its dharma and fulfils its purpose o
the earth. Even a seemingly inert tree is working very hard to perform it
duty as a tree.

'The question is not whether we should act or not, but how to act, and thi
is where the greatest secret to liberation lies.'

As he spoke, a distant rumbling sound disturbed the early morning stillnes.
The animals throughout the plain were becoming restless and agitate
Horses cried out in the distance and the thud of elephants' feet could b
heard as they began to move around and sway from side to side. A breat
of wind, eager to catch hold of Krishna's secret, urged them to be calm an
attune to the voice of the great master. And then, just as suddenly as th
disturbance had begun, everything began to calm down and become sti
again, as He continued.

'It is the spirit in which you act that determines whether you become fre
through your actions or bound and imprisoned by them,' He said, wit
such a force that Arjuna found himself listening with renewed alertness.

'Arjuna,' He said again, with an even greater emphasis in His voice. 'Liste
very carefully to this because it is very important.

'Are you aware that everything in creation is giving itself for the sake c
something else. Every life form instinctively knows it must lay down it
life to sustain another. You know this don't you?'

Arjuna nodded, although he wasn't completely convinced.

'Even a flower blooms for the sake of those who see and smell it, and nev
for itself.' Krishna was determined to get him to understand this gre
truth.

It is the spirit in which you act
that determines whether
you become free through your actions
or whether you become bound
and imprisoned by them.

'The law of selfless giving lies at the very heart of creation,' He sai
emphatically.

Some birds of prey cried out as they flew past, swooping low in the sk
above their heads. Krishna looked up to acknowledge them. 'They kno
how they must live,' He said, pointing to the birds, 'and they have n
confusion about it.'

'Do you think that human beings are exempt from this great law o
creation?' Arjuna shook his head.

'Man has lost sight of his innate knowledge - of how to act out his purpos
on earth. And where harmony rules amongst those who know that sacrific
is the law of life, chaos exists among those who have forgotten.'

'So what is the answer?' Arjuna felt slightly anxious as he strained t
understand what to the animal kingdom and natural world seemed s
obvious.

'How do you act in such a way that ensures you are aligned with creatic
and not opposed to it, then?'

Krishna smiled. He was watching the birds above them dancing and playin
with each other.

Thinking deeply for a moment, He said, 'Let me tell you a story that wi
help you to understand.'

He turned to look into the distance, once again appearing to reach ou
beyond time and space - searching for the means to help His friend fin
clarity and understanding.

'When Brahma created the world,' He said at last, 'He made every creatu
perfectly. He also made perpetual sacrifice. But because the meaning o
sacrifice is very subtle, His creatures couldn't quite understand it and s
they begged Him to explain it clearly to them.

The Creator told them simply, 'Each one of you has your own prescribe
duty to perform, and if you can simply do your own duty, you will find

ecomes like a wish-fulfilling tree for you that will never, ever forsake you.

For by doing your own duty you nourish the Gods, and in turn, they will e pleased and nourish you; taking care of your every need and fulfilling all he desires of your heart, just like the trees of an orchard always wait at he door of spring to shower their abundance of fruit.

f only you can act in this way, solely devoted to your duty, you will find ourself full of happiness and free from desire.'

As He spoke, it was as if they had travelled back in time together, emembering the first moments of creation.

n other words, Arjuna...' Krishna's words gently brought them back into he present.

Strive constantly to perform your own duty - and no-one else's – with the velfare of others always in your mind, never thinking about the outcome of our actions.

No-one should ever abandon their duty, but rather follow it with their vhole heart.'

He paused, waiting to see if Arjuna was absorbing His words. He appeared o be struggling again.

'm saying that you need to act skilfully out of a sense of duty.' He xplained, 'Not for your own sake, but for the good of all, within a spirit of acrifice.

You must perform your duty without preferences or attachment to the esults of your actions, because it is selfish action that leads to exploitation, nanipulation and sorrow.'

He paused, and His face softened.

But you know,' He said, 'those who have found contentment within their wn existence and are completely satisfied within the Self, find that there s stillness in everything they do.

'They don't have any purpose in their actions as such, having no need c
anyone or anything.'

Arjuna felt as though his mind was being turned inside out. Krishna'
words were so beyond his experience and seemed to go almost against th
grain of human nature.

'But with the best will in the world Krishna,' he pleaded. 'This is so har
to do. It is as though one is driven to act in a way that is selfish by som
force outside one's will. Do you know what I mean?

'It's like a fiend that seizes hold of you and pursues you when you try t
escape. A tyrant. What is this power?'

Krishna nodded and smiled knowingly.

'It is the force of desire,' He said, 'and anger, who are like blood brother
both without any trace of compassion. They create turmoil throughout th
whole world.

'Like fire covered by smoke, like a mirror covered by dust, like the unbor
foetus completely surrounded by a membrane, so is the wisdom in ma
covered by the invisible fire of desire, the constant enemy of the Self.

'What people do not really understand is that life has been given to us s
that we can serve creation and not just for the purpose of our own pleasu
and enjoyment.

'People have forgotten this and instead have become slaves to their selfis
desires and anger.

'Because if desire is not satisfied, anger is the inevitable consequence. Desi
is driven by passion and it is this desire which is man's greatest enem
and he really has to fight it day and night.

'First control the senses, as I said before, and then conquer the mind. Whe
you have done this, the intellect will also obey you.'

Like fire covered by smoke,
like a mirror covered by dust,
like the unborn foetus
completely surrounded by a membrane,
so is the wisdom in man
covered by the invisible fire of desire,
the constant enemy of the Self.

Arjuna sighed deeply. Krishna made it all sound so simple, but he knew i
his heart that what He was asking him to do was the hardest task a huma
being could ever undertake.

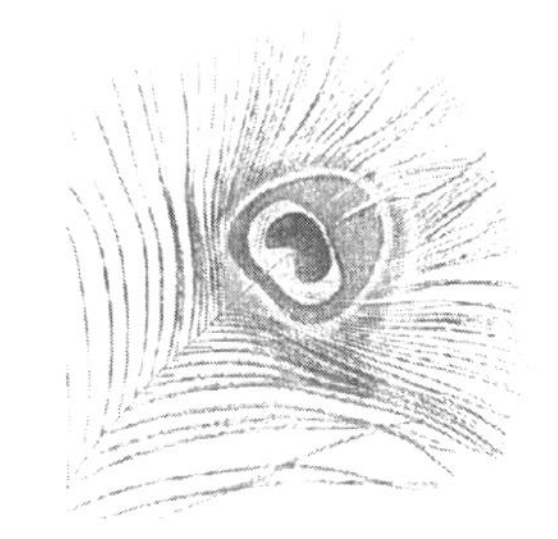

But that still doesn't explain how I can become free through action Arjuna was once again struggling to understand. Krishna looke at him, with eyes full of compassion. He felt the reins tighten i His hands as the horses became restless again, and speaking softly, soothe them back to stillness.

'Arjuna,' He said, trying another approach. 'What you are looking for i your very nature. You already are what you seek.' He paused for a momen 'But do you know why you cannot perceive this truth?'

Arjuna shook his head. 'Of course not,' he thought to himself.

'Because of the turbulence in your mind created by your likes and dislike Preferences, in other words. You judge this action I am asking you to do a 'terrible'. If you judge an act to be horrible or wonderful or anywhere i between the two, that is where your problem will lie.

'These judgements create such turbulence in the mind that they preven us from experiencing real joy and becoming liberated through our actions

He gave Arjuna a few moments to think about what He had said befor continuing.

'And the next trap to avoid is attachment to results.

'People do things because they want to enjoy the results, but they ge attached by imagining the results before and during their actions. Thi means that only half their energy can be available to actually do the actio which in turn means they can only achieve half the result they anticipate and then they are disappointed.

'It's the most difficult thing in the world not to become attached in an way to what you are doing, but if you can put all your energy into th action you won't waste precious time and energy in anticipation of th result.'

Arjuna couldn't hold back. 'That is impossible!' he said. 'Now we are bac where we started. How on earth could I possibly fight without wanting t win?'

If you judge an act
to be horrible or wonderful
or anywhere in between the two,
that is where your problem will lie.

He suddenly caught sight of the army in front of him again and shuddere inside as he reassessed where his duty lay. He could see Bhishma outline against the sun, his great mane of white hair and long beard creating a awesome silhouette as he stood patiently waiting and watching.

He saw his beloved teacher Dronacharya, with his Brahmin's battl standard flying above him, depicting a water jar and golden altar upon deerskin. He was standing beside Bhishma, equally patient and alert. A Arjuna felt their strength and love coming towards him, his eye momentarily filled with tears.

He hung his head and looked at the ground to hide the feelings c overwhelming despair that were beginning to rise inside him again.

'How can I fight them?' he asked himself as the magnitude of his dilemm began to wash over him with renewed force, dragging his spirits back dow

'Arjuna!' Krishna's voice was sharp. He had to move fast to stop him from sinking back into his emotions.

'You must believe me when I tell you that you can do it!'

'But how?' Arjuna's voice was weak and pleading. 'I feel so helpless, I jus don't know how, Krishna.'

'I do not believe this!' Krishna said mockingly, suddenly changing Hi tactics.

'Aren't you supposed to be Dronacharya's best student, admire throughout the three worlds for your great courage and strength? And yo stand here and tell me you feel weak and helpless!'

Arjuna was shocked by the way He was talking to him.

'Do you remember the day Drona asked you and your brothers what yo could see when you looked at the tree?'

Immediately Arjuna's mind went back in time to the more carefree days c his youth. Days spent in intensive training under Drona's expert directio n that day the young princes were practising their archery in the forest. ronacharya asked them all to fix their aim on a bird in the tree in front of hem and to tell him what they could see.

ach brother saw different things. One saw the mountains, the sky and e trees as well as the bird. Another said he could see the sky, the tree and e bird and another saw only the bird and the tree.

see only the eye of one bird.' Arjuna said, such was the astute focus of is mind. Dronacharya beamed at him, recognising the greatness of his tudent.

o you remember how Dronacharya praised you?' Krishna questioned. rjuna nodded reluctantly.

nd is this the same man who stands before me now?'

rjuna hung his head, not knowing what to say. He did remember, and yet could not explain to himself why his strength and courage had suddenly serted him so completely.

'Arjuna, do you not believe that I am going to give you the ways and mean
to achieve the freedom that will enable you to fight in this battle wit
clarity and detachment?'

His words shook Arjuna back to his senses. The great Lord Himself wa
asking if He could be trusted. 'Of course my Lord, forgive me,' he falterec

'There is one sure way to act without attachment, Arjuna.'

As Krishna spoke the air became charged with the atmosphere of Hi
ancient and powerful lineage. Arjuna looked at him, hopeful and expectan
hanging on His every word.

'At all times you must remember Me and dedicate your actions to Me
Krishna said deliberately.

Arjuna looked at him, expecting more of an explanation, before he realise
that he was not going to get one.

'Is that all?' he asked. 'Can it really be that simple?'

'It may sound simple,' Krishna replied patiently, 'but if your mind is restles
and uncontrolled it will be very hard.

'If you are dedicating all your actions to Me, however, you wi
automatically connect with your highest Self which frees the mind fro
the rushing, selfish fever. You will then find yourself easily able to engag
in battle.

'With this approach, you will be able to neutralise the likes and dislik
that disturb your mind and become so free inside yourself that you will n
be concerned about success or failure. You will not be elated by one
disturbed by the other.'

Arjuna thought for a moment. 'That is a freedom that I would dearly lo
to have,' he said to himself. 'But how does it work?' he said out loud.
'If your actions are motivated by selfishness and desire for a particul
outcome, quite simply they will trap you,' Krishna replied. 'But once yo
dedicate everything you do to the Lord, in every moment, then you are n

At all times
you must remember Me
and dedicate your actions
to Me.

doing it for yourself any more, are you?'

Arjuna shook his head. 'So it is your intention that makes the difference he asked.

'Exactly,' said Krishna, stretching out His arm to indicate the armie gathered across the plains.

'If you fight this battle because you want to win for your own glory c dominion over a kingdom, your attachment to the outcome will posses and entrap your mind completely.

'But if you fight only because I ask you to - for My sake alone, without an attachment to either victory or defeat,' He said, 'that action will set yo free.'

They looked at each other for one, timeless moment, locked into a feelin far beyond words. To Arjuna it felt as though Krishna was looking into hi very soul, which was beginning, just beginning, to awaken to another, muc deeper feeling, as yet unnamed...

Chapter Four

THE YOGA OF WISDOM

What's happening now?' snapped Dhritarashtra impatientl 'Why have you stopped?'

Sanjaya was in fact unable to speak, momentaril overwhelmed by emotion. He was sensing the enormity of Krishna's grea affection for Arjuna which seemed incomparable to any other love that h knew.

'Who has ever experienced such a great love as this?' he was thinkin 'And what is moving Krishna - He who is one with the Self, unchangin and eternal - to such depth of compassion?'

To Sanjaya it appeared that Krishna Himself was overcome by His lov for Arjuna and it was this that moved him so much. As tears ran down hi cheeks he was oblivious to the King's impatient remarks, transported as h was to another realm where Kings and courtiers do not exist.

At last, the surge of emotion passed away and he gathered himself bac into the moment.

'Krishna is asking Arjuna,' he said slowly and deliberately, 'If he realise how privileged he is, because these teachings are very ancient and secret

'I first told them to Vivasvan, the God of the Sun,' Krishna is saying, 'bu many ages have passed since then. Then Vivasvan taught it to Manu wh practised it himself and taught it to his son Ishvaku.

'In this way it has been handed down from age to age. Many royal sage knew this yoga after that, but through time the knowledge has been lost.

Arjuna was jolted out of his train of thought as he heard these words an his mind filled with doubt. 'But they were born long before you were!' h said.

'Even our ancestors did not know Vivasvan, so how could you have taugh him?'

Krishna smiled once again before speaking.

'If there is any doubt in your mind that I existed when Vivasvan lived, yo need to know that you and I have passed through many births. I rememb everything in the past and every incarnation I have had, but you have n memory of yours.

'Who I am is unborn and unchanging,' He continued. Arjuna found himse mesmerised by Krishna's eyes. 'Birth and death, which I appear to underg are merely expressions of the power of illusion working through Me.

'I am really formless, Arjun, but when I function in the world of nature fc a special purpose, I act as though I were incarnate.

'For the sake of my devotees I assume human form in order to drive out th darkness of ignorance and to raise the banner of happiness through righteou people. I take birth age after age for this purpose.

'He who knows this is truly wise in this world.'

As Arjuna looked at Him, everything disappeared in that moment and a he was aware of was the sound of these mighty words reverberating in hi ears. Words that seemed to echo into eternity and beyond.

'A person who understands My birth, although I am unborn, wh understands my action although I am above all action, who knows I ar unchanging...who knows me as his own divine Self...

'Breaks through the belief that he is the body and becomes united wit Me. He is never reborn.'

As he gazed at Krishna, his mind dissolved away and the golden chario melted around Him into a halo of light. He could only see and feel th glory of His message.

'Know this also,' Krishna continued. 'In whatever way people are devote to Me, that is how I serve them. All people, Arjuna, follow My path. Jus as the echo's voice returns to you in a cave, or on the top of a mountain, i the same way, I am a witness to all forms of worship.

'I am changeless and beyond all action. Actions do not cling to Me simpl because I have no attachment to their results. Those who understand an

For the sake of my devotees
I assume human form
in order to drive out the
darkness of ignorance
and to raise the banner of happiness
through righteous people.
I take birth, age after age
for this purpose.

practise this truth, live in freedom. You too, can do the same, pursuing a active life but in the manner of those ancient sages.'

Momentarily, Arjuna's understanding was complete, for he not only knew what Krishna was saying, but could feel it in every part of his being. For few brief moments in time no more questions gnawed at his brain or confuse his mind.

But then, as a candle flickers in the wind, he found himself wavering back and forth - in and out of reality, as the unearthly glow around Krishn began to fade away and His voice seemed to lose its great resonance an become normal again. He was back, feeling the earth beneath his feet, onc more aware of the smells and sounds of the battlefield.

Suddenly the sun disappeared behind the clouds and a cool wind brushe across the plain.

He shuddered a little, adjusting to the change as Krishna carried on talking quietly watching Arjuna's reactions.

'The yoga of action is the very highest yoga,' He said, 'and you must try to understand how it works.

'The question that has always confused the greatest Sages,' He continued 'is what is action and what is inaction.

'Its true nature is very difficult to grasp, but I will teach you the secret o action with which you can free yourself.

Action...inaction...Arjuna tried to make sense of Krishna's words. 'Wha does he mean?' he wondered.

Krishna smiled, as He watched Arjuna's struggle and a rush of emotion came over Him. He was reminded that it was only out of His great love for him that He was offering Arjuna these most sacred and secret teachings. Putting His hand on his shoulder, He said, tenderly,

'Remember Arjun that the reason I am telling you all this is because want to help you to heal the conflict in your mind.'

The yoga of action
is the very highest yoga,
and you must try
to understand
how it works.

Arjuna relaxed, acknowledging his teacher's words, and put his hands together to bow to Krishna.

He had pulled himself back together, and renewed by his experience, could feel his mind becoming sharper and more alert.

Bhishma, his grandfather, was looking across at them over the great plains. He stroked his beard thoughtfully and sighed.

'What would I not give to be able to hear what Krishna is saying,' he was thinking. He knew full well how privileged Arjuna was, and wondered how much Arjuna himself recognised what it really meant to be in his position.

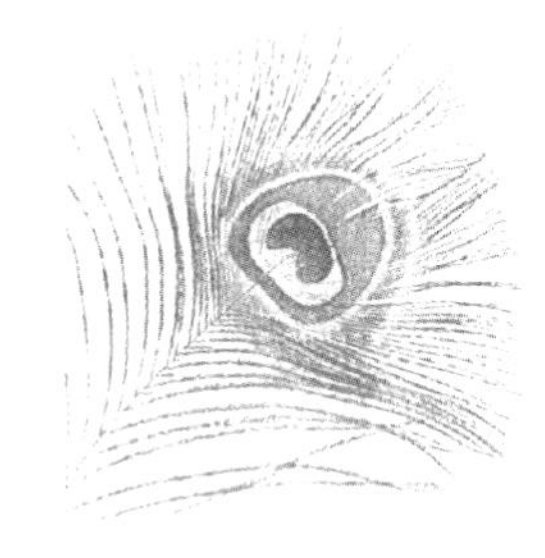

As the sun rose higher into the sky, it took with it the last remnants of early morning mist that previously covered the plains. Krishna surveyed with discerning eyes, the armies of men waiting either side of them thinking deeply about how to help Arjuna to understand this most profound teaching.

'You see all these warriors, horses and elephants?' He said, suddenly seeing a way. Arjuna cast a glance over the scene and nodded.

'They are perfectly still are they not?'

As soon as Krishna said this, Arjuna felt a deep hush descending over the field of Kurukshetra as a dust cloud settled in the distance. The air became motionless and thick as it does just before a storm is about to break. Time seemed to expand around them as Arjuna's awareness became minutely focused upon the silence.

'Listen deeply Arjuna.'

As Krishna spoke He began to weave His web of Yoga Maya, the goddess of illusion, around them and Arjuna became aware of the sound of soft rhythmic drums that seemed to be beating in different tempos.

'What do you hear?' Krishna asked him.

'I hear the sound of a million heartbeats all beating at once,' he answered breathlessly. As he spoke he heard a rushing sound like the wind racing through the trees. 'And the blood as it courses through their veins,' he said and his eyes closed as he listened with every fibre of his being.

'Anything else?' Krishna's voice was strong and powerful.

'I can hear the sound of waves crashing onto the shore as the breath moves in and out of their lungs.

'And a million voices all talking at once!' Arjuna raised his voice in alarm as he became aware of all the thoughts racing through their minds.

'Please stop it Krishna, the sound is deafening me!'

The voices began to fade away as Krishna dissolved His web of illusion and brought Arjuna back into himself.

'Even though we are completely motionless and apparently inactive,' said Krishna, 'yet there is activity in abundance.' Arjuna's face was full of amazement as he opened and refocused his eyes.

'Life is always moving inside us,' He continued, 'and we have no control over it, but most of the time we are completely unaware of this great power of life.'

Arjuna started to speak, but Krishna interrupted him.

'Before you question me further, let me first explain a little more. What I am trying to tell you is that nature is constantly moving through every life form. If you think of a lotus flower that opens when the sun rises and closes as it sets, would you say it is the sun that has that effect on the flower?'

Arjuna thought for a moment before speaking. 'Yes, I would,' he said at last.

'But it isn't the sun Arjuna.' Krishna's eyes were alive and piercing.

'It is the power of nature working through the sun. The very power that created the sun.'

He extended His arm towards the sun to emphasise His point.
'It cannot take any credit for the effect it has on the earth.
Its dharma is to shine, not to worry about how well it shines or if everything is benefiting from its golden rays.'

Krishna looked out beyond the plains as He spoke. 'The whole universe is pervaded by action, so vast is its power. A wise man, although immersed in a life of action, does not expect any fruit; for his only motive is to perform his duty for the benefit of all.

'The wise man, though acting, is constantly offering his action to the place of stillness within him. Acting, without attachment to the outcome, centred in the stillness of his own being, he is free from the bonds of action.

'Content with what comes to him, he is indifferent to pleasure and pain, success or failure and is free in every way.

The wise man, though acting,
is constantly offering his action
to the place of stillness within him.
Acting, without attachment to the outcome,
centred in the stillness of his own being,
he is free from the bonds of action.

'He is like a man who sees his own reflection in the water, yet knows th it is not him. Or like someone boating on a river, who seeing the trees c the bank running past, realises they are stationary.'

He paused for a moment, allowing the images to make an impression c His student. Arjuna nodded his understanding.

'In the same way,' He continued, 'he sees his actions as unreal from th standpoint of the Self. Like the sun that appears to move while rising an setting but actually remains still.

'One who works freely in the spirit of service is free from attachment an becomes one with everything. He sees no difference in the one who give and the one who receives as well as the offering itself. Living for others i peace, love and wisdom, his life becomes divine and everything he does an offering to the Lord.

'There are those who strive for the joy of the Self by offering in this wa and others sacrifice all passions of the mind through self control. Som sacrifice their material possessions, while still others offer the inbreat and the outbreath, or even their intake of food.

'Those who are established in the Self experience that pure and eternall perfect knowledge which is the result of sacrifice. In this state though does not enter, and desire has no place.

'Your goal is to become constantly aware of this power of life workin through you, so that it becomes very clear that you are not the doer of you actions.

'Like the sun, you simply act because it is your nature and your duty to d so, for the benefit of all beings.'

Arjuna pondered His words, as the first glimmerings of understandin began to dawn upon his mind. 'I think I can feel and understand what yo are saying,' he said, 'but how do you do it?'

'Constant effort and awareness,' Krishna replied. He stood back a little i the chariot, taking time to allow the Truth to settle.

Those who are established in the Self
experience that pure
and eternally perfect knowledge
which is the result of sacrifice.
In this state thought does not enter,
and desire has no place.

Duryodhana was fuming with rage. 'Who do they think they are, holding up the entire battle like this?' he shouted insolently at his teacher Dronacharya. 'What sort of time is this to have onversations?' His face was flushed and angry, as he hit his fist on the de of the chariot.

ll his life he had hated the Pandavas. Ever since he could remember they ad been a thorn in his side and he had been tormented by jealousy towards iem. They were always the ones to excel at everything, earning themselves onstant praise and accolade. It seemed there was nothing they could not o or achieve to perfection.

How he had longed for the day when he could openly annihilate them all nd at last rid himself of the bane of his life. His evil mind had thought of othing else both day and night for many years and now, when he at last ad the chance to launch his armies against them, Arjuna was delaying is glory.

rustrated by his inability to start the battle, he yelled at Drona again. Make them start the fighting!'

)ronacharya was well used to Duryodhana's angry tantrums, having nown and taught him since he was a young boy. For years he had watched ie Kauravas and Pandavas fighting with each other and witnessed how alousy had eaten away at Duryodhana to the point of obsession.

He looked at him fiercely. 'Behave like a warrior!' he said. 'You know very ell that we cannot begin until Arjuna blows his conch. No-one can change iis rule of battle. Focus your mind and calm your emotions, so that you an gather your energy for fighting.'

)uryodhana scowled at his teacher. Sullenly he cast his eyes back towards ie distant figures of his mortal enemies, who were still absorbed in onversation.

he atmosphere around Krishna and Arjuna was, in sharp contrast, filled vith a peaceful, gentle quality as Arjuna, in deep humility, sought to absorb ie knowledge that was his privilege to receive. Knowledge that would ee him from all his illusions.

'When you realise this truth Arjuna,' Krishna was saying, 'you will nev
be confused again. You will see clearly that everything in creation is a pa
of you and part of Me.

'Always remember that the goal of all selfless action is liberation ar
spiritual wisdom. Nothing is so holy or so sacred as this knowledge.
cannot be compared to anything just as you cannot compare the flowers
ambrosia to anything else.'

'What you say is true...' began Arjuna.

'Let us not waste any more time on this, Arjuna.' Krishna was determine
to make him understand.

'Listen very carefully now because I am going to tell you the only way b
which knowledge can be possessed.'

It seemed to Arjuna, as he gazed at the face of his master, that He wa
becoming increasingly more radiant the more He spoke. He was struc
once again, as he had been so many times, by the power of His nobilit
There He stood, in the middle of the battlefield, like a beautiful diamon
on a dark sea bed. Still and serene, completely unaffected by H
surroundings.

'Anyone with sincere faith who takes control of the senses,' He was sayin
'will rise to this wisdom. When that wisdom is established in your hea
and the tender shoots of peace start to break through, the light of the Se
will shine out. Then you will see limitless peace wherever you look.

'Once it settles in your heart, you will not be able to believe the great jo
that will spread out from within you in all directions.

'You know,' He said, 'nothing in this world can be compared to the pow
of pure wisdom. Even if you were full to the brim with sins, or drowning i
confusion, they would be blown away like a cloud in a hurricane.'

'Does this mean that wisdom is the highest thing there is?' Arjuna aske

Krishna nodded. 'And there is nothing more sacred,' He said.

'What kind of person attains this kind of knowledge, Krishna?'

'A man of faith, Arjuna,' He replied, 'because someone who is torn by doub
is like a blind man who has no idea of day or night.

'He is not able to distinguish between truth and falsehood, right or wron
Doubt is such a terrible trap for everyone.'

Arjuna knew that this was true. He had experienced himself how dou
completely eclipsed his intellect and poisoned his mind so that he could r
longer see clearly what to do.

'A doubting mind is unhappy in the present or the future,' Krishna adde
reinforcing His point.

'But if you can dedicate your actions in the way I have explained, a
remaining doubts will be destroyed in the fire of your awakening. Th
chains that bind you will fall away and you will find yourself poised i
your true Self at last.

'So stand up Arjuna and completely destroy the doubt that clutches a
your heart!'

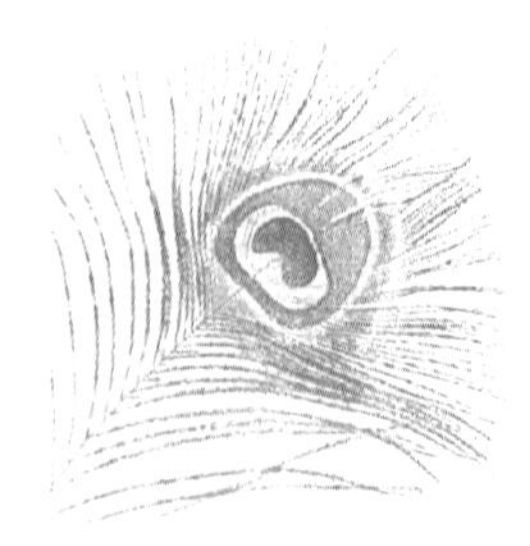

Someone who is torn by doubts
is like a blind man
who has no idea of day or night.
He is not able to distinguish
between truth and falsehood,
right and wrong.

Chapter Five

THE YOGA OF RENUNCIATION OF ACTION

Arjuna squinted against the sun's glare, trying to shake off th
wave of tiredness that was threatening to overcome him. S
much information, so many things to understand. He sighe
deeply, searching for some extra resource of energy with whic
to renew himself. Looking up at Krishna he said,

'You know, if you had just taught me one sure course of action, I woul
have found it a lot easier. But on the one hand you advise renunciation c
actions, and on the other you are praising the superior wisdom of selfles
action. Your words seem inconsistent, so please can you explain to m
once and for all, which one is better?'

Krishna was both pleased and bemused by Arjuna's remarks. He just raise
His eyebrows and smiled.

'Well, the path you show me must be straight and easy to follow and hav
a certain destination, must it not?' Arjuna added quickly.

The Lord of Love nodded wisely. 'It will be as you say Arjun,' He sai
affectionately. 'Listen and I will explain it clearly.'

He paused for a moment before continuing.

'In essence, there is no difference,' He said, 'and both paths lead to freedon
But if I had to choose between the two, I would say that selfless action i
better and easier than renunciation. The state of renunciation is actuall
very hard to reach without performing selfless action.

'Yet for everyone, both wise and ignorant, the yoga of action is very easy t
practise. And through the yoga of selfless action, a person will effortlessl
attain the fruit of renunciation! So you see, the two paths are not reall
different at all.'

'What is a true renunciatie, my Lord?' Arjuna said, still looking for clarity

'Someone who never grieves if they lose something and doesn't care if the
do not get anything, does not need to give up anything as such,' Krishn
replied, 'because his mind has become free from the influence of desire. I
the midst of worldly life, he is free from attachment.'

Krishna looked at him intently.

'For when a person gives up desire, Arjuna, he attains renunciation. Th
renunciation of action and the yoga of action then become joined!

'A person who has realised that these two paths are not different, as th
heavens and the sky are not different, has seen the Self.'

Krishna was very aware of Lord Hanuman's ensign flying above Him a
it flapped against the wood of the pole, almost trying to get His attentio

'Yes, Hanumanji, 'He thought to Himself, 'you are a perfect example
one who is a true renunciate, and yet who uses his knowledge to act wi
pure and selfless devotion.'

Inspired by the image of Hanuman, Krishna continued to explain.

'Those who follow the path of action, who have completely purifie
themselves and conquered their senses and self will, are not tainted b
their actions because they have understood that they are not the doer
those actions.

'The mind becomes purified through selfless action and disciplined throug
meditation. As the senses begin to quieten, you start to see who you real
are.'

'Who you really are...'

The words echoed through the labyrinth of Arjuna's mind. 'Who you reall
are...' There it was again - that familiar flavour of sweet longing. An almos
ancient feeling that seemed to stir so deep inside him...

'When you start to identify with your Real Self, it will become very clea
to you that you are not the one who moves among the sense objects. Eve
while seeing, hearing, touching, smelling, eating and speaking, you will b
aware that you are not the doer. Instead, you will realise that you are onl
a witness to all your actions.'

He grasped the front of the chariot with both hands, holding on firmly a
He spoke. 'Like the captain of a ship,' He said, 'you sit behind the whe

The mind becomes purified
through selfless action
and disciplined
through meditation.
As the senses begin
to quieten down,
you start to see
who you really are.

and observe its movement, but you know you are not driving it because is propelled by another, much greater power.'

He looked at Arjuna with intensity, willing him to understand the imager Arjuna nodded slowly to indicate that he had.

'You know how a lotus leaf is never touched by the water, but seems instea to almost float above it?'

He waited for Arjuna to acknowledge His question.

'In the same way, when you really let go of any attachment to the fruits your actions and instead dedicate them to Me, no sin can ever touch yo

'Your consciousness becomes completely unified and you can li contentedly in your body, the city of nine gates. And when you withdra your mind from external objects, you discover a spring of eternal pea within yourself.'

He glanced up at Hanuman again and smiled as if listening to somethin

'If you are selfishly attached to results, however,' He said cautiously, 'yc become fragmented and bound by everything you do because you will t tied by the knot of desire to the state of enjoying the results of your action

'A wise being performs all actions in the same way, but then complete lets go of them - as if he had not done them at all.

'When you become free from desire in this way you become one with tl Self and concepts such as 'doer' and 'act' simply cease to exist.

'But knowing who you are and continuously thinking about the Self, yc will find that you will begin to merge and settle into it.'

As Krishna began to describe the awakened state, Arjuna could feel onc again the now familiar stirring of recognition deep within him as the worc resonated with the part of him that already knew the truth.

'When the sun rises in the east,' Krishna continued, 'darkness immediate vanishes from the four corners of the earth and so it is when ignorance

And when you
withdraw your mind
from external objects,
you discover
a spring of eternal peace
in yourself.

destroyed and a person has reached harmony in all things.'

Arjuna looked puzzled. 'Can you explain what you mean by 'harmony i all things,' Krishna?' he asked.

Krishna could hardly wait to reply.

'Yes,' He said. 'It means someone who is free from desire and therefor detached. He follows worldly pursuits like everyone else, but at the sam time is completely free inside. He will not rejoice when good things happe or shudder when unpleasantness occurs.'

He paused, to make sure Arjuna understood what He was saying.

'He is truly God, Arjuna,' He said with feeling. 'Is it any wonder that h finds no pleasure in sense objects?'

'What do you mean, Krishna?' Arjuna was confused again.

'Well,' Krishna replied patiently, 'Once the Chakora bird has tasted clea moonbeams among beds of lotus flowers, would it ever want to lick sand?'

Arjuna smiled at the beauty of this imagery and Krishna waited for it t settle into his mind.

'When you have discovered the bliss of the Self, Arjun,' He said at last 'and attained Self-realisation, you will find you will just give up al attachment to, or pursuit of, sense objects quite naturally.'

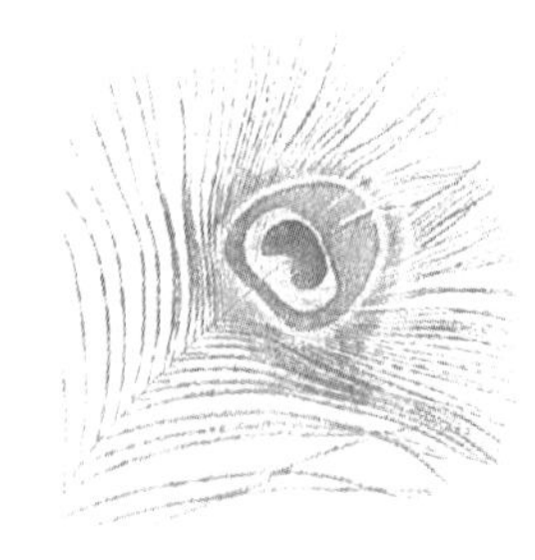

Once the Chakora bird
has tasted
clear moonbeams
among beds of lotus flowers,
would it ever want to lick sand?

Krishna looked at Arjuna's expression and saw that he was findin it hard to believe. 'Your curiosity will make you wonder about thi no doubt,' He said and Arjuna nodded.

'But you know, people who do not know themselves indulge in sens pleasures like a thirsty deer rushes at a mirage in the desert.

'It's important to understand that the happiness gained from enjoying sens objects is actually painful. But people are so deluded by the attractio that they feel that they cannot even live without these pleasures. To suc unfortunate people, pain seems to be the heart of pleasure, but they simpl cannot live without it, just like a fish cannot live without water.'

Arjuna felt slightly shocked by the truth in His words.

'But those who have learned to control their minds,' Krishna continue 'and the physical tendencies of the body, experience only bliss in their heart Their sense of separateness simply vanishes in the same way that the win is lost into the sky.

'When all trace of duality disappears could you say you are all that's left You are united in the embrace of the Lord, and in such a state of union tha only the bliss of the Self remains.

'Shutting out all external sense objects, focusing the attention betwee the eyebrows, equalising the inbreath and the outbreath, thus controllin the mind, senses and intelligence, the sage whose highest aim is freedo and from whom desire and anger have departed, is forever free.'

Arjuna sighed as the longing to experience this state swept over him agai

'How do you become like this?' he asked eagerly.

'First of all you must renounce desire, and once you have done that, yo must concentrate the mind within the body,' Krishna replied.

'With your gaze turned inwards and fixed between the eyebrows, equalis the incoming and outgoing breaths because when you control the breath, He explained, 'the mind becomes stilled in the inner space and desir ceases.'

But those who have learned
to control their minds,
and the physical tendencies of the body,
experience only bliss in their hearts.
Their sense of separateness
simply vanishes in the same way
that the wind is lost
into the sky.

Arjuna was filled with wonder and at the same time relieved, because a last here was a practical method he could easily understand and follow Krishna realised this and smiled.

'Have my words brought you peace of mind?' He asked.

'My Lord!' Arjuna replied. 'You are such a master at understanding th mind and I know you completely understand the way mine works.'

Krishna smiled a secret smile that said nothing and gave nothing away.

'But listen!' Arjuna was now filled with enthusiasm.

'The path you have shown me is indeed like a bridge which makes the rive easier to cross, but it seems to me that for people who are weak, the path o yoga is easier than the path of knowledge. Can you just help me t understand this a little more clearly?'

Sanjaya turned towards the King. He was excited. 'Oh great King,' h said, 'Listen to what Lord Krishna is about to explain to Arjuna. It is a though Krishna has prepared a great spiritual feast for him and we, th guests, have just arrived at the right time.

'Our good fortune is very great, dear master!' Sanjaya was so delighted t be able to hear the discussion between Krishna and Arjuna that he foun himself babbling like an excited child. 'We are like thirsty men who hav found water in the desert.'

Dhritarashtra was unmoved and unaffected by the information.

'Just get on with it,' he snapped impatiently.

Sanjaya understood what was in the King's heart. Blinded as he was by his love for his sons, he could not appreciate the great revelation that they were a party to.

'But how can he understand?' Sanjaya thought sadly. 'How can a blin man see the light of day? Only those who have given up all thought o heaven and earth out of love for Self-realisation can appreciate th sweetness of this knowledge.'

Only those who have given up
all thought of heaven and earth
out of love for Self-realisation
can appreciate the sweetness
of this knowledge.

He dare not say it, however, for fear of offending his beloved master an
instead, turned his divine gaze eagerly back inside himself to experienc
the precious dialogue between Sri Krishna and Arjuna.

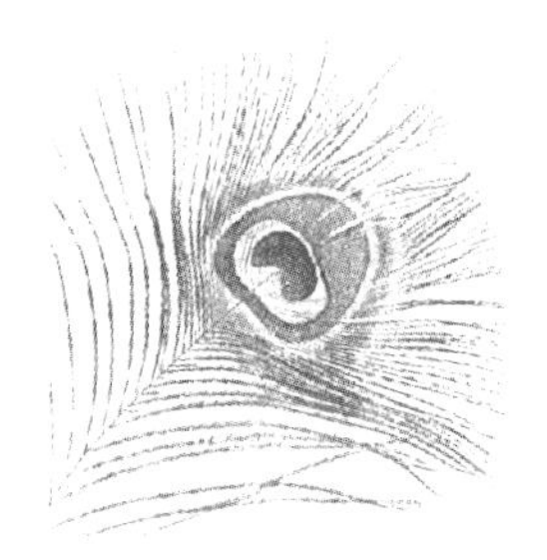

Chapter Six

THE YOGA OF MEDITATION

'Listen Arjuna.' Krishna's voice was, as always, full of patience an understanding, no trace of irritation ruffling His composure, eve though He must have answered this same question many times.

'The yogi and the sannyasin cannot be regarded as different, in the sam way that a person who has been given two names is still the same perso

'Please understand once and for all, Arjun, that a person is considered t be a true yogi if he performs actions with no desire for the fruits. He doe what is right and necessary without concern for the results.'

He could not help wondering how many times it would be necessary t repeat Himself before Arjuna understood. And with the power of thi thought, Arjuna responded unexpectedly as understanding was born insid him.

'Now I understand!' said Arjuna excitedly, 'that if you can perform you duty in the world selflessly, without desiring any reward for yourself, the you are a true renunciate!'

Arjuna smiled broadly, because at last he could see that renunciation an selfless action were the same. Krishna smiled too, with relief, because a last He could take him a step further.

'It's not enough just to renounce the fruits of your actions however, Arjuna, He said. 'You must have a firm control over your mind because it can eithe work for you as your dearest friend, or completely against you as your mos mortal enemy. It all depends on you.

'As you gain control of your mind with the help of the Higher Self, i becomes an ally, but the uncontrolled mind behaves like an enemy.'

As grey clouds were beginning to gather and sweep across the sky and th wind became stronger, Lord Hanuman's flag billowed and flapped loudl above them.

'Heaven and hell exist only in the mind, and the world is a perfect projectio of it. If there is hell in your mind, you could perceive those dark clouds a menacing and threatening, but if there is heaven in your mind, they can b

When the perfectly controlled mind
rests in the Self alone,
free from longing
for all objects of desires,
then it is said,
he is united.

seen as beautiful and exhilarating.'

Arjuna glanced up. So intent was he on Krishna's words, so acute hi
listening, that he had not even noticed the sky darkening, or the storn
clouds gathering on the horizon.

'It's so true,' he thought to himself. 'In this space of peace, nothing ca
touch me.'

He cast his mind back. How long ago was it when he first came onto th
battlefield and saw his friends and relatives in front of him? Five minutes
Five hours? How his mind had reacted to the sight of them! How mucl
control did he have then over the weakness that had seemed to overwheln
him? Did this mean that he was the slave to his mind and not the master

Krishna seemed to read his thoughts.

'Those who have mastered the mind are utterly content and not disturbe
by anything, no matter what it is,' He said quietly.

'The wise are equally friendly towards friends, companions, enemies, peopl
who are indifferent or hateful, saints and sinners alike.'

Arjuna felt suddenly downcast. 'How very far I am from that state,' h
thought sadly.

'How do you do it?' he said, his eyes anxious and questioning.

As he spoke, the sun emerged unexpectedly from behind the clouds, bathin
them both in a dazzling burst of light, although the armies either side wer
still shrouded in shadow.

Krishna looked at Arjuna lovingly.

He sensed the immense longing in Arjuna's heart and secretly knew tha
it would not be very long before the flower of union with God would burs
forth. Of this He was very sure, because Arjuna had glimpsed the abundan
fruit of liberation and nothing would stop him now until he had achieve
it.

You must learn to keep the mind steady through meditation,' He said without betraying His thoughts.

Find somewhere you can be alone, in solitude and establish a clean place of your own to sit. Ideally the seat should be made of cloth, deerskin and Kusha grass, one laid over the other and not too high or too low. Sit firmly, holding your spine, head and neck straight and still, keeping your head looking forward. Balance the inbreath and the outbreath and focus your mind on a single point between the eyebrows to bring it under control.

When the perfectly controlled mind rests in the Self alone, free from longing for all objects of desires, then it is said, 'He is united.'

You will have to practise with great determination not to give up, restraining all the senses from wandering. The goal is to quieten the mind so much that it becomes established in the Self, ceasing to think of anything at all. Every time it wanders, bring it back under control.

You will know when the mind becomes peaceful and harmonised because you will see the Self in everyone and everyone in the Self.'

Arjuna looked puzzled. What did He mean? See the Self in everyone? Krishna continued talking.

To those who have realised that I am in every creature, I am always with them, Arjuna.

They can see that all of life is my manifestation and therefore never become separated from Me. They worship Me in everyone and respond to the joys and sorrows of others as if they were their own.'

He paused, taking a deep breath and looking up at the sky before continuing. This is the very highest state of spiritual union,' He said at last.

Something snapped inside Arjuna. It was all too far above him. How could he, a simple Kshatriya, ever reach such a high spiritual state? He knew how little peace there was in his mind and how difficult it was to control.

'Oh Krishna,' he said, 'this stillness of divine union that you describe is completely beyond me. Not only is the mind restless and turbulent,

t is also powerfully obstinate. Trying to control it is like trying to tame he wind.'

As if in response to His words, the wind cut across the plains with a sudden nd mighty roar, shaking the chariot and disturbing the horses who reared nd strained under Krishna's hand. As soon as it died down again, Krishna nswered him.

Yes, it is true,' He said. 'There is no doubt that the mind is restless and difficult to control.' He tightened His hold on the reins and waited for the horses to become calm again. 'But it can be done, Arjuna,' He said.

How?' Arjuna's voice betrayed his disbelief. Krishna's voice was strong and commanding.

It is possible, through regular practice and detachment, with self control and great determination,' He said with the conviction of one who knew.

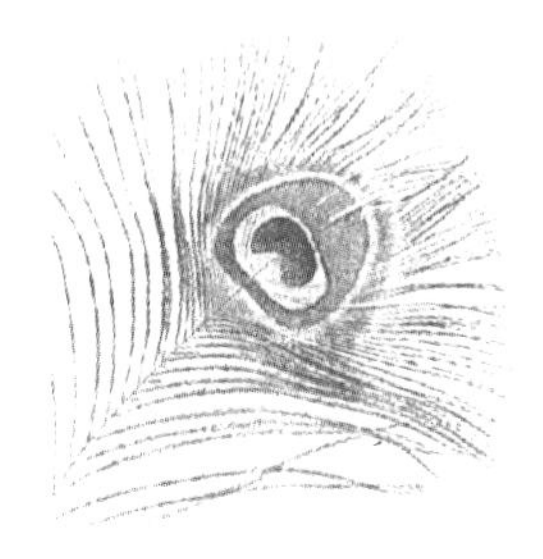

The atmosphere on the plains became very still once again as th wind died down and settled. Arjuna's heart sank with the winc He just could not believe he would ever be able to achieve this kin of control and for a moment panic seized him. What would happen if h was not able to do it?

He turned to his teacher. 'Krishna,' he asked hoarsely, trying to hide hi anxiety.

'What happens to someone who lacks the self-control to master his mind If he wanders off the spiritual path, will he lose the support of both worlds like a cloud scattered across the sky?'

Krishna looked at him, assessing what was going on in his mind, hesitatin to empower any thought of failure.

'Krishna!' Arjuna pleaded with Him, 'you are the only one who can dispe my doubt about this; please tell me.'

Krishna's compassion got the better of Him. He could feel Arjuna' desperation and His heart melted at His devotee's words. His eye softened.

'Arjuna, my son,' He said quietly, His voice infused with love. 'Such person will never be destroyed.'

Arjuna visibly relaxed.

'No-one who does good work can ever come to a bad end,' He continued

'Not in this world or the world to come. Whoever leaves his body befor reaching the highest goal, attains a heavenly state.

'He will stay there for a long time, enjoying the effects of his good deed before taking birth again in a pure and prosperous family where he ca continue where he left off.'

He smiled reassuringly at Arjuna.

The menacing storm clouds had completely vanished from the now clear ky that stretched over the field of Kurukshetra.

Or, he will be reborn into a family of wise, spiritual people; but such a irth in this world is very rare indeed. He will soon remember the knowledge e gained in his former births and can strive for realisation with even more etermination.

Through persistent effort over many lifetimes he will become purified of ll selfish desire and reach the supreme goal of life. He then rises above the scetics with mystic powers and all those who do good deeds.'

He looked Arjuna straight in the eyes.

Arjuna! Become that man!' He said passionately.

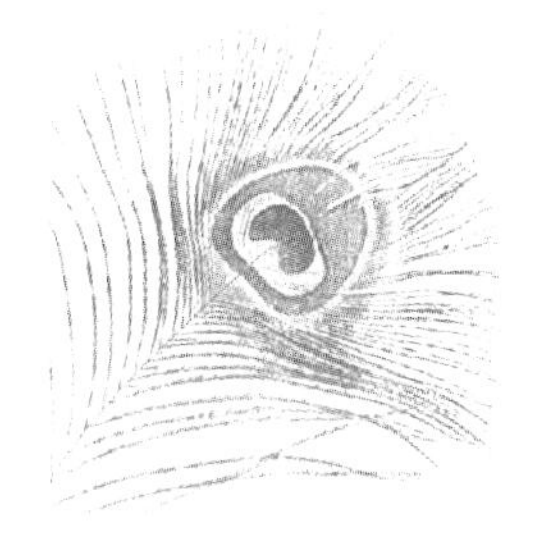

— Part Two —

Living the Gita

John Jones & Savitri MacCuish

The Bhagavad Gita has taug
me many things over the year
not least that it is possible to b
content as a human being an
to be free from emotions of sorrow, self-pity, anger and greed, fear and despair. The Gita teaches about birth and death and the impermanent nature of the body, which can completely free us from the fear of death. In fact, every answer to every problem is contained within its pages.

Eurowalk, through the eyes of the Gita, has taught me to shar the tears of one orphaned child and the smile on the face of another. To notice the raindrops glistening on leaves and to hug grandmother who is sobbing because her children and their children have been pulled from this world into the next, leaving her behind to live on.

I have learned to share the pain of life with people and yet no to be afraid to raise my arms and sing at the wonder of creation. There is a great freedom in feeling your heart skip a beat when the sun takes out its full palette and paints an exquisite picture o farewell over the railway tracks and camps of Birkenau...

Mahatma Gandhi talked about *prayer in action* and to me it has been so important to find a practical application for the great knowledge and wisdom of the Gita. I have found that personal experience is one of the finest ways of bringing the Gita alive inside you. Eurowalk has taught me how to put the teachings of the Gita into action and I have found that it comes alive when yo find a way *to live it.* You must live it and make it your own experience.

Walking across the earth through different seasons, countries, terrains nd borders can change your life, but walking with the Gita as your guide neans that life becomes a magical and enchanting journey. This is truly ur experience.

Mahatma Gandhi said, '*You too can do as I have done, if you bring the ame singleness of purpose that I have brought. The same faith that I brought. It is vithin everyone's reach.*'

I truly believe this and there is no doubt in my mind that the spirit of ne Gita will come to sit on the shoulder of any one of us who cares to are for life.

Savitri

My friendship with the Bhagavad Gita began over twenty years ago while I was an undergraduate at university with Mansukh during the seventies. One cold November day he introduced me to his parents, who exuded a deep feeling of spirituality that was so genuine, tangible and practical that I found it irresistibly attractive. I often heard Mansukh talking about the Gita with his parents. I had struggled with its text myself.

t seemed an unfathomable mystery to me and in spite of all my efforts emained so for several years. Whilst staying with Mum and Dad, as they ecame known to me, in their little terraced house in the Midlands, I first saw Dad consult his Gita. He kept two almost identical books - one had a pale green cover and the other a dark brown one, both carefully wrapped in a meditation shawl. I was struck by the way in which he handled them, with a kind of reverence and respect that I had never see before.

As he unwrapped the little bundle of cloth he seemed transported into another world. To me, he wasn't so much consulting a mere book containing printed pages, as approaching with great humility his belovec spiritual preceptor.

By the soft light of his little butter lamp it was as if his whole body wer drinking in the silent benediction that surrounded him. I felt that I had been privy to a meeting that was intensely personal and yet somehow ancient and noble. This experience made such an impression on me, that I felt prompted to ask him if he would help me to establish a similar relationship with the Gita and to my delight he agreed.

With Dad's help, the Gita's magic began to come alive for me. Experiences and teachings that had remained isolated and disconnected gradually began to resolve themselves into a cohesive picture. Momentary insights took on a new significance in the light of my daily readings and with each new revelation came a sense of freedom and certainty that continues to grow to this day. In 1993 Dad passed away and among the many treasures he left me was one of his precious Gitas. Its pages are yellowed and fragile but wherever I go on Eurowalk that little book goes with me.

It has guided me all over the world, whether walking through the Wes Bank in Palestine, the Shankhill Road in Northern Ireland, or playing football with refugees in Bosnia, the Gita has demonstrated to me that whatever challenges we face, the fundamental answers to life's questions all lie within the heart of the Gita, just waiting for us to be ready to receive them.

John

Contents - Part Two

Living the Gita

by John Jones and Savitri MacCuish

Page No.

The Bhagavad Gita

Chapter One

The Despondency of Arjuna

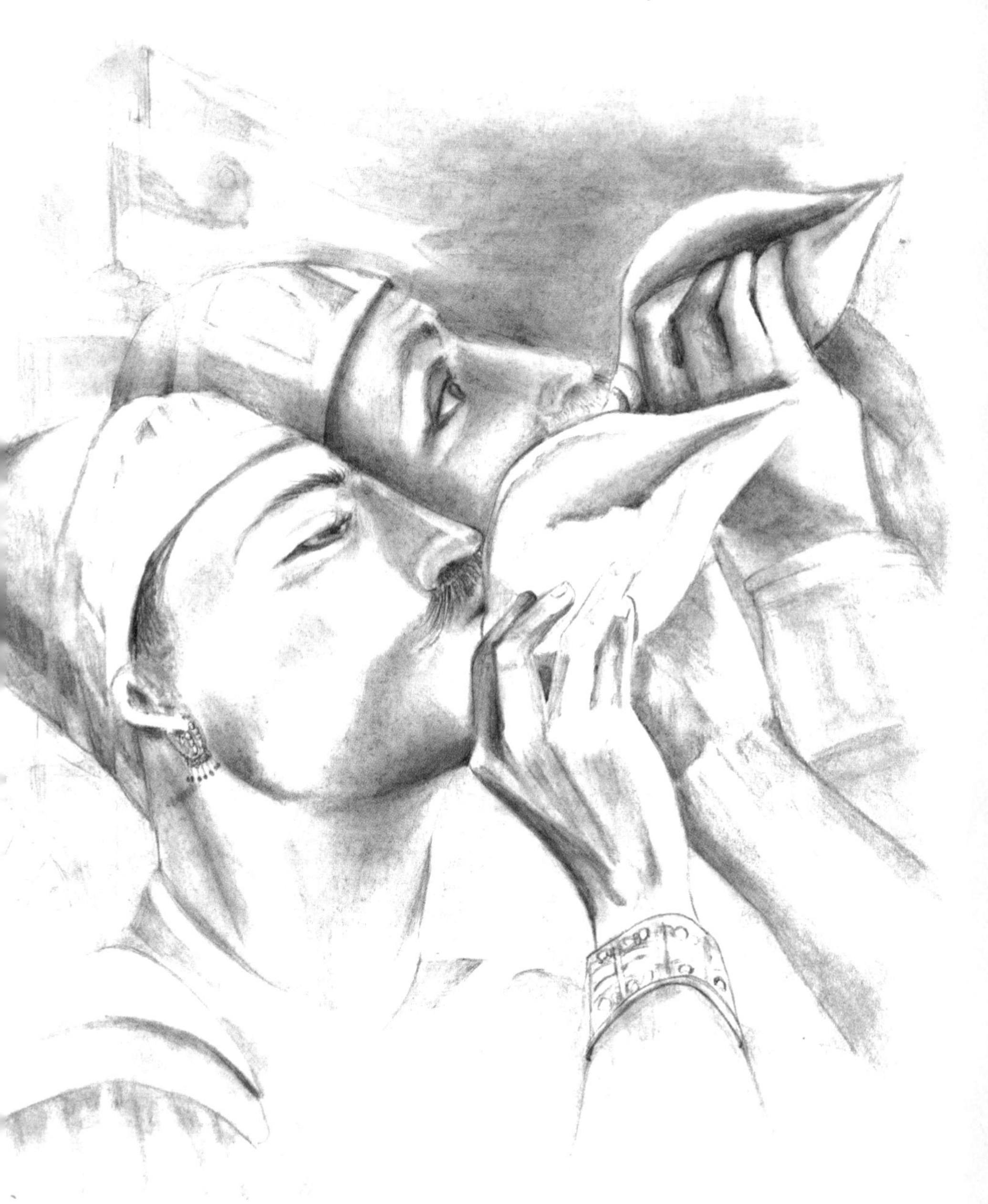

धृतराष्ट्र उवाच
धर्मक्षेत्रे कुरुक्षेत्रे समवेता युयुत्सवः ।
मामकाः पाण्डवाश्चैव किमकुर्वत संजय ॥१॥

Sloka 1
dhritaraashtra uvaacha:
dharma kshetre kuru kshetre
samavetaa yuyutsavaha
maamakaah paandavaas chaiva
kim akurvata sanjaya

1 - King Dhritarashtra said: O Sanjaya, tell me what my sons and the sons of Pandu did as they gathered, ready to fight at the holy place of pilgrimage known as Kurukshetra.

In the Vedic tradition of India, the first word of any great scripture w always give us the key to its central message. The Gita begins with the word, 'Dharmakshetre' which means *the field of dharma.* 'Dharma' mean to live in a way which is true to our higher nature or *real identity* which has nothing to do with the name we are given by our parents. Neither is it related to the job we do, our nationality, or even personality. It is an identity that is deeper and more intrinsic than any of the ways we might normally choose to describe ourselves.

As a royal baby abandoned at birth might grow up in a normal family completely unaware of its birthright, so we too are all unaware of our own real identity. We can go through life completely ignorant of our higher nature and oblivious to the privilege of the freedom that we are born for, hidden from us as it is by ignorance, just as the darkness of a moonless night hides the beauty of a garden. This ignorance, or blindness, is at the root of all our suffering and pain. And so it is fitting that Dhritarashtra, the blind king who represents this ignorance, shoulc speak the first verse of the Gita.

Dharma also means flowing in total synchronicity with the universe, always doing the right thing, in the right place, at the right time. We ca only do this when we are working from our centre, in touch with who w really are.

Kshetra means field, so Dharma-kshetra is the place where a human eing can discover his true nature and hence his purpose. This place ctually exists within the vastness of our own mind, and in Chapter One, 'eda Vyasa, the compiler of the Bhagavad Gita, is describing all the haracters that inhabit 'the holy plain' of the mind. On the one side we ave an army of selfish, negative tendencies, with which we are all amiliar, represented by the Kauravas.

On the other side we have a smaller array of selfless virtues epresented by the Pandavas and perhaps not so familiar to us. The eason the battlefield is referred to as 'holy' is because the mind is ctually a place of great divinity, even though it hosts an army of horoughly undesirable characters. It is the place where realisation of the elf - the Greater Self - can take place, with the help of our virtues.

The Gita makes it clear that it is the ignorant mind, plus the negative raits within us, that are responsible for the suffering in our lives. Another very significant point is that it is also within the mind - the field of action - (karma-kshetra) - that our whole quest of seeking resolution to his suffering begins. This means that in the place where the conflict lies, *here you will find the solution.*

Today

The Gita begins with a question. What happened when the sons of Pandu and Dhritarashtra gathered at Kurukshetra? Similarly, we prepare to begin our journey together with an enquiry: What has brought me to this point in my life? As you ask yourself this question, be grateful for the opportunity hat this now presents to you.

संजय उवाच
दृष्ट्वा तु पाण्डवानीकं व्यूढं दुर्योधनस्तदा ।
आचार्यमुपसंगम्य राजा वचनमब्रवीत् ॥२॥

पश्यैतां पाण्डुपुत्राणामाचार्य महतीं चमूम् ।
व्यूढां द्रुपदपुत्रेण तव शिष्येण धीमता ॥३॥

Slokas 2 - 3
sanjaya uvaacha:
drishtvaa tu paandavaaneekam
vyoodham duryodhanas tadaa
aachaaryam upasangamya
raajaa vachanam abraveet

pasyaitaam paandu putraanaam
aachaarya mahateem chamoom
vyoodhaam drupada putrena
tava sishyena dheemataa

2 - Sanjaya said: Having seen the Pandava army arrayed in battle formation, King Duryodhana approached his teacher and said,
3 - O my teacher, look at this great army of the Pandavas, so magnificently arranged by your gifted disciple, the son of Drupada!

Duryodhana, Dhritarashtra's eldest son, is the first participant in the battle to speak. Aggressive, arrogant and boastful, he has little or no respect for his teachers and elders and in this verse, although he acknowledges the Pandavas are a formidable adversary, he is really scoffing at them. This is what the mind will do to us when we try to be good and virtuous. It will tell us we are *doing really well* - when we are not - just to mislead us and it will also make us very attached to tendencies that actually imprison us. The ego loves to react and counter-react and it can be very clever in the process. For our purposes, we can see that when we give vent to our negative tendencies, *and express them* - as Duryodhana does, it creates suffering and pain in our lives.

Today

When you embark on this spiritual journey, be aware of the flippant nature of the mind and watch out for thoughts like, 'I don't know why I am bothering with this because it's all a waste of time.' Instead say to the mind, 'This is the most important thing that has ever happened to me.'

अत्र शूरा महेष्वासा भीमार्जुनसमा युधि ।
युयुधानो विराटश्च द्रुपदश्च महारथः ॥४॥

धृष्टकेतुश्चेकितानः काशिराजश्च वीर्यवान् ।
पुरुजित्कुन्तिभोजश्च शैब्यश्च नरपुङ्गवः ॥५॥

युधामन्युश्च विक्रान्त उत्तमौजाश्च वीर्यवान् ।
सौभद्रो द्रौपदेयाश्च सर्व एव महारथाः ॥६॥

Slokas 4 - 6
atra sooraa maheshv aasaa
bheemaarjuna samaa yudhi
yuyudhaano viraatas cha
drupadas cha mahaa rathaha

dhrishtaketus chekitaanaha
kaasiraajas cha veeryavaan
purujit kuntibhojas cha
saibyas cha nara pungavaha

yudhaamanyus cha vikraanta
uttamaujaas cha veeryavaan
saubhadro draupadeyaas cha
sarva eva mahaa rathaha

4 & 5 - *There are great heroes and mighty archers, equal in battle to Bhima and Arjuna, Yuyudhana and Virata and the great chariot fighter Draupada. See also Drishtaketu, Chekitana, the valiant King of Kasi, Purujit, Kuntibhoja, and the great leader of men Saibya.*
6 - *They also have the courageous Yudhamanyu, the very powerful Uttamaujas, Subhadra's son and the sons of Draupadi; these are all great warriors and chariot fighters.*

Duryodhana lists the warriors in the Pandava army and acknowledges their presence and strength although not in order to admire them, but rather to *undermine* them. In the same way, the ego will always look at ou positive efforts and do the same, telling us not to bother being nice, kinc or generous to people, simply because they will not appreciate it. The ego-mind is so quick to judge and will say things like, 'See! I told you kindness doesn't pay!' If it could only wait, however, the results would soon show that kindness really *does* pay. The ego also stops us from seein that the only real values in life are peace, joy and inner security, which is why the fragmented ego-mind needs to be transformed into one unified mind.

Today

Don't give negative tendencies any space! Be patient with yourself and others, giving time for goodness to emerge.

अस्माकं तु विशिष्टा ये तान्निबोध द्विजोत्तम ।
नायका मम सैन्यस्य संज्ञार्थं तान्ब्रवीमि ते ॥७॥

भवान्भीष्मश्च कर्णश्च कृपश्च समितिंजयः ।
अश्वत्थामा विकर्णश्च सौमदत्तिस्तथैव च ॥८॥

Slokas 7 - 8

asmaakam tu visishtaa ye
taan nibodha dvijottama
naayakaa mama sainyasya
samjnaartham taan braveemi te

bhavaan bheeshmas cha karnas cha
kripas cha samitim jayaha
asvatthaamaa vikarnas cha
saumadattis tathaiva cha

7 - I'll tell you, who are the best of brahmins and the highest of the twice born, the names of our leaders who are equally distinguished.
8 - People like yourself and Bhishma, Karna and Kripa, Aswatthama, Vikarna and Jayadratha, the son of Somadatta.

Duryodhana is feeling insecure because of the great magnitude of the Pandava forces, so he quickly starts to praise his own army in order to boost his self confidence. It is always a sign of fear when a leader starts to panic and say things to bolster his own morale. In the same way, the ego will happily enumerate its good qualities, never skimping on detail to tell us how clever we are and what a powerful intellect we have and how we can beat anybody in an argument. But Duryodhana's words have no real power or strength behind them.

Today

Dronacharya is referred to as 'the twice born.' The one born again in spirit. Start today feeling that you have been born again and are just beginning this journey with a renewed sense of freshness and lightness.

अन्ये च बहवः शूरा मदर्थे त्यक्तजीविताः ।
नानाशस्त्रप्रहरणाः सर्वे युद्धविशारदाः ॥९॥

Sloka 9
anye cha bahavah sooraa
mad arthe tyakta jeevitaaha
naanaa sastra praharanaaha
sarve yuddha visaaradaaha

9 - And many other heroes and well trained warriors who are ready to give their lives - all for me.

Duryodhana is now starting to boast that all these brave warriors are willing to give up their lives *just for him*, when really he should be feeling ashamed. He is responsible for the fact that his whole dynasty is about to be destroyed, but in his arrogance he puffs himself up with pride. The ego will give up anything to save itself and the more threatened it feels, the more sacrifices it is willing to make.

Today

Recognise that there are many obstacles on this path, but that each one of them will be easily overcome eventually. The first obstacle that you face will be the ego, which will always say that it is not possible. Do not believe it!

अपर्याप्तं तदस्माकं बलं भीष्माभिरक्षितम् ।
पर्याप्तं त्विदमेतेषां बलं भीमाभिरक्षितम् ॥१०॥

Sloka 10
aparyaaptam tad asmaakam
balam bheeshmaabhir~akshitam
paryaaptam tvidam eteshaam
balam bheemaabhir~akshitam

10 - Our army is unlimited and perfectly protected by grandfather Bhishma whereas theirs is small and insignificant under Bhima's protection.

Duryodhana is trying to reassure himself that what they are doing is right and convincing himself at the same time that they are more powerful than the Pandavas. A person on the wrong side will always boost their own ego. Bhishma, one of the greatest warriors that ever lived, represents one of our most powerful and cherished qualities. The one that is so brave and strong, that we can always depend on to stand up for us, to fight to defend and protect our interests. No matter how kind or reassuring our tendency may be however, it will always cause us problems if we are against dharma.

Today

Remember that the mind is so arrogant that it will never admit defeat and will always think that it is in control and cannot be beaten. That is its nature.

अयनेषु च सर्वेषु यथाभागमवस्थिताः ।
भीष्ममेवाभिरक्षन्तु भवन्तः सर्व एव हि ॥११॥

तस्य संजनयन्हर्षं कुरुवृद्धः पितामहः ।
सिंहनादं विनद्योच्चैः शङ्खं दध्मौ प्रतापवान् ॥१२॥

ततः शङ्खाश्च भेर्यश्च पणवानकगोमुखाः ।
सहसैवाभ्यहन्यन्त स शब्दस्तुमुलोऽभवत् ॥१३॥

Slokas 11 - 13

ayaneshu cha sarveshu
yathaa bhaagam avasthitaaha
bheeshmam evaabhir~akshantu
bhavantah sarva eva hi

tasya sanjanayan harsham
kuru vriddhah pitaamahaha
simha naadam vinadyoch~chaih
sankham dadhmau prataapavaan

tatah sankhaas cha bheryas cha
panavaanaka gomukhaaha
sahasaivaabhya~hanyanta
sa sabdas tumulo 'bhavat

11 - All of you must now take your positions and give full support to Bhishma.
12 - Then Bhishma, the mighty great-grandfather of the Kauravas, in order to please Duryodhana, roared like a lion and blew his conch shell very loudly.
13 - Hearing this, all the Kurus began sounding their conches, cowhorns, tabors and trumpets, creating a tremendous noise.

Bhishma starts off the battle by roaring loudly and sounding his conch shell. Similarly, when the ego starts to panic, you can be sure it will always make a noise to show its strength. The result will be chaos and confusion as the power of our vices wash over us like a tidal wave, just as a football team who realise they are losing will start to argue with each other, a sure sign that they *will* lose.

Today

The Kauravas conches represent all the desires and noise that the mind and ego make. When the conches of your mind blow be aware that they awaken the ego's defence system and you become reactive and defensive like a strutting peacock. So today, refuse to give strength to the ego when it throws up excuses for not being quiet.

ततः श्वेतैर्हयैर्युक्ते महति स्यन्दने स्थितौ ।
माधवः पाण्डवश्चैव दिव्यौ शङ्खौ प्रदध्मतुः ॥१४॥

Sloka 14
tatah svetair hayair yukte
mahati syandane sthitau
maadhavah paandavas chaiva
divyau sankhau pradadhmatuhu

14 - Then Madhava and Arjuna, standing in their magnificent chariot drawn by white horses, also blew their divine conches.

Sanjaya uses Krishna's name Madhava which represents victory. By using this name Sanjaya predicts Arjuna's victory right from the start.

Today

It is time to be courageous and to stand up to the challenges in your life!

पाञ्चजन्यं हृषीकेशो देवदत्तं धनंजयः।
पौण्ड्रं दध्मौ महाशङ्खं भीमकर्मा वृकोदरः॥१५॥

अनन्तविजयं राजा कुन्तीपुत्रो युधिष्ठिरः।
नकुलः सहदेवश्च सुघोषमणिपुष्पकौ॥१६॥

काश्यश्च परमेष्वासः शिखण्डी च महारथः।
धृष्टद्युम्नो विराटश्च सात्यकिश्चापराजितः॥१७॥

द्रुपदो द्रौपदेयाश्च सर्वशः पृथिवीपते।
सौभद्रश्च महाबाहुः शङ्खान्दध्मुः पृथक्पृथक्॥१८॥

स घोषो धार्तराष्ट्राणां हृदयानि व्यदारयत्।
नभश्च पृथिवीं चैव तुमुलो व्यनुनादयन्॥१९॥

Slokas 15 - 19
paanchajanyam hrisheekeso
devadattam dhananjayaha
paundram dadhmau mahaa sankham
bheema karmaa vrikodaraha

anantavijayam raajaa
kuntee putro yudhishthiraha
nakulah sahadevas cha
sughosha manipushpakau

kaasyas cha parameshv aasaha
sikhandee cha mahaa rathaha
dhrishtadyumno viraatas cha
saatyakis chaaparaajitaha

drupado draupadeyaas cha
sarvasah prithivee pate
saubhadras cha mahaa baahuhu
sankhaan dadhmuh prithak prithak

sa ghosho dhaartaraashtraanaam
hridayaani vyadaarayat
nabhas cha prithiveem chaiva
tumulo 'bhyanunaadayan

15 - Krishna blew his conch known as Panchajanya, while Arjuna blew Devadatta and the mighty Bhima blew the huge conch Paundra.
16 - King Yudhishthira, the son of Kunti, blew Anantavijaya and Nakula and Sahadeva blew the Sughosha and Manipushpaka.
17 - The supreme archer the King of Kasi, the great warrior Sikhandi, Dhrishtadyumna, Virata and the unbeatable Satyaki;
18 - Drupada, all the sons of Draupadi and Subhadra's son with the mighty arms - all blew their conches.
19 - The deafening sound filled heaven and earth with such a roar that it tore at the hearts of the Kauravas.

Just as the stars fade when the sun rises, all the Kauravas' war-like sounds are completely silenced by Krishna's conch and those of the Pandavas. At the moment when we realise the truth about our mind, the very realisation of that truth silences the mind totally. We then get a glimpse of the peace that exists in our real nature. This is what is symbolised here by Krishna's conch. Over and over again the Gita emphasises that voluntary surrender to our Higher Self is the most important gesture we can ever make in our life, so that all the forces of good can be allowed to continue to bring us back into balance.

Today

Blow the conches of all the different virtues within you. Be generous, kind, loving, peaceful and humble, and let the very act of focusing on these qualities still the restless mind. If you find it hard to manage all these qualities, then just focus on one or two, like generosity with humility.

अथ व्यवस्थितान्दृष्ट्वा धार्तराष्ट्रान्कपिध्वजः ।
प्रवृत्ते शस्त्रसंपाते धनुरुद्यम्य पाण्डवः ॥२०॥
हृषीकेशं तदा वाक्यमिदमाह महीपते ।

अर्जुन उवाच
सेनयोरुभयोर्मध्ये रथं स्थापय मेऽच्युत ॥२१॥

यावदेतान्निरीक्षेऽहं योद्धुकामानवस्थितान् ।
कैर्मया सह योद्धव्यमस्मिन्रणसमुद्यमे ॥२२॥

योत्स्यमानानवेक्षेऽहं य एतेऽत्र समागताः ।
धार्तराष्ट्रस्य दुर्बुद्धेर्युद्धे प्रियचिकीर्षवः ॥२३॥

Slokas 20 - 23
atha vyavasthitaan drishtvaa
dhaartaraashtraan kapi dhvajaha
pravritte sastra sampaate
dhanur udyamya paandavaha
hrisheekesam tadaa vaakyam
idam aaha mahee pate

arjuna uvaacha:
senayor ubhayor madhye
ratham sthaapaya me 'chyuta

yaavad etaan nireekshe 'ham
yoddhu kaamaan avasthitaan
kair mayaa saha yoddhavyam
asmin rana samudyame

yotsyamaanaan avekshe 'ham
ya ete 'tra samaagataaha
dhaartaraashtrasya durbuddher
yuddhe priya chikeershavaha

20 - Then Arjuna, sitting in his chariot flying the flag of Lord Hanuman, having seen Duryodhana's forces drawn up in battle array, raised his bow and turning to Lord Krishna said,
21 & 22 - O Hrishikesha (Lord of the Earth), please place my chariot between the two armies so that I can clearly see who I have to fight when the battle begins.
23 - I want to see those who have come here to fight wishing to please the evil-minded Duryodhana.

Arjuna asks Krishna to show him exactly who he is up against. Each one of us has an enemy, although we may not know who or what it is, and we have to appeal to the highest part of ourselves to show us where this obstacle to our progress really lies. We need to ask specifically, 'What things that please the mind do I have to fight?' For a serious seeker, this question arises as a questing from deep inside and a search for understanding beyond the conditions we experience.

Today

Take the trouble to ask the universe to show you what you have to fight and be assured that you will be shown.

संजय उवाच
एवमुक्तो हृषीकेशो गुडाकेशेन भारत।
सेनयोरुभयोर्मध्ये स्थापयित्वा रथोत्तमम् ॥२४॥

भीष्मद्रोणप्रमुखतः सर्वेषां च महीक्षिताम्।
उवाच पार्थ पश्यैतान्समवेतान्कुरूनिति ॥२५॥

Slokas 24 - 25
sanjaya uvaacha:
evam ukto hrisheekeso
gudaakesena bhaarata
senayor ubhayor madhye
sthaapayitvaa rathottamam

bheeshma drona pramukhataha
sarveshaam cha mahee kshitaam
uvaacha paartha pasyaitaan
samavetaan kuroon iti

24 - Sanjaya said: As Arjuna commanded, Lord Krishna drove his chariot and placed it between the two armies.
25 - In front of Bhishma, Drona and all the kings of the earth He said, 'Behold all the Kurus assembled here, Arjuna!'

Once we have asked the question, we realise we have a battle on our hands! Krishna immediately responds to Arjuna's request with a seemingly harmless remark, His only utterance in Chapter One. It is an all-important one however, because He deliberately draws Arjuna's attention to the Kauravas and the forces of darkness. In other words, once we have asked the Lord to show us our selfishness - He will!

Today

Accept whatever the universe chooses to give you as a gift, whether it be happiness or sadness. For only in this acceptance will the answer to your question become clear.

तत्रापश्यत्स्थितान्पार्थः पितॄनथ पितामहान् ।
आचार्यान्मातुलान्भ्रातॄन् पुत्रान्पौत्रान्सखींस्तथा ॥२६॥

श्वशुरान्सुहृदश्चैव सेनयोरुभयोरपि ।
तान्समीक्ष्य स कौन्तेयः सर्वान्बन्धूनवस्थितान् ॥२७॥
कृपया परयाविष्टो विषीदन्निदमब्रवीत् ।

Slokas 26 - 27
tatraapasyat sthitaan paarthaha
pitrin atha pitaamahaan
aachaaryaan maatulaan bhraatrin
putraan pautraan sakheems tathaa

svasuraan suhridas chaiva
senayor ubhayor api
taan sameekshya sa kaunteyaha
sarvaan bandhoon avasthitaan
kripayaa parayaavishto
visheedann idam abraveet

26 & 27 - As he stood there, Arjuna could see fathers and grandfathers, teachers, uncles, brothers, sons and grandsons, friends and also his fathers-in-law and well wishers. Seeing his friends and relatives standing before him as his enemies, Arjuna became overwhelmed by confusion and pity, saying,

Arjuna is standing on his own with Krishna by his side as he surveys all his attachments. What is the first thing we do when we arrive at the altar of the Lord? We close our eyes. We can compare this moment to the start of our meditation practice. When we close our eyes we can be alone with God in a place where we can see clearly what is happening. It is a place of stillness and quiet where we can observe clearly. This is when the Kauravas start to appear!

Today

Watch yourself closely. Observe yourself in happiness or irritation. Just observe, do not judge and take no action.

अर्जुन उवाच
दृष्ट्वेमं स्वजनं कृष्ण युयुत्सुं समुपस्थितम् ॥२८॥

सीदन्ति मम गात्राणि मुखं च परिशुष्यति ।
वेपथुश्च शरीरे मे रोमहर्षश्च जायते ॥२९॥

गाण्डीवं स्रंसते हस्तात्त्वक्चैव परिदह्यते ।
न च शक्नोम्यवस्थातुं भ्रमतीव च मे मनः ॥३०॥

Slokas 28 - 30
arjuna uvaacha:
drishtvemam sva janam krishna
yuyutsum samupasthitam

seedanti mama gaatraani
mukham cha parisushyati
vepathus cha sareere me
roma harshas cha jaayate

gaandeevam sramsate hastaat
twak chaiva paridahyate
na cha saknomy avasthaatum
bhramateeva cha me manaha

28 & 29 - Arjuna said: O Krishna, having seen my own people wanting to fight, my limbs are weak, my mouth is dry, my body trembles and my hair stands on end.
30 - My skin is burning and the Gandiva bow slips from my hand. I can't even stand and my mind is reeling.

Arjuna is in shock! As soon as we start to clearly see our habit patterns, fears, desires and anger, we realise they have always been there. We have never thought of them as enemies, but rather as treasured parts of ourselves which we have cultivated and even *nurtured* for our own survival. They are like old friends to us, even though they actually constitute the very *source* of our suffering. We may not have recognised them before, but once spotted, our first impulse will be to run! We may start to show strange symptoms and even become ill rather than face and deal with the inner turmoil it creates, because we simply do not have the courage to face ourselves. But the truth is, there is *nowhere to hide* because the problems of the mind will always be with us until we are prepared to deal with them.

Today

At first it is difficult to realise just how little control you sometimes have. You may have noticed this yesterday in your observations. Accept this truth, and affirm to yourself, 'I have the courage to change my life because I know I am never on my own.'

निमित्तानि च पश्यामि विपरीतानि केशव ।
न च श्रेयोऽनुपश्यामि हत्वा स्वजनमाहवे ॥३१॥

Sloka 31
nimittaani cha pasyaami
vipareetaani kesava
na cha sreyo 'nupasyaami
hatvaa sva janam aahave

31 - O Kesava, I see bad omens and misfortune resulting from destroying my own people in battle!

Here come all the excuses as the mind begins to squirm and tries to wriggle out of the situation. Of course there are bad omens - bad for the ego! It is like trying to give up a bad habit like smoking. The mind will use every trick in the book to persuade us that it will not be the best thing for us and that there really cannot be any good in it!

Today

In your heart of hearts you know those things about you that are negative. When the mind tries to trick you and says, 'You don't really need to change this,' be honest and affirm, 'Oh yes I do!'

न काङ्क्षे विजयं कृष्ण न च राज्यं सुखानि च ।
किं नो राज्येन गोविन्द किं भोगैर्जीवितेन वा ॥३२॥

येषामर्थे काङ्क्षितं नो राज्यं भोगाः सुखानि च ।
त इमेऽवस्थिता युद्धे प्राणांस्त्यक्त्वा धनानि च ॥३३॥

Slokas 32 - 33
na kaankshe vijayam krishna
na cha raajyam sukhaani cha
kim no raajyena govinda
kim bhogair jeevitena vaa

yeshaam arthe kaankshitam no
raajyam bhogaah sukhaani cha
ta ime 'vasthitaa yuddhe
praanaams tyaktvaa dhanaani cha

2 & 33 - O Krishna! I do not desire victory, kingdom or even pleasures. Vhat use is a kingdom, O Govinda, or happiness or even life itself when all hose for whom we would desire a kingdom are standing before us?

At the sight of his relatives, Arjuna, overwhelmed by his own owerlessness and confusion, lets his bow slip from his hand because he o longer has the strength to hold it. This symbolises the disempowering f our self-will. Once we have decided to face ourselves, then the things hat come up from the depths of our mind can be so strong that they ompletely take our power away from us unless we know how to handle hem. We can feel this same kind of dejection and it takes *great courage* nd every ounce of resolution and strength we can find to face this onfrontation.

Today

\rjuna refers to Krishna as 'Govinda', which literally means, 'Winner of the Vorld' because at that particular moment he certainly didn't feel like inning anymore. He is disempowering himself, because he cannot face the b he has to do. This is exactly what we do: we disempower ourselves at very turn. Affirm to yourself, 'Just being on this journey is enough to uarantee me a place on the finishing line. I will win!'

आचार्याः पितरः पुत्रास्तथैव च पितामहाः ।
मातुलाः श्वशुराः पौत्राः श्यालाः सम्बन्धिनस्तथा ॥३४॥

एतान्न हन्तुमिच्छामि घ्नतोऽपि मधुसूदन ।
अपि त्रैलोक्यराज्यस्य हेतोः किं नु महीकृते ॥३५॥

Slokas 34 - 35
aachaaryaah pitarah putraas
tathaiva cha pitaamahaaha
maatulaah svasuraah pautraaha
syaalaah sambandhinas tathaa

etaan na hantum ich~chhaami
ghnato 'pi madhusoodana
api trailokya raajyasya
hetoh kim nu mahee krite

34 - Teachers, fathers, sons, grandfathers, maternal uncles, fathers-in-law, grandsons, brothers-in-law and other relatives are ready to give up their lives and properties. Why should I want to kill them?
35 - Even if they kill me, I am not prepared to fight them even for the sake of dominion over the three worlds, let alone for this earth, O Madhusudana.

All of a sudden Arjuna has changed his mind and decided he doesn't want to fight any more! It is all too much and Arjuna would 'rather die' than face the situation. The opposition seems too great and he feels inadequate and impotent. Arjuna echoes all our sentiments at this point, when we realise that the enemy we must fight is ourselves. But where can you run to get away from yourself?

The mind will try anything to dissuade us from engaging in any confrontation with our desires and habits, saying things like, 'What is the use of doing all this serious stuff?' and, 'You will never be happy without all the things you enjoy. In the end you will not be happy because you won't have the things you enjoy now! Why should you want to fight these tendencies when they have given you so much enjoyment in the past?' The weight of knowing what we have to do can sometimes be too much nd can make us give up before we have started. But here Arjuna has nother issue. He says, 'I do not desire victory, kingdom or even leasures... Even if it means I will have complete control over myself, I o not want to lose this.' In other words he cannot cope!

We all know that there are things in our life which we know are not ood for us and yet we still carry on. Here Krishna is referred to as Madhusudana' - the killer of the demon, Madhu. It is telling us that we eed to ask for help to strike at the demon ego.

oday

ecognise that there are some things that do not improve with leaving. ake a list of those things that are real sore points in your life like all those ttachments you cannot let go of; the things that make you angry. You can uarantee that underneath them there will be something you don't really ant to give up.

निहत्य धार्तराष्ट्रान्नः का प्रीतिः स्याज्जनार्दन ।
पापमेवाश्रयेदस्मान् हत्वैतानाततायिनः ॥३६॥

तस्मान्नार्हा वयं हन्तुं धार्तराष्ट्रान्स्वबान्धवान् ।
स्वजनं हि कथं हत्वा सुखिनः स्याम माधव ॥३७॥

Slokas 36 - 37
nihatya dhaartaraashtraan naha
kaa preetih syaaj janaardana
paapam evaasrayed asmaan
hatvaitaan aatataayinaha

tasmaan naarhaa vayam hantum
dhaartaraashtraan sa baandhavaan
sva janam hi katham hatvaa
sukhinah syaama maadhava

36 & 37 - O Krishna, what joy could we possibly find in killing Dhritarashtra's sons? We ourselves will become sinners if we kill these men even if they are evil. How could we ever be happy again after killing our own people, O Madhava?

The ego is throwing up any argument it can at this stage, saying, 'What joy will there be when all these tendencies and pleasures are gone?' Joy for the ego-mind that is! 'It is wrong and even sinful,' it tells us as the excuses become more and more absurd.

Today

Don't make excuses for your habit patterns. Instead, recognise it is within your power to change your habits. You just have to want to do it.

यद्यप्येते न पश्यन्ति लोभोपहतचेतसः ।
कुलक्षयकृतं दोषं मित्रद्रोहे च पातकम् ॥३८॥

कथं न ज्ञेयमस्माभिः पापादस्मान्निवर्तितुम् ।
कुलक्षयकृतं दोषं प्रपश्यद्भिर्जनार्दन ॥३९॥

Slokas 38 - 39
yadyapyete na pasyanti
lobhopahata chetasaha
kula kshaya kritam dosham
mitra drohe cha paatakam

katham na jneyam asmaabhihi
paapaad asmaan nivartitum
kula kshaya kritam dosham
prapasyadbhir janaardana

38 & 39 - Although these men are overpowered by greed and see no fault in killing us, their own family, or quarrelling with friends, why should we, who can see the crime in destroying a family, engage in this evil, O Janardana?

Now the excuses become more subtle and sneaky. The mind says,

Surely the fact that I will always try to bring you down is no reason to get t me? After all, isn't it a kind of self-violence to hurt yourself? And aren't ou against that sort of thing?'

Today

All reasoning is suspect if the ignorant mind is involved. Have none of it! Choose a habit pattern that is a particular issue for you and replace it with its opposite. If you cannot think of one, choose generosity, which always works.

कुलक्षये प्रणश्यन्ति कुलधर्माः सनातनाः ।
धर्मे नष्टे कुलं कृत्स्नमधर्मोऽभिभवत्युत ॥४०॥

Sloka 40
kula kshaye pranasyanti
kula dharmaah sanaatanaaha
dharme nashte kulam kritsnam
adharmo 'bhibhavaty uta

40 - When a family is destroyed, its time-honoured religious traditions perish and the spiritual foundations for life are lost, causing the whole family to lose its sense of unity.

The mind says, 'Surely there is a way you can have your spiritual values and still let me have my own way? Isn't there some value in tradition? Otherwise, all the good you have ever done will perish with the rest and we will not stand together! '

Today

If you had to say that you stand for one value in life, what would it be? Truthfulness? Happiness? Helping others? If you have difficulty finding a value to attribute to yourself, perhaps you need to give yourself one. Choose any positive value and spend some time today putting it into action.

अधर्माभिभवात्कृष्ण प्रदुष्यन्ति कुलस्त्रियः ।
स्त्रीषु दुष्टासु वार्ष्णेय जायते वर्णसंकरः ॥४१॥

संकरो नरकायैव कुलघ्नानां कुलस्य च ।
पतन्ति पितरो ह्येषां लुप्तपिण्डोदकक्रियाः ॥४२॥

Slokas 41-42
adharmaa~bhibhavaat krishna
pradushyanti kula striyaha
streeshu dushtaasu vaarshneya
jaayate varna sankaraha

sankaro narakaayaiva
kula ghnaanaam kulasya cha
patanti pitaro hyeshaam
lupta pindodaka kriyaaha

41 - O Krishna, where there is no sense of family unity, the women become immoral, and with the corruption of women, society's laws break down.
42 - As the social fabric crumbles, society is plunged into chaos, which is hell for the family and for those who have destroyed the family as well. The ancestors of such corrupt families also suffer, without the aid of their descendant's devotional offerings of food and water.

The mind is babbling now and saying, 'If we allow ourselves to go down this road, then the consequences for those around and closest to us will be catastrophic.' However, while everything the ego-mind is saying is true, it only has a *tenuous* connection to what is really going on. We all have a habit of doing this and tend to make connections that are unjustified and have little to do with the real problems we are facing. This is known as the 'blame anything' syndrome.

At these times of confrontation, the mind will always present hundreds of convincing and eloquent arguments as to why we should run away. Everyone experiences these moments many times in their life, in missed chances, failures and disappointments. But we will not miss, fail or be disappointed if we are able to face up to our problems with more *faith in ourselves.*

In one respect Arjuna is right, and this is the rather disturbing way in which the mind tricks us. It is true that society generates its own problems by changing its standards and values, but you cannot use this as an excuse for not being incisive when a situation needs action. In reality, Arjuna is getting away from the point and trying to shift the balance elsewhere.

Today

Try to be clear in what you are doing and not distracted. You will find that you will be able to accomplish far more if you keep distractions to one side and just focus on the tasks you have to do.

दोषैरेतैः कुलघ्नानां वर्णसंकरकारकैः ।
उत्साद्यन्ते जातिधर्माः कुलधर्माश्च शाश्वताः ॥४३॥

उत्सन्नकुलधर्माणां मनुष्याणां जनार्दन ।
नरकेऽनियतं वासो भवतीत्यनुशुश्रुम ॥४४॥

अहो बत महत्पापं कर्तुं व्यवसिता वयम् ।
यद्राज्यसुखलोभेन हन्तुं स्वजनमुद्यताः ॥४५॥

यदि मामप्रतीकारमशस्त्रं शस्त्रपाणयः ।
धार्तराष्ट्रा रणे हन्युस्तन्मे क्षेमतरं भवेत् ॥४६॥

Slokas 43 - 46
doshair etaih kula ghnaanaam
varna sankara kaarakaih
utsaadyante jaati dharmaaha
kula dharmaas cha saasvataaha

utsanna kula dharmaanaam
manushyaanaam janaardana
narake niyatam vaaso
bhavateety anususruma

aho bata mahat paapam
kartum vyavasitaa vayam
yad raajya sukha lobhena
hantum sva janam udyataaha

yadi maam aprateekaaram
asastram sastra paanayaha
dhaartaraashtraa rane hanyus
tan me kshemataram bhavet

43 & 44 - We have repeatedly heard that those who destroy the timeless spiritual foundations of the family and society violate the unity of life and dwell indefinitely in hell.
45 - Surely, if we are prepared to kill our own relatives out of greed for the pleasure of such a kingdom, it is a dreadful sin!
46 - I would be happier if the sons of Dhritarashtra, with weapons in hand, should kill me in battle whilst I remain unarmed and unresisting.

Now Arjuna comes up with a very flimsy argument as a reason not to
ght: 'Surely if I do all this, I will never forgive myself!' Guilt is a very
fficult emotion to live with, but in this case, the guilt is not warranted.
e says he would rather be killed himself, because by now he is talking
mself into *any* argument, simply because it requires far too much effort
fight.

day

*e joyful and happy in knowing that through Arjuna's experience you are
arning to avoid all the pitfalls he fell into.*

संजय उवाच
एवमुक्त्वार्जुनः संख्ये रथोपस्थ उपाविशत् ।
विसृज्य सशरं चापं शोकसंविग्नमानसः ॥४७॥

Sloka 47
sanjaya uvaacha:
evam uktvaarjunah sankhye
rathopastha upaavisat
visrijya sa saram chaapam
soka samvigna maanasaha

*7 - Sanjaya said: Arjuna spoke these words, his heart overwhelmed by
rrow. Throwing down his bow and arrows, he sat down in his chariot.*

Arjuna is like every one of us. Although brave and courageous, when
aced with the ultimate challenge he becomes dejected, impotent and
earful. The forces of darkness which constitute our selfish desires and
elf-will always threaten to overwhelm us with feelings of depression,
neliness, rejection and pain. But in reality any negative state is an
ndulgence. The Gita urges us to 'stand up and fight' against these
endencies and not to give in to lethargy and despair. Instead we are
sked to believe in and empower our virtues. The problem is that we
end to lose *faith in ourselves* and our ability to overcome the negativity
ithin us. Everyone feels this intrinsic lack - a feeling of inadequacy and

unworthiness which seems to exist almost at the substratum of our consciousness. It is the bottom line belief for every human being who h not realised the truth of who they are. Whenever we find ourselves confronted by a situation that is very difficult or overwhelming, this negative belief is triggered inside us. We begin to feel limited, vulnerabl isolated and lonely, painfully aware of our mortality, tormented by those around us who appear to be better than us. This sense of being incomplete actually represents the fundamental problem of humankinc and arises out of a *mistaken sense of identity*. In other words, *it simply isn't true*. The Gita's vision is that our identification with our mind, body and emotions is incorrect. This mistaken identity is fraught with limitations and frailties which do not really belong to us. It is as if in a dream we commit a crime and feel the guilt and fear of a fugitive when in reality the crime and resultant guilt belong not to us, but to the dream.

Arjuna epitomises our human state and here in the Gita, Lord Krishr takes the opportunity to show us all that far from being limited, isolated and inadequate, we are in fact completely limitless, immortal and divine at one with the whole of creation and therefore capable of absolutely *anything*. At the end of Chapter One we see Arjuna overwhelmed by grie and anguish at his apparent inadequacy, throwing down his bow Gandiv which represents the arrogant self-will, and surrendering to his Higher Self - Lord Krishna. Now that he has cast away the ego-mind, Krishna ca help him to see the truth of who he really is.

Om tat sat iti
sreemad bhagavad geetaa su
upanishad su
brahmavidyaayaam
yoga shastre
sree krishna arjuna samvaade

arjuna vishaada yogo naama
prathamo 'dhyaayaha

Thus in the
glorious Bhagavad Gita,
the cream of the Upanishads,
the science of the Eternal,
the scripture of Yoga,
the dialogue between Sri Krishna and Arjuna,

ends the first discourse entitled
The Despondency of Arjuna

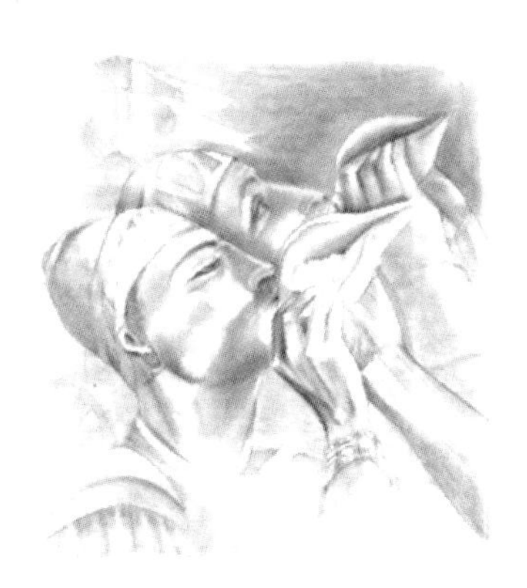

Chapter Two

The Yoga of Knowledge

संजय उवाच
तं तथा कृपयाविष्टमश्रुपूर्णाकुलेक्षणम् ।
विषीदन्तमिदं वाक्यमुवाच मधुसूदनः ॥१॥

श्री भगवानुवाच
कुतस्त्वा कश्मलमिदं विषमे समुपस्थितम् ।
अनार्यजुष्टमस्वर्ग्यमकीर्तिकरमर्जुन ॥२॥

क्लैब्यं मा स्म गमः पार्थ नैतत्त्वय्युपपद्यते ।
क्षुद्रं हृदयदौर्बल्यं त्यक्त्वोत्तिष्ठ परंतप ॥३॥

Slokas 1 - 3
sanjaya uvaacha:
tam tathaa kripayaavishtam
asru poornaaku~lekshanam
visheedantam idam vaakyam
uvaacha madhusoodanaha

sree bhagavaan uvaacha:
kutas tvaa kasmalam idam
vishame samupasthitam
anaarya jushtam asvargyam
akeerti karam arjuna

klaibyam maa sma gamah paartha
naitat tvayy upapadyate
kshudram hridaya daurbalyam
tyaktvottishtha parantapa

1 - Sanjaya said: When Krishna saw Arjuna overcome with self pity, his eye blurred with tears of despair, He said,
2 - Where has this shameful cowardice come from? It doesn't befit you and will certainly not lead you towards a state of liberation.
3 - It doesn't suit you to give in to this degrading weakness, Arjuna. Stand up, O Parantapa - scorcher of foes. Wake up and be courageous!

Up until now Krishna has remained silent, allowing Arjuna to express all his many arguments for not being able to fight his relatives. (While w

·e full of ourselves, there is no room for the Lord.) But realising that he not convincing Krishna, Arjuna sinks into despair. Now the ego is arting to give in and sense defeat and there is space for Krishna to ›me in to help him.

This is one of the most important moments in the Gita.

Whenever we find ourselves overwhelmed by circumstances in life,we ill inevitably reach a point like this, where the ego has to step aside and e find ourselves forced to appeal to a higher power for help. And when ıe tears come - the Lord comes. But it is interesting to notice how rishna deals with Arjuna. He doesn't offer him soft words or kind hrases to gently reassure and comfort him, because He knows full well ıat this will never work on this state of mind. Instead his words are arsh, in order to shock him out of it, simply because self-pity degrades ho we are and diminishes our potential. Words that can make you ırink can also be empowering.

Arjuna has disempowered himself so much that Krishna has to give ım some power back. 'Stand up and fight!' is a statement of npowerment. We can almost hear Krishna saying, 'I will always support ›u, but I will never support your illusions.'

The Lord within us simply will not tolerate any indulgence in self-pity, ecause it allows all kinds of unworthy thoughts to enter our mind. houghts that turn us from a prince among warriors, like Arjuna, into a arful weakling who refuses to fight. We actually have infinite resources ithin us to meet any challenges in life, as long as we remember *to ask the ord for His help.*

›day

s you read these words, take in their meaning, then close your eyes and firm to yourself, 'the quality I wish to change has no more power to affect e.'

अर्जुन उवाच
कथं भीष्ममहं संख्ये द्रोणं च मधुसूदन ।
इषुभिः प्रति योत्स्यामि पूजार्हावरिसूदन ॥४॥

गुरूनहत्वा हि महानुभावान्
श्रेयो भोक्तुं भैक्ष्यमपीह लोके ।
हत्वार्थकामांस्तु गुरूनिहैव
भुञ्जीय भोगान्रुधिरप्रदिग्धान् ॥५॥

न चैतद्विद्मः कतरन्नो गरीयो
यद्वा जयेम यदि वा नो जयेयुः ।
यानेव हत्वा न जिजीविषाम-
स्तेऽवस्थिताः प्रमुखे धार्तराष्ट्राः ॥६॥

Slokas 4 - 6

arjuna uvaacha:
katham bheeshmam aham sankhye
dronam cha madhusoodanaha
ishubhih pratiyotsyaami
poojaarhaav ari soodana

guroon ahatvaa hi mahaanubhaavaan
sreyo bhoktum bhaikshyam apeeha loke
hatvaartha kaamaams tu guroon ihaiva
bhunjeeya bhogaan rudhira pradigdhaan

na chaitad vidmah kataran no gareeyo
yad vaa jayema yadi vaa no jayeyuhu
yaan eva hatvaa na jijeevishaamas
te 'vasthitaah pramukhe dhaartaraashtraaha

4 - Arjuna said: Madhusudana - how can I ever bring myself to fight with Bhishma and Drona who are worthy of worship?
5 & 6 - I don't even know if it would be better for us to conquer them, or fo them to conquer us. I would rather live as a beggar than kill these great and worthy souls who are my teachers. If I kill them with desire for wealth, everything we enjoy will be tainted by their blood. Why would we want to live if we killed the sons of Dhritarashtra?

As soon as Krishna intervenes, Arjuna's arguments begin again. When the mind is full of despondency, it will swing back and forth like a pendulum and give good strong arguments against doing what we really have to do. Arjuna is looking at the situation in an emotional way, which always clouds true understanding, however rational it may appear to be. It is very reasonable not to want to kill your loved ones, but when those relatives are out to get *you*, it is more logical to fight! In the same way, we have no choice but to confront those elements within us that we dearly love, but which are actually obstructing our pathway towards discovering our true Selves.

Today

Is there a habit or tendency you know you must overcome, but feel unable to confront? Decide to start today to become free from it.

कार्पण्यदोषोपहतस्वभावः
पृच्छामि त्वां धर्मसंमूढचेताः ।
यच्छ्रेयः स्यान्निश्चितं ब्रूहि तन्मे
शिष्यस्तेऽहं शाधि मां त्वां प्रपन्नम् ॥७॥

Sloka 7

kaarpanya doshopahata svabhaavaha
prich~chhaami tvaam dharma sammoodha chetaaha
yach chhreyah syaan nischitam broohi tan me
sishyas te 'ham saadhi maam tvaam prapannam

7 - I am paralysed by weakness and utterly confused about my duty. I beg you to tell me exactly what to do. I am your disciple and have fallen at your feet. Please teach me.

Arjuna at last recognises Krishna as his teacher. In this moment he surrenders self-will and becomes receptive to universal will. Here is where the Srimad Bhagavad Gita really begins as Sri Krishna can now teach him. This verse tells us that if we wish to learn we must first empty ourselves of our misconceptions and actually realise that we might not have the answer to our problems. Only then are we likely to be open enough for the answer to become clear to us.

Today

Learn to listen more to what others have to say to you, and to what your real needs are.

न हि प्रपश्यामि ममापनुद्याद्
यच्छोकमुच्छोषणमिन्द्रियाणाम् ।
अवाप्य भूमावसपत्नमृद्धं
राज्यं सुराणामपि चाधिपत्यम् ॥८॥

संजय उवाच
एवमुक्त्वा हृषीकेशं गुडाकेशः परंतपः।
न योत्स्य इति गोविन्दमुक्त्वा तूष्णीं बभूव ह ॥९॥

Slokas 8 - 9
na hi prapasyaami mamaapanudyaad
yach chhokam uch~chhoshanam indriyaanaam
avaapya bhoomaav asapatnam riddham
raajyam suraanaam api chaadhipatyam

sanjaya uvaacha:
evam uktvaa hrisheekesam
gudaakesah parantapaha
na yotsya iti govindam
uktvaa tooshneem babhoova ha

8 - I cannot see any way to dispel this great sorrow of mine which saps my vitality; even if I were to obtain unrivalled prosperity and royal power on earth or sovereignty over the Gods.
9 - Sanjaya said: Having addressed Hrishikesa in this way, Arjuna said, 'I will not fight' and then became silent.

After his moment of clarity, Arjuna finds himself once again overwhelmed by a fresh wave of emotion. Even the senses do not suppor us when we are in a state and in his sorrow he just cannot see things learly. Sanjaya still upholds him however, calling him, 'Hrishikesa' which neans, 'conqueror of sleep.' It also means 'thick headed' and with this louble entendre, he is saying that even he who has conquered sleep can t times be thick headed.

Today

When the mind realises that it is threatened, it fights back with tenacity. Today, when the mind reacts against your suggestion that you do something positive, just affirm to yourself, 'I do want to be positive. Please mind, do not disturb me with your distractions.'

तमुवाच हृषीकेशः प्रहसन्निव भारत ।
सेनयोरुभयोर्मध्ये विषीदन्तमिदं वचः ॥१०॥

Sloka 10
tam uvaacha hrisheekesaha
prahasann iva bhaarata
senayor ubhayor madhye
visheedantam idam vachaha

10 - Then, O Great King, as they stood between the two armies, Krishna as f smiling, turned to the grief stricken Arjuna and said,

Krishna's smile is telling us something very beautiful. He doesn't add o Arjuna's sorrow by looking sad, but instead speaks to him through the anguage of the heart - His smile. He is demonstrating to us that no natter what is happening around us, we need to smile. And there is great visdom in this. When the police came to arrest Gandhi after his famous alt march, he just calmly picked up his bundle and walked out of the ashram smiling. No sadness or grief, no anger or hatred. Like Krishna, he infected everyone with his smile, even though he had no idea whether he would even come back alive.

Today

Whatever happens to you today, just smile. Remember that an outward smile soon reflects an inner smile.

श्री भगवानुवाच
अशोच्यानन्वशोचस्त्वं प्रज्ञावादांश्च भाषसे।
गतासूनगतासूंश्च नानुशोचन्ति पण्डिताः ॥११॥

Sloka 11
sree bhagavaan uvaacha:
asochyaan anvasochas tvam
prajnaa vaadaams cha bhaashase
gataasoon agataasooms cha
naanusochanti panditaaha

11 - Lord Krishna said: Although your words sound wise, you are grieving for those who should not be grieved for. The wise grieve neither for the living nor the dead.

Krishna's words are all embracing, but at the same time they come lik a bombshell to Arjuna. He tells him his 'wisdom' is misplaced, although logical, and then hits right at the very root of his problem. All our understanding and spiritual practice should be based on the knowledge of the immortal Self. This verse therefore contains the whole of the Gita's message; the highest and most sacred knowledge that a human being can ever absorb in a lifetime. Like a pearl dropped into the consciousness of our mind, we could almost pass it by and not realise its importance.

Today

Krishna is saying to us 'All your problems, all your worries, all your anxieties arise simply because you are looking at the world, in a particular way. Change your view point, change the basic way you see the world to one of truth, and all these problems are problems no more.'
So today, choose an anxiety, a worry, a problem and look at it from all sides - you will find that whatever is worrying you is in the future. In this moment it doesn't actually exist. Now just say to yourself, 'How am I now?'

Actually, you will find that you are fine!

न त्वेवाहं जातु नासं न त्वं नेमे जनाधिपाः ।
न चैव न भविष्यामः सर्वे वयमतः परम् ॥१२॥

Sloka 12
na tvevaaham jaatu naasam
na tvam neme janaadhipaaha
na chaiva na bhavishyaamaha
sarve vayam atah param

2 - There has never been a time when you and I and these Kings did not xist, nor will there ever be a time when we cease to be.

Krishna inverts the whole view that Arjuna has of the world. He puts is problem in the context of a universal stage instead of the small, ersonal agenda that Arjuna is tied to. It seems such a little thing to say, There was never a time when you and all these Kings did not exist,' but hat great consequences. These words shake our very souls, shake us out f the slumber of attachment to our own petty, personal agendas.

Today

ut your own problems into a larger arena. Ask yourself, 'In comparison to he thousands of people that die every day from malnutrition, or lack of ygiene or water, or those caught up in violence or war, how big are my roblems?'

o one stage further. Consider that there might be a deeper reason why this roblem is there for you. Just remember, as someone once said, 'Every roblem has a gift for you in its hands. We seek our problems because we eed their gifts.'

देहिनोऽस्मिन्यथा देहे कौमारं यौवनं जरा ।
तथा देहान्तरप्राप्तिर्धीरस्तत्र न मुह्यति ॥१३॥

Sloka 13
dehino 'smin yathaa dehe
kaumaaram yauvanam jaraa
tathaa dehaantara praaptir
dheeras tatra na muhyati

13 - Just as the same person inhabits the body from childhood and youth to old age, in the same way he attains another body at the time of death. A wise man is not disturbed by these changes.

Krishna here speaks of the transmigration of the Soul, from one life to another; the concept of re-incarnation, that you and I will be born again, that we have been born over and over again, until we have reached this point in space and time. But deeper than this is the recognition that every moment is like a kind of re-birth. And all through this there is something about us that never changes - that essential sense of 'I-ness' that defines who you are. If this is true, surely one of the most important things that we can ever do in our lives is to realise the preciousness of each moment, to carry the spark of our awareness into each moment, to allow it to arise, without judgement. If we can do this, then our whole life is filled with so much bliss.

Today

If you want to touch God, be in the moment. Carry something with you or around your neck that will remind you constantly of the importance of being in the moment. It should be something that is not so small that it won't be noticed. In fact, something that continually gets in the way will work even better! At first you be will annoyed at this irritating stone in your pocket. Eventually you will be grateful for its presence in your life!

मात्रास्पर्शास्तु कौन्तेय शीतोष्णसुखदुःखदाः ।
आगमापायिनोऽनित्यास्तांस्तितिक्षस्व भारत ॥१४॥

यं हि न व्यथयन्त्येते पुरुषं पुरुषर्षभ ।
समदुःखसुखं धीरं सोऽमृतत्वाय कल्पते ॥१५॥

नासतो विद्यते भावो नाभावो विद्यते सतः ।
उभयोरपि दृष्टोऽन्तस्त्वनयोस्तत्त्वदर्शिभिः ॥१६॥

Slokas 14 - 16
maatraa sparsaas tu kaunteya
seetoshna sukha duhkha daaha
aagamaapaayino 'nityaas
taams titikshasva bhaarata

yam hi na vyathayanty ete
purusham purusharshabha
sama duhkha sukham dheeram
so 'mritatvaaya kalpate

naasato vidyate bhaavo
naabhaavo vidyate sataha
ubhayor api drishto 'ntas
tvanayos tattva darsibhihi

14 - O Son of Kunti, physical sensations like heat and cold, pain and pleasure come and go and never last, like the appearance and disappearance of summer and winter. One must learn to endure them patiently, O Bharata.
15 - In fact, a person who is not affected by these sensations, staying balanced in pain and pleasure, is truly wise and fit for immortality.
16 - Nothing impermanent is real, for reality lies only in the eternal. The seers have realised the certainty of this truth.

Krishna often talks about pairs of opposites like joy and pain, or loss and gain. It is the nature of the world we live in that sensations just come and go. The world is ever changing, and Krishna says to Arjuna, please endure these sensations patiently or bravely. Krishna is alluding to something deeper here. All our lives we have been searching for happiness, for an even better feeling. Now Krishna is saying that this ver search is flawed. What we are looking for is not happiness, nor is it sadness. It is not even in the same spectrum of experience.

Today

Remember, each moment is precious. Remember this when you are happy and joyful, and yes, also when you are sad or in pain.

अविनाशि तु तद्विद्धि येन सर्वमिदं ततम् ।
विनाशमव्ययस्यास्य न कश्चित्कर्तुमर्हति ॥१७॥

Sloka 17
avinaasi tu tad viddhi
yena sarvam idam tatam
vinaasam avyayas~yaasya
na kaschit kartum arhati

17 - Know that That which pervades the universe is indestructible and no one can destroy what is everlasting.

This verse is filled with comfort and reassurance. There is a part of us that cannot be touched by anything and we need to *discover* this part of ourselves, because it belongs to *our true nature.*

Today

Courage, self-confidence, and self-empowerment all arise from the knowledge that there is part of you that is always safe and unassailable. Make sure that you spend even a few minutes every day making contact with that part of you that is untouchable. You will find that self-empowerment will never again be a problem for you.

अन्तवन्त इमे देहा नित्यस्योक्ताः शरीरिणः ।
अनाशिनोऽप्रमेयस्य तस्माद्युध्यस्व भारत ॥१८॥

Sloka 18
antavanta ime dehaa
nityasyoktaah sareerinaha
anaasino 'prameyasya
tasmaad yudhyasva bhaarata

18 - The body is mortal, although inhabited by the eternal, and will come to an end. Therefore fight, Arjuna!

Krishna makes the distinction to Arjuna that what he thinks is himself is only the body, which is subject to decay. The true Self is subtle and indestructible.

Today

Krishna says to Arjuna that this body is only the vehicle of your real nature, so why get attached to it? Very often in life we are afraid to do something because of what might happen. Once we realise that the body is impermanent we know that there is no reason at all why we should ever hesitate. After all, every hesitation is a precious moment wasted. So, don't wait to do the important things in life. When was the last time you said to someone important to you how much they actually mean to you? Why are we sometimes so afraid to say the things that matter?

य एनं वेत्ति हन्तारं यश्चैनं मन्यते हतम् ।
उभौ तौ न विजानीतो नायं हन्ति न हन्यते ॥१९॥

Sloka 19
ya enam vetti hantaaram
yas chainam manyate hatam
ubhau tau na vijaaneeto
naayam hanti na hanyate

19 - One person thinks himself to be the slayer and another believes he is the slain, but neither of them understands that the embodied Self can neither kill nor be killed.

People who think in terms of slayer and slain only relate to the body. The body, however, cannot move even one limb without that which lives within the body - our awareness - which is our true nature.

Today

Recognise the importance of silence in your life. If you continually seek noise, in order to drown out the longing for that sense of completeness, then you will never ever hear that quiet inner voice that is the sweet balm of the spirit. As has been said, 'Be still and know that I am God.' Find time today to re-affirm that connection with the depth of your being. Sit quietly for a while and just be still, or go for a quiet walk in nature.

न जायते म्रियते वा कदाचि-
न्नायं भूत्वा भविता वा न भूयः।
अजो नित्यः शाश्वतोऽयं पुराणो
न हन्यते हन्यमाने शरीरे ॥२०॥

Sloka 20
na jaayate mriyate vaa kadaachin
naayam bhootvaa bhavitaa vaa na bhooyaha
ajo nityah saasvato 'yam puraano
na hanyate hanyamaane sareere

0 - The Self is not born and does not die at any time. Unborn, eternal and ncient, the Self does not die when the body dies.

The Self has always existed and will never die. It does not incarnate, it nly resides at the deepest level of our being. It is not touched by the hanges that take place in the world, and always remains in its state of eace.

ōday

ecognise that the same peace that exists deep within your own being also esides within all beings. With this understanding you realise that it is not ossible to hurt anyone at this level, nor can anyone ever hurt you. There is wonderful prayer. It simply says, 'May all beings be at peace. May all eings find the true peace which lies in their own hearts.'

वेदाविनाशिनं नित्यं य एनमजमव्ययम ।
कथं स पुरुषः पार्थ कं घातयति हन्ति कम ॥२१॥

Sloka 21
vedaavinaasinam nityam
ya enam ajam avyayam
katham sa purushah paartha
kam ghaatayati hanti kam

21 - O Partha, how can anyone who knows that the soul is indestructible, ternal, birthless and imperishable, kill anyone or cause anyone to kill?

Krishna says it clearly enough here. How is it possible for you to kill or o be killed? It is only the body that dies.

Today

Be comforted. At the deepest level you cannot be hurt - the rest is just xperience.

वासांसि जीर्णानि यथा विहाय
नवानि गृह्णाति नरोऽपराणि ।
तथा शरीराणि विहाय जीर्णा-
न्यन्यानि संयाति नवानि देही ॥२२॥

Sloka 22
vaasaamsi jeernaani yathaa vihaaya
navaani grihnaati naro 'paraani
tathaa sareeraani vihaaya jeernaa
nyanyaani samyaati navaani dehee

22 - Just as a person puts on new clothes and casts away the old ones, the soul casts off worn out bodies and takes on new ones.

Krishna uses the analogy of a garment to describe the process of taking on and relinquishing a body.

We all feel happy when we buy a new coat. We also have no problems about throwing it away when we have finished with it. When we get to the end of our lives, it is only when we have not resolved everything that we feel regret.

Today

If you lived each day as if it were your last day on this planet you would make sure that you finished it without any regret. Today try to complete everything you begin. Leave as little as possible undone.

नैनं छिन्दन्ति शस्त्राणि नैनं दहति पावकः ।
न चैनं क्लेदयन्त्यापो न शोषयति मारुतः ॥२३॥

अच्छेद्योऽयमदाह्योऽयमक्लेद्योऽशोष्य एव च ।
नित्यः सर्वगतः स्थाणुरचलोऽयं सनातनः ॥२४॥

Slokas 23 - 24
nainam chhindanti sastraani
nainam dahati paavakaha
na chainam kledayanty aapo
na soshayati maarutaha

ach~chhedyo 'yam adaahyo 'yam
akledyo 'soshya eva cha
nityah sarva gatah sthaanur
achalo 'yam sanaatanaha

23 - Weapons cannot touch the Self. Fire cannot burn it, water cannot wet it, neither can it be dried by the wind.
24 - The Self cannot be pierced or cut by weapons, burned, made wet or dried; it is eternal, everlasting and infinite, standing on the motionless foundations of eternity.

Something cannot be touched if it is subtler than the one who touches. Matter cannot touch spirit, and so there is nothing in the physical plane that can affect us at this deep level.

Today

Again Krishna is re-iterating the importance of maintaining the connection with your deeper Self if you wish to experience the indestructible nature of the spirit. Be constant in your spiritual quest.

अव्यक्तोऽयमचिन्त्योऽयमविकार्योऽयमुच्यते ।
तस्मादेवं विदित्वैनं नानुशोचितुमर्हसि ॥२५॥

Sloka 25
avyakto 'yam achintyo 'yam
avikaaryo 'yam uchyate
tasmaad evam viditvainam
naanusochitum arhasi

25 - It is said that the soul is unmanifest, inconceivable and unchanging. Having understood this, there is no cause to grieve.

Grief comes from attachment to people, places and things. The Self does not manifest in any place in the material world. It is beyond time and cannot be perceived. Understanding this truth, we should not grieve.

Today

Grief arises out of the disintegration of the personality when it suffers a shock. All of the boundaries between the different roles that we play in life are shocked when we suffer loss or pain. Consequently we find it difficult to relate to each other. From the central point, however, where the Self resides, we are not touched by any of this. All emotions are modified by the overwhelming realisation of the continual flow of consciousness from moment to moment. Then there is just peace. No grief, no sadness, just peace.

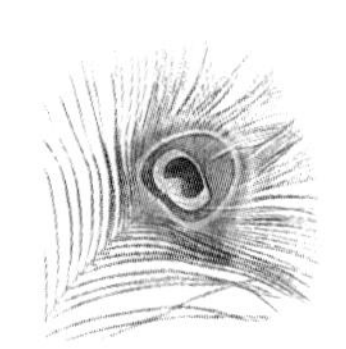

अथ चैनं नित्यजातं नित्यं वा मन्यसे मृतम् ।
तथापि त्वं महाबाहो नैनं शोचितुमर्हसि ॥२६॥

जातस्य हि ध्रुवो मृत्युर्ध्रुवं जन्म मृतस्य च ।
तस्मादपरिहार्येऽर्थे न त्वं शोचितुमर्हसि ॥२७॥

Slokas 26 - 27
atha chainam nitya jaatam
nityam vaa manyase mritam
tathaapi tvam mahaa baaho
nainam sochitum arhasi

jaatasya hi dhruvo mrityur
dhruvam janma mritasya cha
tasmaad aparihaarye 'rthe
na tvam sochitum arhasi

26 - And even if you believed the Self to be continually taking birth and dying, O mighty Arjuna, you still should not grieve.
27 - Death is inevitable for the living; birth is inevitable for the dead. Since these are unavoidable, you should not grieve.

Knowing that death is inevitable doesn't really help us with grief when it happens, but *realising it* is a completely different situation. Krishna's words are not just words meant to satisfy the mind. They carry a power that can bring this realisation to your life, if you will allow it.

Today

Just for once, put all of your doubts and all of your questions to one side. Ask your higher Self, ask God, to let you have the realisation that you need. It won't come with flashing lights and a fanfare, but with a sense of affirmation of everything that you know to be right.

अव्यक्तादीनि भूतानि व्यक्तमध्यानि भारत।
अव्यक्तनिधनान्येव तत्र का परिदेवना ॥२८॥

Sloka 28
avyaktaadeeni bhootaani
vyakta madhyaani bhaarata
avyakta nidhanaany eva
tatra kaa paridevanaa

28 - All living beings are unmanifest at first and then attain manifestation O Bharata. When the end comes they are once again unmanifest, so what is there to mourn about?

The real world is like a dream. You go to sleep, all sorts of things happen, and then you wake up and realise that none of it was real. Lord Krishna is saying that there's no need to grieve, simply because as in a dream the events presented in front of us are *not real. We* are the only ones who make it real.

Today

The mind has a mysterious way of allowing us to perceive things as staying the same, even though they can be quite different from day to day. If you are with someone everyday, you will probably not notice how they change over a period of months. Similarly with the changes in the seasons; it is only when a dramatic, fast change takes place, like the leaves in bud, or flowers filling a tree, that they are noticed. Today take time to look at a plant or a flower closely. Leave aside your perceptions and really see it.

आश्चर्यवत्पश्यति कश्चिदेन-
माश्चर्यवद्वदति तथैव चान्यः।
आश्चर्यवच्चैनमन्यः शृणोति
श्रुत्वाप्येनं वेद न चैव कश्चित्॥२९॥

Sloka 29
aascharya vat pasyati kaschid enam
aascharya vad vadati tathaiva chaanyaha
aascharya vach chainam anyah srinoti
srutvaapy enam veda na chaiva kaschit

'9 - Some see this as a wonder, and some describe it as a wonder, still others ear of this as a wonder, but no one knows or understands it.

You will find there are very few people who centre themselves in the elf, because it is something very rare. Those who do, however find life otally amazing. Those who are not centred in the Self can be shown and old about it, but they won't even be able to hear what you say.

'oday

)on't judge other people because they do not have a certain insight into life hat you might possess. It is possible that they have insights that you do not ave! Accept people as they are. Everyone is unique and has something pecial to offer.

देही नित्यमवध्योऽयं देहे सर्वस्य भारत।
तस्मात्सर्वाणि भूतानि न त्वं शोचितुमर्हसि॥३०॥

Sloka 30
dehee nityam avadhyo 'yam
dehe sarvasya bhaarata
tasmaat sarvaani bhootaani
na tvam sochitum arhasi

30 - This Self, which exists in everyone, is eternally indestructible O 3harata, therefore you should not grieve for anyone.

Every living thing has consciousness. That is the nature of the onenes of God. The added advantage that we have is that we are *conscious*, which allows us to be aware of this consciousness. Consciousness can be perceived in the space between our thoughts where there is nothing but *awareness.* In this space we can truly experience the oneness of all things.

Today

Choose a mantra, like 'I am peaceful'. Repeat it, and watch your thoughts slowly fade until there is just stillness. Reside in this stillness until a thought arises again. Whenever a thought arises, repeat the mantra until it fades away into stillness. In this way learn to experience the spaciousness between each thought.

स्वधर्ममपि चावेक्ष्य न विकम्पितुमर्हसि ।
धर्म्याद्धि युद्धाच्छ्रेयोऽन्यत्क्षत्रियस्य न विद्यते ॥३१॥

यदृच्छया चोपपन्नं स्वर्गद्वारमपावृतम् ।
सुखिनः क्षत्रियाः पार्थ लभन्ते युद्धमीदृशम् ॥३२॥

Slokas 31 - 32
sva dharmam api chaavekshya
na vikampitum arhasi
dharmyaad dhi yuddhaach chhreyo 'nyat
kshatriyasya na vidyate

yadrich~chhayaa chopapannam
svarga dvaaram apaavritam
sukhinah kshatriyaah paartha
labhante yuddham eedrisam

31 - Considering your dharma you should not tremble. For certainly there is nothing higher for a warrior than a righteous war.
32 - Happy indeed are the warriors, Arjuna, called to fight in such a battle that opens the doors of heaven to them.

Dharma is anything that takes us closer to the Self, to God. Adharma is that which takes us away from the peacefulness of the Self. Krishna is

sking us to choose actions that take us closer to this state of peacefulness
ıstead of actions that take us into anger or emotional disturbance.

Today

n our heart of hearts we often know what is right or wrong for us. Intuition
vill often tell us. Yet just as often we refuse to listen to it and instead we are
driven by the wanting mind. Today listen to your intuition and follow it
hrough.

अथ चेत्त्वमिमं धर्म्यं संग्रामं न करिष्यसि ।
ततः स्वधर्मं कीर्तिं च हित्वा पापमवाप्स्यसि ॥३३॥

Sloka 33
atha chet tvam imam dharmyam
sangraamam na karishyasi
tatah sva dharmam keertim cha
hitvaa paapam avaapsyasi

33 - But if you don't fight when it is your duty to do so, you will lose your honour and incur demerit.

'Demerit' is defined as following adharmic activities that take us away
rom God, like selfish desires and tendencies. The whole purpose of our
ncarnation, in fact, is to clear our negative tendencies and free ourselves
rom the hold they have over us.

Today

n the same way, there are times when we have to stand up for what is right
and not be a witness to negativity. If you are in tune, your intuition will tell
you what to do, what to say, and who to say it to. Never let it be said of you
hat you did nothing whilst there was something important to do.

अकीर्तिं चापि भूतानि कथयिष्यन्ति तेऽव्ययाम् ।
संभावितस्य चाकीर्तिर्मरणादतिरिच्यते ॥ ३४॥

Sloka 34
akeertim chaapi bhootaani
kathayishyanti te 'vyayaam
sambhaavitasya chaakeertir
maranaad atirichyate

34 - People will continually recall your dishonour and for one who has been honoured, dishonour is worse than death.

If we find ourselves strengthened by other people's opinions, we will also find that we can be weakened by them.

Today

Write down any projected opinions that you think other people may hold about you and put them into a river to let them float away or bury them in the ground. Allow the true You to emerge, untainted by other's opinions and feel the freedom and joy of just being yourself.

भयाद्रणादुपरतं मंस्यन्ते त्वां महारथाः ।
येषां च त्वं बहुमतो भूत्वा यास्यसि लाघवम् ॥ ३५॥

Sloka 35
bhayaad ranaad uparatam
mamsyante tvaam mahaa rathaaha
yeshaam cha tvam bahu mato
bhootvaa yaasyasi laaghavam

35 - The great warriors who have held you in such high esteem will think you have withdrawn out of fear and will consider you to be insignificant.

Despite the fact that Arjuna is one of the greatest warriors of all time, he still cannot afford to rest on his laurels and judge his success by previous achievements. Success or liberation depends entirely on what we do *now.*

Today

Ve can often miss opportunities to help each other. When you meet omebody, do you really know with any sense of certainty that you will ever neet them again? What you do NOW matters, so do something today to nake this day special for others.

अवाच्यवादांश्च बहून्वदिष्यन्ति तवाहिताः ।
निन्दन्तस्तव सामर्थ्यं ततो दुःखतरं नु किम् ॥३६॥

Sloka 36
avaachya vaadaams cha bahoon
vadishyanti tavaahitaaha
nindantas tava saamarthyam
tato duhkhataram nu kim

36 - Your enemies will ridicule your strength and slander you. What could e more painful than this?

Krishna uses the pain of being laughed at to spur Arjuna into action. We, in our ignorance, think that we can escape action - but we cannot. Physical pain can be endured, but what could be more painful than not loing what you are supposed to do?

Today

What is the point of having talents if you don't use them? If you have a gift n life make use of it. Don't hide it away so that no one ever finds out how ich you really are.

हतो वा प्राप्स्यसि स्वर्गं जित्वा वा भोक्ष्यसे महीम्।
तस्मादुत्तिष्ठ कौन्तेय युद्धाय कृतनिश्चयः ॥३७॥

Sloka 37
hato vaa praapsyasi svargam
jitvaa vaa bhokshyase maheem
tasmaad uttishtha kaunteya
yuddhaaya krita nischayaha

37 - O Son of Kunti, either you will be killed on the battlefield and attain heaven or, having conquered, you shall enjoy the earth. Therefore, stand up Arjuna, resolved to fight!

Krishna is telling Arjuna that win or lose, he will always gain because he is on the side of goodness. Krishna's call to us all is to let go of our sadness and despondency about facing our challenges in life and to be determined to play out the game as best we can. Arjuna needed to understand that he was fighting on Krishna's behalf, not his own. In the same way, we all need to remember that we personally have nothing to do with the battle we find ourselves facing and that the responsibility lies solely with the Lord.

Today

Make your life count, NOW! Do something special for someone.

सुखदुःखे समे कृत्वा लाभालाभौ जयाजयौ।
ततो युद्धाय युज्यस्व नैवं पापमवाप्स्यसि ॥३८॥

Sloka 38
sukha duhkhe same kritvaa
laabhaalaabhau jayaajayau
tato yuddhaaya yujyasva
naivam paapam avaapsyasi

38 - Seeing the same in pleasure and pain, profit and loss, victory and defeat, fight for the sake of the battle, and you will be freed from bad repercussions.

If you find life is a stormy sea, you need to know how to ride the waves nd stay unaffected by different mental reactions. In this verse, Krishna ives us the way to remain calm and poised throughout any circumstance make your mind the same in pleasure, pain, profit, loss, defeat or ictory.

Today

low with life, regardless of what is happening around you and offer all your ctions and experiences to the Lord, be they compliments or criticisms, leasure or pain.

एषा तेऽभिहिता सांख्ये बुद्धिर्योगे त्विमां शृणु ।
बुद्ध्या युक्तो यया पार्थ कर्मबन्धं प्रहास्यसि ॥३९॥

Sloka 39
eshaa te 'bhihitaa saankhye
buddhir yoge tvimaam srinu
buddhyaa yukto yayaa paartha
karma bandham prahaasyasi

39 - So far, you have heard the intellectual explanation of Sankhya Yoga, O artha. Now let Me tell you how to apply this wisdom that will enable you to reak through all the bonds of karma.

There are two aspects to Sankhya Yoga. Theory *(Sankhya)* and practice *Yoga)*. Now Krishna will explain how to attain the wisdom He has been lescribing and apply the theory to our everyday lives.

Today

Ve all take time to nurture our bodies with food, drink, and sleep and to urture our minds with books, conversation, writing, and ideas. But when lo we ever take time to nourish our spirit? This is by far the greatest of the hree and should be given a lot more time than it is. So make sure today hat you make time to nourish your spirit.

नेहाभिक्रमनाशोऽस्ति प्रत्यवायो न विद्यते ।
स्वल्पमप्यस्य धर्मस्य त्रायते महतो भयात् ॥४०॥

Sloka 40
nehaabhikrama naaso 'sti
pratyavaayo na vidyate
svalpam apyasya dharmasya
traayate mahato bhayaat

40 - No effort is ever wasted in these practices, nor is there any failure. Even a little effort towards spiritual awareness will protect you from great danger.

Krishna reassures us that even the smallest effort to practise this yoga will go a long way.

Today

Just do whatever you can to remember God.

व्यवसायात्मिका बुद्धिरेकेह कुरुनन्दन ।
बहुशाखा ह्यनन्ताश्च बुद्धयोऽव्यवसायिनाम् ॥४१॥

Sloka 41
vyavasaayaatmikaa buddhir
ekeha kuru nandana
bahu saakhaa hyanantaas cha
buddhayo 'vyavasaayinaam

41 - Those who are completely resolute and one-pointed towards their goal attain singleness of purpose, Arjuna. For those who lack resolution, whose minds are wavering and unsteady, the choices and decisions in life are endless and have many branches.

This verse shows us that through being consistent and one-pointed, we can avoid self-sabotage. Without single mindedness, however, our energy will be dissipated and wasted. With a firm mind there is only *one* decision and *one* goal.

ǒday

'ave total conviction about your goal and then nothing can stop you.

यामिमां पुष्पितां वाचं प्रवदन्त्यविपश्चितः ।
वेदवादरताः पार्थ नान्यदस्तीति वादिनः ॥४२॥

कामात्मानः स्वर्गपरा जन्मकर्मफलप्रदाम् ।
क्रियाविशेषबहुलां भोगैश्वर्यगतिं प्रति ॥४३॥

भोगैश्वर्यप्रसक्तानां तयापहृतचेतसाम् ।
व्यवसायात्मिका बुद्धिः समाधौ न विधीयते ॥४४॥

Slokas 42 - 44
yaam imaam pushpitaam vaacham
pravadanty avipaschitaha
veda vaada rataah paartha
naanyad asteeti vaadinaha

kaamaatmaanah svarga paraa
janma karma phala pradaam
kriyaa visesha bahulaam
bhogaisvarya gatim prati

bhogaisvarya prasaktaanaam
tayaapahrita chetasaam
vyavasaayaatmikaa buddhihi
samaadhau na vidheeyate

2 - Ignorant people are very attached to the flowery words of the
criptures and delight in the letter of the law, saying there is nothing else,
) Partha.
3 - Full of selfish desires, their idea of heaven is their own enjoyment, and
hey are addicted to a myriad of activities to attain pleasure and power.
4 - Those whose minds are attached to pleasure and power are not able to
neditate one-pointedly and to enjoy Samadhi.

Krishna here describes those who will never become free. A heart full of selfish desires simply cannot see the divine. Rama, the principle of abiding joy, and Kama (selfish desire), cannot live side by side. We have to relinquish all our cravings.

Today

When we look at ourselves, we often see those things in ourselves that we would rather not see. Consequently we tend not to bother to look. It is quit important to realise that we all have selfish desires unless we are truly Self-realised or enlightened. What we have to do, however, is to deal with one issue at a time. To look at all of our problems at once is too much and will get us nowhere. However, a strategy of systematic self-appraisal and introspection will enable you to make an in-road into the problems of the mind.

Choose a desire or personality trait that you don't like and decide that you will deal with this one today. Make a point of affirming to yourself in the morning that this is the quality that you are going to work with. Then whenever this problem (ego, anger, reactiveness, pride, etc.) arises, replace this quality with its opposite. You will soon see that by taking this stance, you will become far more aware of your psychological makeup and far more in control of it.

त्रैगुण्यविषया वेदा निस्त्रैगुण्यो भवार्जुन ।
निर्द्वन्द्वो नित्यसत्त्वस्थो निर्योगक्षेम आत्मवान् ॥४५॥

Sloka 45
trai gunya vishayaa vedaa
nistrai gunyo bhavaarjuna
nirdvandvo nitya sattva stho
niryoga kshema aatmavaan

45 - The scriptures describe the three modes of nature (the gunas). Be free from the gunas, Arjuna, indifferent towards the pairs of opposites, self controlled, without any sense of duality, free from thoughts or wanting to get or keep anything, remaining centred in your true Self.

The three Gunas are the building blocks of all nature. Raja-guna Rajas) is the mode of action, where all things begin. It is the creative rinciple and is represented by the power of springtime. Sattva-guna Sattva) is the mode of purity, the still mode that exists when everything in flower and strong. It is represented by summertime. Tama-guna Tamas) represents the inherent nature of all things to dissolve back into ne cycles of creation, ready for the next cycle. Krishna asks Arjuna to be ree from the power of the gunas, and to reside only in sattva-guna centred in your own Self). This is an important statement. Up to now rishna has said how we will be when we have achieved our goal, but this his first real instruction. Live in sattva-guna, i.e. live in the mode of urity, where the things that you do are conducive to the spirit.

oday

ry to eat food that is sattvic today. Exclude food that is too rich or spicy, or ood that has been left for more than two hours after cooking.

यावानर्थ उदपाने सर्वतः संप्लुतोदके ।
तावान्सर्वेषु वेदेषु ब्राह्मणस्य विजानतः ॥४६॥

Sloka 46
yaavaan artha udapaane
sarvatah samplutodake
taavaan sarveshu vedeshu
braahmanasya vijaanataha

6 - To one who knows the truth, the Scriptures are about as useful as a eservoir in a flood.

If you are alive, do you need a book to tell you that you are? An nlightened being doesn't need to read books on enlightenment!

oday

Whether you feel lazy, passionate or pure and sincere, don't let it get in the ay of who you really are.

कर्मण्येवाधिकारस्ते मा फलेषु कदाचन।
मा कर्मफलहेतुर्भूर्मा ते सङ्गोऽस्त्वकर्मणि॥४७॥

Sloka 47
karmany evaadhikaaras te
maa phaleshu kadaachana
maa karma phala hetur bhoor
maa te sango 'stvakarmani

47 - You have the right to work, but never to the results. Never allow yourself to be motivated by the fruits of your actions, nor should you be attached to inaction.

All of us fall in the spectrum somewhere between these two states. We are either too involved in our work, or, at the other end of the spectrum we avoid work whenever possible. To be sattvic in the way that we work, we need to be full of energy, and yet not upset if the results don't turn out the way that we want.

Today

Try and find a balance in your life with everything that you do. If you are working too hard, just remember that on their deathbed, no one ever wishe that they had spent more time in work. No one is indispensable! Similarly, you are caught up in being lazy, remember that the result of living in the mode of tamas, just as living in the mode of rajas, is always pain.

योगस्थः कुरु कर्माणि सङ्गं त्यक्त्वा धनंजय।
सिद्ध्यसिद्ध्योः समो भूत्वा समत्वं योग उच्यते॥४८॥

Sloka 48
yoga sthah kuru karmaani
sangam tyaktvaa dhananjaya
siddhy asiddhyoh samo bhootvaa
samatvam yoga uchyate

48 - Do everything centred in that equanimity, free from all selfish attachments and indifferent to success or failure. Yoga is equanimity of mind Arjuna.

With equanimity there is no need to worry about the outcome of your :tions. This equipoise leads to self-knowledge and total self-confidence ıd this confidence helps any action to succeed.

ɔday

'hen you are complimented or feeling self-satisfied with an achievement, ɜ grateful, but quickly let it go. Similarly, if you are criticised, accept it, •view your action, learn from it and then let it go.

दूरेण ह्यवरं कर्म बुद्धियोगाद्धनंजय।
बुद्धौ शरणमन्विच्छ कृपणाः फलहेतवः ॥४९॥

Sloka 49
doorena hyavaram karma
buddhi yogaad dhananjaya
buddhau saranam anvich~chha
kripanaah phala hetavaha

9 - Seek refuge in this wisdom O Dhananjaya! Those who are motivated by ıe fruits of their actions are miserly indeed.

When we are caught up in the fruits of our actions we forget one ındamental rule. We are not in control! Very often the universe throws spanner in the works. If we are caught in the expectation of how we 'ant things to turn out then the end result will be only pain and upset.

ɔday

'ou have every right to plan ahead and organise things. Just don't get ɔught up in thinking that just because it is organised it will turn out that •ay. So today, plan your day. Write a list of things to do, and at the bottom •rite 'God Willing.'

बुद्धियुक्तो जहातीह उभे सुकृतदुष्कृते।
तस्माद्योगाय युज्यस्व योगः कर्मसु कौशलम् ॥५०॥

Sloka 50
buddhi yukto jahaateeha
ubhe sukrita dushkrite
tasmaad yogaaya yujyasva
yogah karmasu kausalam

50 - He whose wisdom is established in equanimity casts off both good and bad karma in this life. Therefore devote yourself to the discipline of yoga, for yoga is skill in action.

If you can act with wisdom, then you do not create waves with your action. We tend to forget that our actions have good and bad implications for other beings. With skilful actions we make no waves and only bring good to all beings.

Today

Always act for the highest good and you will not go far wrong.

कर्मजं बुद्धियुक्ता हि फलं त्यक्त्वा मनीषिणः।
जन्मबन्धविनिर्मुक्ताः पदं गच्छन्त्यनामयम् ॥५१॥

Sloka 51
karma jam buddhi yuktaa hi
phalam tyaktvaa maneeshinaha
janma bandha vinirmuktaaha
padam gach~chhanty anaamayam

51 - Enjoying equanimity of mind, the wise who have renounced the fruits of their actions and are freed from the bondage of rebirth, go to a place that is free from pain.

Again, Krishna is hinting that living in the mode of sattva is the key. Living in this mode you become free from pain of all kinds, and your actions are selfless.

Today

Do something today for someone else and don't let them know about it.

यदा ते मोहकलिलं बुद्धिर्व्यतितरिष्यति ।
तदा गन्तासि निर्वेदं श्रोतव्यस्य श्रुतस्य च ॥५२॥

श्रुतिविप्रतिपन्ना ते यदा स्थास्यति निश्चला ।
समाधावचला बुद्धिस्तदा योगमवाप्स्यसि ॥५३॥

Slokas 52 - 53
yadaa te moha kalilam
buddhir vyatitarishyati
tadaa gantaasi nirvedam
srotavyasya srutasya cha

sruti vipratipannaa te
yadaa sthaasyati nischalaa
samaadhaav achalaa buddhis
tadaa yogam avaapsyasi

52 - Once your mind overcomes the confusion of duality you become indifferent to things you have heard and are yet to hear.
53 - When your mind is no longer disturbed by conflicting opinions and becomes still and centred, you will attain the self-realised state of complete union (perfect yoga).

Once we become indifferent to the siren call of the senses and have no taste for things that used to give us pleasure, (like pizza and chips), we will know that we are growing spiritually. Sense organs are the antennae through which the world's signals creep in and disturb the mental pool. The steady flow of stimuli only agitate the mind. Perfect yoga is a state where, although the sense organs are letting in stimuli, inner serenity is not disturbed.

Today

Look at everything you know. Write down a list of all the subjects you are knowledgeable in and all those you wish to learn more about. Then just sit still and know that the true You is beyond this duality of past and future and exists purely in this one, present, living moment.

अर्जुन उवाच
स्थितप्रज्ञस्य का भाषा समाधिस्थस्य केशव ।
स्थितधीः किं प्रभाषेत किमासीत व्रजेत किम् ॥५४॥

Sloka 54
arjuna uvaacha:
sthita prajnasya kaa bhaashaa
samaadhi sthasya kesava
sthita dheeh kim prabhaasheta
kim aaseeta vrajeta kim

54 - Arjuna said: Tell me about the man of steady wisdom, Krishna, who is always aware of the Self. How does he speak? How does he sit? How does h move?

Arjuna, no longer under the influence of his hysteria, is taking an active interest in the discussion. Being a practical man, he wants to know if he will be able to live so vigorously in the outside world once he has attained this great goal of life. He is curious to know fully the condition of the wise man before actually accepting the theory and trying to live it. 'Man of steady wisdom' means one who has, through direct realisation, come to experience and live his Godly Self.

Today

Ask the question that Arjuna has asked Krishna. How can you recognise a being who is living in that wisdom? Put a sincere plea out to the universe. You won't be ignored.

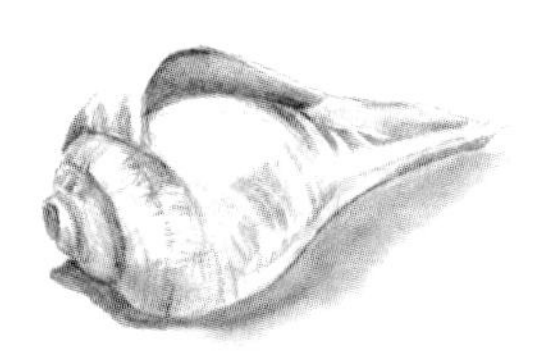

श्री भगवानुवाच
प्रजहाति यदा कामान्सर्वान्पार्थ मनोगतान् ।
आत्मन्येवात्मना तुष्टः स्थितप्रज्ञस्तदोच्यते ॥५५॥

दुःखेष्वनुद्विग्नमनाः सुखेषु विगतस्पृहः ।
वीतरागभयक्रोधः स्थितधीर्मुनिरुच्यते ॥५६॥

Slokas 55-56
sree bhagavaan uvaacha:
prajahaati yadaa kaamaan
sarvaan paartha mano gataan
aatmany evaatmanaa tushtaha
sthita prajnas tadochyate

duhkheshv anudvigna manaaha
sukheshu vigata sprihaha
veeta raaga bhaya krodhaha
sthita dheer munir uchyate

55 - Lord Krishna said: He who leaves behind all desires of the mind, utterly content in the Self alone, lives in wisdom.
56 - Free from lust, fear and anger, he is not agitated by misfortune, nor does he hanker after pleasure.

These opening stanzas of Krishna's reply are a brilliant summary of everything we need to know about the man of wisdom. An ignorant mind creates a breeding ground for desires and when we overcome ignorance, we become desireless. A desire is the ignorant mind's attempt to *create* a state of happiness. The wise man goes beyond these false glimpses of happiness, to experience the true bliss of the Self.

Today

Every time you feel happy today, ask yourself, 'What part of me is happy?' You will find that at moments of happiness, you reach inside and touch part of yourself. It is this touch that creates the happiness that we experience. And the best way to create this sense? Be generous. It is impossible to give from the heart and not feel happiness.

यः सर्वत्रानभिस्नेहस्तत्तत्प्राप्य शुभाशुभम् ।
नाभिनन्दति न द्वेष्टि तस्य प्रज्ञा प्रतिष्ठिता ॥५७॥

Sloka 57
yah sarvatraana~bhisnehas
tat tat praapya subhaasubham
naabhinandati na dveshti
tasya prajnaa pratishthitaa

57 - No longer bound by selfish attachments, neither rejoicing at good fortune, nor disliking bad, their wisdom is steady.

Detachment is not in itself the way to a perfect life, because duties need to be upheld. By its very nature, life is a mixture of good and bad and if we embrace the good and reject the bad, we are not living intelligently.

Today

Whatever happens to you today, whether you see it as good or as bad, just say to yourself, 'Is that so?'... In this way you are treating all things equally, with the same emotional balance of mind.

यदा संहरते चायं कूर्मोऽङ्गानीव सर्वशः ।
इन्द्रियाणीन्द्रियार्थेभ्यस्तस्य प्रज्ञा प्रतिष्ठिता ॥५८॥

Sloka 58
yadaa samharate chaayam
koormo 'ngaaneeva sarvasaha
indriyaa~neendriyaar~thebhyas
tasya prajnaa pratishtitaa

8 - The man of steady wisdom can draw in the senses at will like a tortoise ithdraws its limbs into its shell.

Identifying with the ego, we are plagued by desires for sense objects nd have strong emotional attachments to them. Transcending the ego, e come face to face with our divinity where everything else just melts way. The five senses are known as the five avenues of knowledge - but nly if you can control them. If you can withdraw the senses every time ou are tempted, you are free!

oday

emember that just taking up one sense withdrawal means all the rest will ollow. It doesn't necessarily have to be the hardest one, either!

विषया विनिवर्तन्ते निराहारस्य देहिनः ।
रसवर्जं रसोऽप्यस्य परं दृष्ट्वा निवर्तते ॥५९॥

Sloka 59
vishayaa vinivartante
niraahaarasya dehinaha
rasa varjam raso 'pyasya
param drishtvaa nivartate

59 - Even though people abstain from sense objects, they still crave them, ut these cravings all disappear once they experience union with the Lord.

It is not enough to restrain the senses through prayer, meditation and fasting, because the power of our desires and our attachment to them will still be there. What we have to do is to become more attracted to the divine - so that everything else becomes irrelevant.

Today

It is important to practise pratyahara- the art of internalising the senses, traditionally shown as a tortoise withdrawing its limbs.
Here's an exercise to help you:
Close your eyes.
Note where your awareness lies, i.e. behind your eyelids.
Step back from that in your mind.
Now open your eyes and focus on an object.
Now step back from that in your mind.
Cultivate this art of 'seeing' rather than 'looking'.

यततो ह्यपि कौन्तेय पुरुषस्य विपश्चितः ।
इन्द्रियाणि प्रमाथीनि हरन्ति प्रसभं मनः ॥६०॥

तानि सर्वाणि संयम्य युक्त आसीत मत्परः ।
वशे हि यस्येन्द्रियाणि तस्य प्रज्ञा प्रतिष्ठिता ॥६१॥

Slokas 60 - 61
yatato hyapi kaunteya
purushasya vipaschitaha
indriyaani pramaatheeni
haranti prasabham manaha

taani sarvaani samyamya
yukta aaseeta mat paraha
vase hi yasyendriyaani
tasya prajnaa pratishthitaa

60 - The stormy senses can even carry away the mind of a man who is striving for wisdom.
61 - But the wise subdue the senses by keeping their minds fixed on Me. For those whose senses are controlled, that wisdom stands firm.

It's very easy for the chaotic mind to dwell on the sense objects and ven a highly evolved seeker has to be constantly vigilant. It is not ossible to overcome these tendencies by willpower and abstinence lone. The key is to fix your mind on the Lord - all the time - and then all ast mental and emotional tendencies and attachments can be radicated.

Today

Vhatever inspires you in life, whatever lifts you up, use this as a focus. At he highest level you should keep your thoughts on God at all times, but if ou can't manage this then focus on someone who inspires you to greater hings.

ध्यायतो विषयान्पुंसः सङ्गस्तेषूपजायते ।
सङ्गात्संजायते कामः कामात्क्रोधोऽभिजायते ॥६२॥

क्रोधाद्भवति संमोहः संमोहात्स्मृतिविभ्रमः ।
स्मृतिभ्रंशाद्बुद्धिनाशो बुद्धिनाशात्प्रणश्यति ॥६३॥

Slokas 62 - 63
dhyaayato vishayaan pumsaha
sangas teshoopajaayate
sangaat sanjaayate kaamaha
kaamaat krodho 'bhijaayate

krodhaad bhavati sammohaha
sammohaat smriti vibhramaha
smriti bhramsaad buddhi naaso
buddhi naasaat pranasyati

52 - If a man keeps thinking about the sense objects, attachment is born; attachment breeds desire and from desire anger is born.
53 - Anger confuses the mind, which in turn disturbs memory. When memory fails, discrimination is lost and then you are lost and your life is an utter waste.

This is an astounding verse. To know how anger arises is probably one of the most useful things that you will find in the whole of the Srimad Bhagavad Gita. To know that at the root of all anger is simply attachment to some sense object or other and that desires are a breeding ground for anger is a most liberating fact. It becomes very clear that it is attachment that has to be dealt with before any of the other problems we have in life can be addressed. In fact, just by dealing with this one issue, all the others will fade away anyway.

Today

If something annoys you today, ask yourself ,'What is it that I am attached to here? Is it something physical? Is it my pride? Is it the way that I am seeing the situation?' Then let it go. See the anger dissolve as the attachment goes.

रागद्वेषवियुक्तैस्तु विषयानिन्द्रियैश्चरन् ।
आत्मवश्यैर्विधेयात्मा प्रसादमधिगच्छति ॥६४॥

प्रसादे सर्वदुःखानां हानिरस्योपजायते ।
प्रसन्नचेतसो ह्याशु बुद्धिः पर्यवतिष्ठते ॥६५॥

Slokas 64 - 65
raaga dvesha viyuktais tu
vishayaan indriyais charan
aatma vasyair vidheyaatmaa
prasaadam adhigach~chhati

prasaade sarva duhkhaanaam
haanir asyopajaayate
prasanna chetaso hyaasu
buddhih paryavatishthate

64 & 65 - The wise, who have controlled the mind and have self restraint, move amidst the world of the senses free from attachment and aversion and attain the tranquillity in which all sorrows end. The intellect quickly becomes steady when the mind is tranquil.

Krishna says that a wise being can be in the world, but not be
istracted by it. An egotistical scholar once went to a famous monk and,
ying to catch him out said 'Don't you ever do anything but meditate?'.
'he monk replied, 'What is there to meditate upon?'At this the scholar
houted out 'So, you don't even meditate?' The monk just replied, 'But
hen am I ever distracted?'

oday

*)on't be distracted by what the world throws at you. Instead, make a point
f doing whatever comes in front of you without hesitation.*

नास्ति बुद्धिरयुक्तस्य न चायुक्तस्य भावना ।
न चाभावयतः शान्तिरशान्तस्य कुतः सुखम् ॥६६॥

Sloka 66
naasti buddhir ayuktasya
na chaayuktasya bhaavanaa
na chaabhaavayatah saantir
asaantasya kutah sukham

*6 - The uncontrolled mind, however, is far from wise. It cannot meditate
r concentrate, which means there can be no peace. How can you be happy
vithout peace?*

We need to do things that create equanimity, in a way that allows the
self to emerge. There is no peace in a mind that is reacting to
everything that happens, so make wise decisions and control your
eactions with a sense of one-pointed determination.

Today

*Happiness is an active state. Be happy! Think and pretend you are, even if
you cannot feel it and soon it will become a reality. With an inner smile, we
can cope with life without judgement or reactions.*

इन्द्रियाणां हि चरतां यन्मनोऽनुविधीयते ।
तदस्य हरति प्रज्ञां वायुर्नावमिवाम्भसि ॥६७॥

तस्माद्यस्य महाबाहो निगृहीतानि सर्वशः ।
इन्द्रियाणीन्द्रियार्थेभ्यस्तस्य प्रज्ञा प्रतिष्ठिता ॥६८॥

Slokas 67 - 68
indriyaanaam hi charataam
yan mano 'nuvidheeyate
tad asya harati prajnaam
vaayur naavam ivaambhasi

tasmaad yasya mahaa baaho
nigriheetaani sarvasaha
indriyaa~neendriyaar~thebhyas
tasya prajnaa pratishthitaa

67 - When the mind runs after the wandering senses, it carries away better judgement as the wind carries away a ship on the waters.
68 - You should therefore, O mighty-armed one, (Mahabaho), use all your power to completely withdraw the senses from the sense objects so that your wisdom can remain firm.

The mind will only be as steady as the senses are and if even one sense is attached to the material world, it will draw the others with it. The mind can only be steady when the senses are restrained through self-control.

Today

It is said that the tortoise represents the quality of pratyahara (sense withdrawal), and the yoga posture named after it is said to be particularly effective in helping you to control the senses. Practise this posture today.

या निशा सर्वभूतानां तस्यां जागर्ति संयमी ।
यस्यां जाग्रति भूतानि सा निशा पश्यतो मुनेः ॥६९॥

Sloka 69
yaa nisaa sarva bhootaanaam
tasyaam jaagarti samyamee
yasyaam jaagrati bhootaani
saa nisaa pasyato munehe

69 - What seems like night to others is a state of awakening to the self-controlled man; and what the world calls day is the night of ignorance to the sage who knows the Self.

The ignorant mind cannot perceive the world as it really is. It projects its own imperfections onto it, like a child looking through a coloured window pane believes the world to be made up of that colour. With spiritual eyes, we can see and experience the world as it truly is.

Today

To appreciate this verse it is useful to actually make the effort to be awake when the rest of the world around you is asleep. It is recommended that those learning the science of meditation should arise early at about 4.30 and practise yoga and meditation when the vibrations of the world are more peaceful. This is certainly a habit that you should cultivate. The earlier you can get up, the greater the result will be.

आपूर्यमाणमचलप्रतिष्ठं
समुद्रमापः प्रविशन्ति यद्वत् ।
तद्वत्कामा यं प्रविशन्ति सर्वे
स शान्तिमाप्नोति न कामकामी ॥७०॥

Sloka 70
aapooryamaanam achala pratishtham
samudram aapah pravisanti yadvat
tadvat kaamaa yam pravisanti sarve
sa saantim aapnoti na kaama kaamee

70 - A wise man is not disturbed by the incessant flow of desires, and obtains peace just as the ocean remains still when being filled by countless rivers. But not so the man who is full of desires.

The subjective mind processes and the objective mind *observes*. If we can become an objective observer to our desires, they can come and go, but we have a choice as to whether we get caught up in them or not.

Today

Take a step back and become a silent witness.

विहाय कामान्यः सर्वान् पुमांश्चरति निःस्पृहः ।
निर्ममो निरहंकारः स शान्तिमधिगच्छति ॥७१॥

Sloka 71
vihaaya kaamaan yah sarvaan
pumaams charati nihsprihaha
nirmamo nirahankaaraha
sa saantim adhigach~chhati

71 - He who lives free from longing for anything, free from all personal desires, and with no individual sense of 'me' and 'mine', experiences peace.

Krishna talks about there being no identification between myself and the possessions I have. With freedom there is no need to achieve anything, for what else needs to be achieved? There is no need to possess anything, for what else could be possessed? In this state there is only peace. A peace that nothing can destroy.

Today

When you come across something that the mind wants (like an ice cream, or some other sense object), just ask yourself, 'what do I really want here?' You might be surprised at the answer that the mind throws out. Persevere though. Say 'No, it's not that...' for every thought that the mind throws at you. Eventually the mind will let you see that you never really wanted that thing, it was only the mind that desired it. Underneath, you will realize that you have everything you could ever need.

एषा ब्राह्मी स्थितिः पार्थ नैनां प्राप्य विमुह्यति।
स्थित्वाऽस्यामन्तकालेऽपि ब्रह्मनिर्वाणमृच्छति ॥७२॥

Sloka 72
eshaa braahmee sthitih paartha
nainaam praapya vimuhyati
sthitvaasyaam anta kaale 'pi
brahma nirvaanam rich~chhati

72 - This is the ultimate, divine state and on experiencing this, there is no more confusion. Establishing yourself into this awareness at the time of death, you will merge into the oneness of God.

Krishna promises that if we absorb ourselves into Him at the moment of our death, then we will merge with Him. The only way that you can ever achieve this is if you are always absorbing yourself into Him, so that it becomes a habit. Then you are guaranteed to reach His abode.

Today

Start the day meditating on the presence of God; before eating, offer all of your food to God; before working, ask for His blessings on what you are doing, and when you finish the day's work, thank Him for all you have been able to achieve. Finally, let your last thought be of resting in His vast presence. Surely you will be!

Om tat sat iti
sreemad bhagavad geetaa su
upanishad su
brahmavidyaayaam
yoga shastre
sree krishna arjuna samvaade

saankhya yogo naama
dviteeyo 'dhyaayaha

Thus in the
glorious Bhagavad Gita,
the cream of the Upanishads,
the science of the Eternal,
the scripture of Yoga,
the dialogue between Sri Krishna and Arjuna,

ends the second discourse entitled:

The Yoga of Knowledge

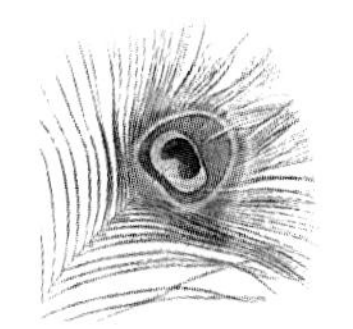

Chapter Three

The Yoga of Action

अर्जुन उवाच
ज्यायसी चेत्कर्मणस्ते मता बुद्धिर्जनार्दन ।
तत्किं कर्मणि घोरे मां नियोजयसि केशव ॥१॥

व्यामिश्रेणेव वाक्येन बुद्धिं मोहयसीव मे ।
तदेकं वद निश्चित्य येन श्रेयोऽहमाप्नुयाम् ॥२॥

Slokas 1 - 2
arjuna uvaacha:
jyaayasee chet karmanas te
mataa buddhir janaardana
tat kim karmani ghore maam
niyojayasi kesava

vyaamisreneva vaakyena
buddhim mohayaseeva me
tad ekam vada nischitya
yena sreyo 'ham aapnuyaam

1 - *Arjuna said: O Janardana, if you believe that knowledge is better than action, why do you ask me to engage in this terrible act?*
2 - *I am confused O Kesava; can you give me just one clear way to attain the highest goal?*

In Chapter Two Arjuna has been instructed in the science of Self-knowledge, in which it becomes clear to him that when you have steady wisdom, nothing in the universe can touch you. The great inner resolve and strength that it brings takes you beyond harm.

On the one hand, Krishna is asking Arjuna to fight, but on the other, in Arjuna's mind, he is almost negating the whole process by saying, 'All these people in front of you have existed before and will exist again.'

What is the point then? Arjuna thinks. Why bother? He is confused - and so his question is a very sensible one. But Krishna's whole purpose in approaching this teaching is to apply shock tactics to Arjuna that will turn the whole system upside down. By giving him the teachings of Chapter Two He is saying to him, 'Look. This isn't a problem any more.

[T]his is something you have to do.'

The whole of Chapter Three is Krishna's response to Arjuna's question, [i]n order to clarify what the result of action is, and why it is that correct [a]ction is the only way. When following the path of Self-discovery, we often [b]ecome confused by the attraction of the spiritual world. It can make us [n]eglect our duties in life. Confusion arises because we don't know which [i]s better and it takes a while to realise that there is no difference!

Today

[W]hat is the most joyous thing you could do, that is also the most practical?

श्री भगवानुवाच
लोकेऽस्मिन्द्विविधा निष्ठा पुरा प्रोक्ता मयानघ ।
ज्ञानयोगेन सांख्यानां कर्मयोगेन योगिनाम् ॥३॥

Sloka 3
sree bhagavaan uvaacha:
loke 'smin dvi vidhaa nishthaa
puraa proktaa mayaanagha
jnaana yogena saankhyaanaam
karma yogena yoginaam

3 - Lord Krishna said: Since ancient times I have given the world two paths [A]rjuna. Sankhya Yoga, which is the intuitive path of spiritual knowledge, [a]nd Karma Yoga, the active path of selfless service.

Krishna explains to Arjuna that there are different ways of [a]pproaching spirit. Some people are very practical and just get on with [t]hings (doers), and others are more intellectual and think a lot [(]thinkers). Both will take you where you want to go. Mother Teresa is a [p]erfect example of someone whose practical actions have brought her [g]reat wisdom. When she received the Nobel Peace Prize, she came down [o]ff the rostrum and was stopped by a tearful woman who appealed to her [f]or help because her baby was dying. She turned to her, smiled with great [c]ompassion and said, 'The Lord has given you a beautiful gift. If He wants you to give it back to him, please do so with grace.' Not an intellectual woman, it is working with the poor and dying that has given her this depth of wisdom.

Today

Ask yourself: 'Am I a thinker or a doer?' If you are a doer, spend some time thinking! If you are a thinker - do more than usual!

न कर्मणामनारम्भान्नैष्कर्म्यं पुरुषोऽश्नुते ।
न च संन्यसनादेव सिद्धिं समधिगच्छति ॥४॥

न हि कश्चित्क्षणमपि जातु तिष्ठत्यकर्मकृत् ।
कार्यते ह्यवशः कर्म सर्वः प्रकृतिजैर्गुणैः ॥५॥

Slokas 4 - 5
na karmanaam anaarambhaan
naishkarmyam purusho 'snute
na cha sannyasanaad eva
siddhim samadhigach~chhati

na hi kaschit kshanam api
jaatu tishthaty akarma krit
kaaryate hyavasah karma
sarvah prakriti jair gunaih

4 - *You cannot attain freedom by non-action or by renunciation of action.*
5 - *Nobody can exist without performing action because of the three-fold qualities we attract to us from the material world.*

Krishna is just saying, 'Well, even if you wanted to just think and spend your life in contemplation - you can't!' We have to act, according to the qualities of nature - the gunas. (The gunas have been mentioned in Chapter Two, verse 45.)

ꟷoday

ꞌhe next time you sit still, perhaps in a pause between sips of tea, listen to he beat of your heart. Notice the flow of your breath, the colours around ou. Everything is in motion and you cannot stop acting.

कर्मेन्द्रियाणि संयम्य य आस्ते मनसा स्मरन्।
इन्द्रियार्थान्विमूढात्मा मिथ्याचारः स उच्यते ॥६॥

Sloka 6
karmendriyaani samyamya
ya aaste manasaa smaran
indriyaarthaan vimoodhaatmaa
mithyaachaarah sa uchyate

- Those that sit still, trying to abstain from action, but allowing their ninds to dwell on the objects of the senses, are not considered to be sincere eekers of truth.

This verse is telling us that we are deluding ourselves if we think we re achieving something, when in actual fact we are not. For example, if ou are washing the dishes, but not focused on what you are doing, you re wasting your energy.

Today

ꞌhoose one simple act and do it with the utmost sincerity, as if it were the nost sacred thing in your life. It could be putting a cup away in a cupboard. ngage fully and do it with feeling.

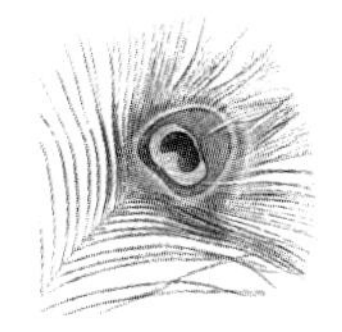

यस्त्विन्द्रियाणि मनसा नियम्यारभतेऽर्जुन ।
कर्मेन्द्रियैः कर्मयोगमसक्तः स विशिष्यते ॥७॥

Sloka 7
yas tvindriyaani manasaa
niyamyaarabhate 'rjuna
karmendriyaih karma yogam
asaktah sa visishyate

7 - But those who control the senses and engage themselves in the practice of Karma Yoga excel.

You will notice that when you practise acting with deep sincerity, the mind becomes quiet. The greater the sincerity, the quieter the mind and the less the pull from attractions around you. This is where Karma Yoga begins. In order to infuse every action with sincerity, it is necessary to begin at the start of the day.

Today

Make your first action sincere and you will slowly find that this focusing will percolate through into everything else in your life.

नियतं कुरु कर्म त्वं कर्म ज्यायो ह्यकर्मणः ।
शरीरयात्रापि च ते न प्रसिद्ध्येदकर्मणः ॥८॥

यज्ञार्थात्कर्मणोऽन्यत्र लोकोऽयं कर्म बन्धनः ।
तदर्थं कर्म कौन्तेय मुक्तसङ्गः समाचर ॥९॥

Slokas 8 - 9
niyatam kuru karma tvam
karma jyaayo hyakarmanaha
sareera yaatraapi cha te
na prasiddhyed akarmanaha

yajnaarthaat karmano 'nyatra
loko 'yam karma bandhanaha
tad artham karma kaunteya
mukta sangah samaachara

8 - You have to act, O Arjuna, even to maintain your body. Perform your duty because action is better than inaction.
9 - Work should be performed as a sacrifice to God. Otherwise such work binds you to the material world. Therefore act always for Him and you will be free from bondage, O Kaunteya. Make all your actions selfless and free from personal gain.

Krishna is saying that we must perform our duty and do it well, so that we add to life rather than take from it. All actions should be done as a dedication to the very highest.

Today

Choose the task you least prefer to do first. Do it with love. This will help you to see things more equally.

सहयज्ञाः प्रजाः सृष्ट्वा पुरोवाच प्रजापतिः ।
अनेन प्रसविष्यध्वमेष वोऽस्त्विष्टकामधुक् ॥१०॥

देवान्भावयतानेन ते देवा भावयन्तु वः ।
परस्परं भावयन्तः श्रेयः परमवाप्स्यथ ॥११॥

Slokas 10 - 11
saha yajnaah prajaah srishtvaa
purovaacha prajaapatihi
anena prasavishyadhvam
esha vo 'stvishta kaama dhuk

devaan bhaavayataanena
te devaa bhaavayantu vaha
parasparam bhaavayantaha
sreyah param avaapsyatha

10 - At the time of creation, Prajapati, the Lord of all Creatures said, 'Sacrifice to God and be happy, for this will bring the fulfilment of all your desires.
11 - 'Through sacrifice you cherish the Gods and they cherish you. Thus loving one another, you reap the very highest.'

The Creator gave us sacrifice as a gift saying, 'I am giving you the opportunity to give, because when you do, you will find great peace and happiness.' Sacrifice means giving part of your time, energy and space fo the benefit of others. We often say, 'that was a great sacrifice,' meaning that there was nothing in it for us. Sacrifice is about giving up the conce of 'I' and acting selflessly. As St. Francis used to say so beautifully, the more you give, the greater the happiness you can receive. It is actually impossible to give and be unhappy.

When we practise the Law of Sacrifice, nature itself will come into harmony with us. Closed doors open and unexpected obstacles are removed.

Today

Give! At every opportunity.

इष्टान्भोगान्हि वो देवा दास्यन्ते यज्ञभाविताः ।
तैर्दत्तानप्रदायैभ्यो यो भुङ्क्ते स्तेन एव सः ॥१२॥

यज्ञशिष्टाशिनः सन्तो मुच्यन्ते सर्वकिल्बिषैः ।
भुञ्जते ते त्वघं पापा ये पचन्त्यात्मकारणात् ॥१३॥

Slokas 12 - 13
ishtaan bhogaan hi vo devaa
daasyante yajna bhaavitaaha
tair dattaan apradaayaibhyo
yo bhunkte stena eva saha

yajna sishtaasinah santo
muchyante sarva kilbishaih
bhunjate te tvagham paapaa
ye pachanty aatma kaaranaat

12 - Nourished by your spirit of selfless service, the gods will satisfy all your needs, but anyone who enjoys these without offering selfless acts in return is a thief.

3 - Preparing food for others releases you from previous karma, but if you repare food just for yourself, you add to your karma.

When we practice the Law of Sacrifice, many gifts of happiness and eace come to us. These also have to be offered back as a sacrifice, therwise we are taking a free gift. Peace will not stay with us if we don't se our gifts to make others happy, because they are only given to us to se for the benefit of all. One who serves - a devotee - is forever feeding ack into the cycle of creation and is thereby released from all kinds of ast karma*.

Remember a time in your life when you carried a great weight on your houlders. Imagine it is suddenly taken from you and you feel strangely ree. Imagine the joy as the capstone comes off the well and the waters of oy flow out. Time spent in self-gratification adds more weight to your houlders and doesn't bring you joy, whereas practising the Law of acrifice, brings tremendous inner freedom.

oday

Valk out into the garden and affirm: 'I am a free being'. Feel all of your esponsibilities being lifted and taken away. Now imagine that feeling nagnified a thousand times.

अन्नाद्भवन्ति भूतानि पर्जन्यादन्नसंभवः ।
यज्ञाद्भवति पर्जन्यो यज्ञः कर्मसमुद्भवः ॥१४॥

Sloka 14
annaad bhavanti bhootaani
parjanyaad anna sambhavaha
yajnaad bhavati parjanyo
yajnah karma samudbhavaha

4 - All living creatures are nourished by food and food is nourished by rain. The rain is the result of selfless sacrifice and sacrifice is brought into being y action.

* *see glossary*

There is a natural order of cause and effect that this verse describes, showing that all of nature is affected by acts of sacrifice. It is easy to see and appreciate the cycle of harmony in nature, because it is external and all around us. The sun rises and sets, the tides ebb and flow, and everything is in accord with everything else. We all need to allow ourselves to fit into the harmonious cycles of nature by living according to her laws. In fact, we simply must live according to these laws.

When we break the cycle and step outside these natural laws, disharmony occurs on a grand scale. Living outside the Law of Sacrifice for instance, human beings take the view that everyone is out for themselves and therefore the community will suffer. On the other hand, when people live for the community, it creates total harmony.

Today

Be aware that the money you have may be satisfying your desires, but what good is it doing to the whole community? Take an interest in the community. What can you do?

कर्म ब्रह्मोद्भवं विद्धि ब्रह्माक्षरसमुद्भवम् ।
तस्मात्सर्वगतं ब्रह्म नित्यं यज्ञे प्रतिष्ठितम् ॥१५॥

Sloka 15
karma brahmodbhavam viddhi
brahmaakshara samudbhavam
tasmaat sarva gatam brahma
nityam yajne pratishthitam

15 - Understand Arjuna that every selfless act originates from the Creator of all things, and so the way to establish yourself in Him is through your self-sacrifice.

Because the Law of Sacrifice is given as a gift from God, the very nature of God is a sacrifice. Acts of sacrifice therefore, will situate you in God's heart, because they draw your nature towards God.

ōday

ïve someone a gift - and examine your own feelings. Enjoy the instant of :illness within your own being.

एवं प्रवर्तितं चक्रं नानुवर्तयतीह यः ।
अघायुरिन्द्रियारामो मोघं पार्थ स जीवति ॥१६॥

Sloka 16
evam pravartitam chakram
naanuvartayateeha yaha
aghaayur indriyaaraamo
mogham paartha sa jeevati

6 - All of life revolves around this great Law of Sacrifice. Those who do not ɔllow it, choosing instead to indulge in the senses for personal pleasure lone, have wasted their life.

Sacrifice means 'to make sacred'. If we do not perform sacrifice, we .ve outside the natural harmony and can never find our purpose in life. Vhen we are selfish, our actions tend to be acquisitive, which make us eactive, angry and greedy. Our eternal nature is obscured and the result an only be misery. We will find ourselves caught in all kinds of ınpleasant interactions which can become a self-perpetuating cycle.)nce you stop the wheel and reverse the process, the cycle of harmony tarts and you will feel peace. Forgiveness is an even deeper aspect of this aw and a great act of sacrifice. It is said in mystical circles to be the best lefence against any negative energy.

Today

\pply the Law of Forgiveness and affirm you will make it an important part f your life. Try to look at somebody who has hurt you in a completely lifferent way. See beyond their actions and into the heart of the person. 'ou could imagine them as a small child, because it is easy to forgive a hild.

यस्त्वात्मरतिरेव स्यादात्मतृप्तश्च मानवः ।
आत्मन्येव च संतुष्टस्तस्य कार्यं न विद्यते ॥१७॥

नैव तस्य कृतेनार्थो नाकृतेनेह कश्चन ।
न चास्य सर्वभूतेषु कश्चिदर्थव्यपाश्रयः ॥१८॥

Slokas 17 - 18
yas tvaatma ratir eva syaad
aatma triptas cha maanavaha
aatmany eva cha santushtas
tasya kaaryam na vidyate

naiva tasya kritenaartho
naakriteneha kaschana
na chaasya sarva bhooteshu
kaschid artha vyapaasrayaha

17 - He who delights only in the Self, finds satisfaction in the Self and is centred in the Self, has no more need to act.
18 - There is no reason or purpose in acting or not acting, and no dependence on anyone for any purpose.

A being of steady wisdom, as described in Chapter Two, lives outside the Law of Duty because they are fully satisfied and do not need anything. Nothing matters any more.

Today

Go out into nature and stand among the trees. Look at the sky and the earth and consider all the things that you have ever done. Ask yourself, 'What do these really matter now? How is it now?'

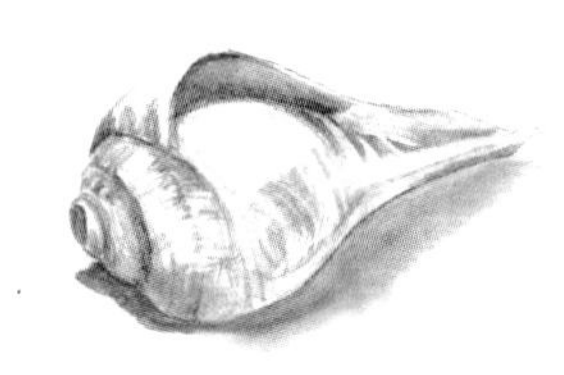

तस्मादसक्तः सततं कार्यं कर्म समाचर ।
असक्तो ह्याचरन्कर्म परमाप्नोति पूरुषः ॥१९॥

कर्मणैव हि संसिद्धिमास्थिता जनकादयः ।
लोकसंग्रहमेवापि संपश्यन्कर्तुमर्हसि ॥२०॥

यद्यदाचरति श्रेष्ठस्तत्तदेवेतरो जनः ।
स यत्प्रमाणं कुरुते लोकस्तदनुवर्तते ॥२१॥

Slokas 19 - 21
tasmaad asaktah satatam
kaaryam karma samaachara
asakto hyaacharan karma
param aapnoti poorushaha

karmanaiva hi samsiddhim
aasthitaa janakaadayaha
loka sangraham evaapi
sampasyan kartum arhasi

yad yad aacharati sreshthas
tat tad evetaro janaha
sa yat pramaanam kurute
lokas tad anuvartate

9 - So perform your duty without attachment. If you can do things without lesiring results for yourself, you will achieve the very highest state.
0 - King Janaka and many others have attained perfection through action lone. You too should follow this path of action, keeping in mind the velfare of others.
1 - Whatever a great man does the whole world follows. Whatever tandards he sets, the whole world takes as his example.

In our actions we need to try to attain the peace and stillness that arises out of sacrifice. It shows non-attachment. Everything we do should benefit humanity and great beings will always show us the way by performing such actions. Always aspire to be an example to others, by displaying the positive attributes of humanity such as love, generosity and kindness.

Today

Always uphold yourself and your values and never betray yourself. If you witness an unjust act - speak out!

न मे पार्थास्ति कर्तव्यं त्रिषु लोकेषु किंचन ।
नानवाप्तमवाप्तव्यं वर्त एव च कर्मणि ॥२२॥

यदि ह्यहं न वर्तेयं जातु कर्मण्यतन्द्रितः ।
मम वर्त्मानुवर्तन्ते मनुष्याः पार्थ सर्वशः ॥२३॥

उत्सीदेयुरिमे लोका न कुर्यां कर्म चेदहम् ।
संकरस्य च कर्ता स्यामुपहन्यामिमाः प्रजाः ॥२४॥

Slokas 22 - 24
na me paarthaasti kartavyam
trishu lokeshu kinchana
naanavaaptam avaaptavyam
varta eva cha karmani

yadi hyaham na varteyam
jaatu karmany atandritaha
mama vartmaanuvartante
manushyaah paartha sarvasaha

utseedeyur ime lokaa
na kuryaam karma ched aham
sankarasya cha kartaa syaam
upahanyaam imaah prajaaha

2 - O Partha, there is nothing in the three worlds for Me to do, nor is there ıything I need to attain, but I still engage in action.
3 - For if I, who is inexhaustible, did not act, everyone would follow my cample.
4 - If I ever stopped performing action, I would be the cause of confusion ıd chaos. These worlds would perish and all creatures would be destroyed.

Krishna is telling us that even though He has no need to act, He does! ı fact action is inherent in every minute part of creation. Krishna is mply saying that we have no choice in the matter.

oday

hink of someone great that you admire and respect and then think about problem you have to resolve. Ask yourself how they would do it. How ould Gandhi approach your relationship problem?

सक्ताः कर्मण्यविद्वांसो यथा कुर्वन्ति भारत ।
कुर्याद्विद्वांस्तथासक्तश्चिकीर्षुर्लोकसंग्रहम् ॥२५॥

Sloka 25
saktaah karmany avidvaamso
yathaa kurvanti bhaarata
kuryaad vidvaams tathaasaktas
chikeershur loka sangraham

25 - While the unwise act from attachment to action O Arjuna, the wise ac without any attachment, for the welfare of the world.

Every action a realised being performs has a magical quality to it, because they do ordinary things without attachment and in accordance with the Law of Sacrifice. People around them become purified because even a little bit of knowledge can be used to help a great deal of people. If you can make ordinary actions resonate with God's love, people will be drawn to you. They will want to know why you are so peaceful and happy So Krishna is telling us not to try to change people, but just to go about our normal duties in the right way.

Today

Krishna is saying that a wise act is always for the well-being of all. Be wise today and do things that help others improve the quality of their lives or make them happy. Don't wait until someone has gone before you realise how much they mean to you.

न बुद्धिभेदं जनयेदज्ञानां कर्मसङ्गिनाम् ।
जोषयेत्सर्वकर्माणि विद्वान्युक्तः समाचरन् ॥२६॥

Sloka 26
na buddhi bhedam janayed
ajnaanaam karma sanginaam
joshayet sarva karmaani
vidvaan yuktah samaacharan

6 - One should not unsettle the mind of a person who is attached to action, ut rather compassionately help them to engage in all actions whilst himself cting as an example.

If you are in a position of responsibility or teaching people, you must nake sure they are always engaged in activity. A wise teacher will always nake his students word hard. Otherwise, if left to their own devices, they ill follow destructive actions that will not lead them to freedom.

oday

ook at your free time. What will you do? If the mind is lazy you will issipate energy which in turn creates weakness. Even relaxation should be ctive, by engaging the mind.

प्रकृतेः क्रियमाणानि गुणैः कर्माणि सर्वशः ।
अहंकारविमूढात्मा कर्ताहमिति मन्यते ॥२७॥

Sloka 27
prakriteh kriyamaanaani
gunaih karmaani sarvasaha
ahankaara vimoodhaatmaa
kartaaham iti manyate

7 - He whose mind is confused by egoism imagines, 'I am the doer', hereas in fact all actions are carried out by the three qualities of nature he gunas).

All the activities we engage in are forced upon us by the three gunas. By practising the Law of Sacrifice, the gunas will enforce actions which are of the highest nature (sattvic). If we do not practise this law the othe two gunas will apply (tamas and rajas). In other words, forget about being the 'doer' because all your actions are controlled by the laws of nature.

Today

Sit by a window and look out at nature. Try to have a deep sense of gratitude for what the world has presented to you. Gratitude helps you to appreciate the oneness of nature and moves your awareness into a sattvic space. You see things as they are and not as you would wish them to be.

तत्त्ववित्तु महाबाहो गुणकर्मविभागयोः ।
गुणा गुणेषु वर्तन्त इति मत्वा न सज्जते ॥२८॥

प्रकृतेर्गुणसंमूढाः सज्जन्ते गुणकर्मसु ।
तानकृत्स्नविदो मन्दान्कृत्स्नविन्न विचालयेत् ॥२९॥

Slokas 28 - 29
tattva vit tu mahaa baaho
guna karma vibhaagayoho
gunaa guneshu vartanta
iti matvaa na sajjate

prakriter guna sammoodhaaha
sajjante guna karmasu
taan akritsna vido mandaan
kritsna vinna vichaalayet

28 - But those who know the truth, O Arjuna, understand the relationship between the gunas and action and are not attached.
29 - Those who are deluded by the qualities of material nature become attached to material activities. Those who understand these truths should not disturb the minds of those who do not know any better.

The wise can discriminate between actions which are always beneficia and those which are not. You cannot, however, enforce your view on nother, but instead can help them to reach a similar understanding. You must discover it for yourself. It is important always to *inspire* and *uplift* hose who do not know and never to unsettle them.

Today

When you meet a friend, say something uplifting that makes them feel good about themselves. Do the same to someone you do not necessarily get on with so well.

मयि सर्वाणि कर्माणि संन्यस्याध्यात्मचेतसा ।
निराशीर्निर्ममो भूत्वा युध्यस्व विगतज्वरः ॥३०॥

Sloka 30
mayi sarvaani karmaani
sannyasyaa~dhyaatma chetasaa
niraaseer nirmamo bhootvaa
yudhyasva vigata jvaraha

30 - Dedicating all actions to Me, meditating on the Supreme Spirit, becoming free from the wishing and selfishness fever, you must fight!

The most useful thing that anyone can do is to make themselves effective in this life and to work. Effectiveness arises out of a lack of personal agenda and a sincere wish to help all beings equally. Effectiveness does, however, require discipline. Be steadfast in your search and affirm, 'I am working here only for you, dear Lord'. Think of God and all selfish desires will burn away. Krishna admonishes Arjuna to fight. Again and again we need to be reminded.

Today

Dedicate this day to the greatest good of the world and to God. Affirm: 'I stand in the presence of God and have nothing to gain apart from His presence.' Be active, positive and powerful and focus on empowering your strengths. Look inside yourself for a quality which you consider 'weak' and resolve to strengthen that quality.

ये मे मतमिदं नित्यमनुतिष्ठन्ति मानवाः ।
श्रद्धावन्तोऽनसूयन्तो मुच्यन्ते तेऽपि कर्मभिः ॥३१॥

ये त्वेतदभ्यसूयन्तो नानुतिष्ठन्ति मे मतम् ।
सर्वज्ञानविमूढांस्तान्विद्धि नष्टानचेतसः ॥३२॥

Slokas 31 - 32
ye me matam idam nityam
anutishthanti maanavaaha
sraddhaavanto 'nasooyanto
muchyante te 'pi karmabhihi

ye tvetad abhyasooyanto
naanutishthanti me matam
sarva jnaana vimoodhaams taan
viddhi nashtaan achetasaha

31 - Whoever constantly practises this teaching of Mine, with pure faith and without complaint, is released from karma.
32 - But those who, out of envy, disregard these teachings and misunderstand everything, become lost and are the cause of their own suffering.

Krishna is being blunt here. If you want to experience peace and love then trust Him. Don't complain at the tasks He offers you. Practise being in His presence and He will free you. But if you are caught up in the cycle of emotional attachment remember that the outcome is always pain. Peace always comes with freedom from attachment.

Today

Ask yourself, 'Am I living up to my own values?' If you feel a beautiful sense of freedom, achievement, success and self-esteem, you are. If you are not, Krishna is inviting you to practise the Law of Sacrifice and Karma Yoga - action with sacrifice.

सदृशं चेष्टते स्वस्याः प्रकृतेर्ज्ञानवानपि ।
प्रकृतिं यान्ति भूतानि निग्रहः किं करिष्यति ॥३३॥

Sloka 33
sadrisam cheshtate svasyaaha
prakriter jnaanavaan api
prakritim yaanti bhootaani
nigrahah kim karishyati

33 - All beings act according to their own nature, even the wise. Why try to force anything to be otherwise?

One of the greatest challenges that we have as human beings is seeing a situation from someone else's point of view. If we could accept that people see the world differently from us and adapt accordingly, then we would find that most of the problems and challenges we have with other people would vanish in an instant.

Today

Be yourself. You have everything you need and are totally unique. We are all individuals in the eyes of God.

इन्द्रियस्येन्द्रियस्यार्थे रागद्वेषौ व्यवस्थितौ ।
तयोर्न वशमागच्छेत्तौ ह्यस्य परिपन्थिनौ ॥३४॥

श्रेयान्स्वधर्मो विगुणः परधर्मात्स्वनुष्ठितात् ।
स्वधर्मे निधनं श्रेयः परधर्मो भयावहः ॥३५॥

Slokas 34 - 35
indriyas~yendriyas~yaarthe
raaga dveshau vyavasthitau
tayor na vasam aagach~chhet
tau hyasya paripanthinau

sreyaan sva dharmo vigunaha
para dharmaat svanushthitaat
sva dharme nidhanam sreyaha
para dharmo bhayaavahaha

34 - It is natural for the senses to be attracted to that which is pleasant and to reject the unpleasant, but you must not come under the power of these two forces because they are your enemies.
35 - It is better to perform your own duty imperfectly, than someone else's perfectly. In fact, it is better to die in one's own duty, because following someone else's path is dangerous.

We think we are free because we have a choice in our actions, but in reality we are bound by the things we do and do not like. These preferences are an inhibitor of Self-realisation, the root of our attachments.

We can only become free when we have completely overcome preference and aversion. With this freedom, it becomes very easy to express oneself in the world as we are. With preferences, however, you will find you will want to do the things that *other* people do. Krishna is saying, 'Do act, but make it *your* action,' which it cannot be if we find ourselves bound by preferences.

Today

If you have a habit that you really like - give it up today! You will soon find out how attached you are by the effort or lack of effort it takes to do this.

अर्जुन उवाच
अथ केन प्रयुक्तोऽयं पापं चरति पूरुषः ।
अनिच्छन्नपि वार्ष्णेय बलादिव नियोजितः ॥३६॥

श्री भगवानुवाच
काम एष क्रोध एष रजोगुणसमुद्भवः ।
महाशनो महापाप्मा विद्ध्येनमिह वैरिणम् ॥३७॥

धूमेनाव्रियते वह्निर्यथादर्शो मलेन च ।
यथोल्बेनावृतो गर्भस्तथा तेनेदमावृतम् ॥३८॥

आवृतं ज्ञानमेतेन ज्ञानिनो नित्यवैरिणा ।
कामरूपेण कौन्तेय दुष्पूरेणानलेन च ॥३९॥

Slokas 36 - 39
arjuna uvaacha:
atha kena prayukto 'yam
paapam charati poorushaha
anich~chhann api vaarshneya
balaad iva niyojitaha

sree bhagavaan uvaacha:
kaama esha krodha esha
rajo guna samudbhavaha
mahaasano mahaa paapmaa
viddhy enam iha vairinam

dhoomenaavriyate vahnir
yathaadarso malena cha
yatholbenaavrito garbhas
tathaa tenedam aavritam

aavritam jnaanam etena
jnaanino nitya vairinaa
kaama roopena kaunteya
dushpoorenaanalena cha

36 - Arjuna said: What force is it that compels us to act selfishly Varshneya? Even against our own will and desire to act for the good of all?

37 - Lord Krishna said: It is the force of desire, which later shows itself as anger, arising from raja-guna, which is the all-consuming enemy.
38 & 39 - Like fire covered by smoke, like a mirror covered by dust, like the unborn foetus completely surrounded by a membrane, so too is the wisdom in man covered by the insatiable fire of desire, the mortal enemy of the Self, O Kaunteya.

Attachment leads to desire, which leads to anger. Anger means you are lost! It is again our desires which are our greatest enemy (Chapter Two verse 63). They cloud our vision making us lose sight of our goals and purpose in life.

Today

Do you ever feel angry? Next time you do, stop and ask yourself, 'What do I really want? Is it selfish?' If it is, apply the Law of Sacrifice! (Chapter Three verses 10 & 11).

इन्द्रियाणि मनो बुद्धिरस्याधिष्ठानमुच्यते ।
एतैर्विमोहयत्येष ज्ञानमावृत्य देहिनम् ॥४०॥

Sloka 40
indriyaani mano buddhir
asyaadhishthaanam uchyate
etair vimohayaty esha
jnaanam aavritya dehinam

40 - This desire lives in your senses, emotions and intellect, covers the real knowledge of your Self and bewilders you.

Our desires live in our emotions and thoughts but not in pure awareness, which is the experience of the NOW. Desire can never affect pure awareness, because desire is always rooted in how we want something to be or in remembering how it was. Desire cannot exist in the here and now. We need therefore, to engage the mind in the present.

Today

Go out and walk in nature. It has an amazing power to bring us into harmony with who we are and to free us from our illusions and misconceptions. Walk them off!

तस्मात्त्वमिन्द्रियाण्यादौ नियम्य भरतर्षभ ।
पाप्मानं प्रजहि ह्येनं ज्ञानविज्ञाननाशनम् ॥४१॥

Sloka 41
tasmaat tvam indriyaany aadau
niyamya bharatarshabha
paapmaanam prajahi hyenam
jnaana vijnaana naasanam

41 - Therefore O Arjuna, best of the Bharatas, stop desires by controlling the senses and slay this destroyer of Self-knowledge.

The strength of a person's mind and will is measured by how much control they have over their desires. The more desires are regulated, the more that person will be able to be in control of themselves. You have to make a conscious decision to gain control over desires and until you do, you will not actually realise how weak your will is.

Today

More and more, western society is being dominated by greed, sensuality and power. When these desires fill your life, then your whole life comes to depend on their presence. Like the man who was found eating chillies one after the other. When asked why, he replied, 'I just keep going in the hope that the next one will be sweet.' What a silly point of view - our desires cause us nothing but pain in the end. So why don't we stop 'eating the chillies?' The fact is that our mental muscles are so flabby that they don't have the strength to resist the ego. So today make a commitment to say no to one desire, no matter what the outcome is.

इन्द्रियाणि पराण्याहुरिन्द्रियेभ्यः परं मनः ।
मनसस्तु परा बुद्धिर्यो बुद्धेः परतस्तु सः ॥४२॥

एवं बुद्धेः परं बुद्ध्वा संस्तभ्यात्मानमात्मना ।
जहि शत्रुं महाबाहो कामरूपं दुरासदम् ॥४३॥

Slokas 42 - 43
indriyaani paraany aahur
indriyebhyah param manaha
manasas tu paraa buddhir
yo buddheh paratas tu saha

evam buddheh param buddhvaa
samstabhyaatmaanam aatmanaa
jahi satrum mahaa baaho
kaama roopam duraasadam

42 - They say that the senses are higher than the body, the mind higher than the senses, the intellect is above the mind and above the intellect is the Self.
43 - Therefore, knowing your real nature to be beyond the material world, the mind and the senses, you should steady the mind by correct practice and thus with strength conquer desire.

The reason the senses have so much power over us is because we identify with them. But our real nature is much higher than the senses, emotions, feelings and thoughts. Our real nature is experienced in moments of pure awareness and then even the senses work for, rather than against, us.

Today

Pick up a flower. Hold it in your hand and look at it very carefully, bringing all your attention to yourself in the present. Continue to observe the flower. Suddenly you will notice the flower becomes more vivid, the scent more powerful, and the colours around you stronger. The senses aid and work with you, because the awareness acts through the senses like a lens. Unless you practise these things, you will never be able to increase your inner strength.

Om tat sat iti
sreemad bhagavad geetaa su
upanishad su
brahmavidyaayaam
yoga shastre
sree krishna arjuna samvaade

karma yogo naama
triteeyo 'dhyaayaha

Thus in the
glorious Bhagavad Gita,
the cream of the Upanishads,
the science of the Eternal,
the scripture of Yoga,
the dialogue between Sri Krishna and Arjuna,

ends the third discourse entitled
The Yoga of Action

गीतोपनिषद्

Chapter Four

The Yoga of Wisdom

श्री भगवानुवाच
इमं विवस्वते योगं प्रोक्तवानहमव्ययम् ।
विवस्वान्मनवे प्राह मनुरिक्ष्वाकवेऽब्रवीत् ॥१॥

एवं परम्पराप्राप्तमिमं राजर्षयो विदुः ।
स कालेनेह महता योगो नष्टः परंतप ॥२॥

स एवायं मया तेऽद्य योगः प्रोक्तः पुरातनः ।
भक्तोऽसि मे सखा चेति रहस्यं ह्येतदुत्तमम् ॥३॥

Slokas 1 - 3
sree bhagavaan uvaacha:
imam vivasvate yogam
proktavaan aham avyayam
vivasvaan manave praaha
manur ikshvaakave 'braveet

evam paramparaa praaptam
imam raajarshayo viduhu
sa kaaleneha mahataa
yogo nashtah parantapa

sa evaayam mayaa te 'dya
yogah proktah puraatanaha
bhakto 'si me sakhaa cheti
rahasyam hyetad uttamam

1 - Lord Krishna said: I told this eternal secret to Vivasvan, the Sun God, who taught it to Manu, the first man. Manu in turn taught it to his son Ikshvaku.
2 - Thus, O Arjuna, was the science of yoga passed from teacher to disciple through the ages and received by many eminent sages.
3 - I am now giving you this ancient science because you are my devotee as well as my friend.

Sri Krishna is saying that He is the ultimate source beyond and behind all things and that He instructed the secrets of this yoga to Vivasvan at the dawn of time.

Planets are not just massive bodies in the heavens, they are considered to have a life of their own. Also, the sun is symbolic of our very Self - implying that our Self was taught these laws of harmony at the moment of our creation. We have just forgotten them.

Sri Krishna goes on to say that the sun taught this yoga to the very first man and that he, in turn, taught it to others. This science was then passed down from teacher to student until it was lost.

Today

God is telling us He is reflected in all things. Sit today in silence until you touch the inner source and then get up and work.

अर्जुन उवाच
अपरं भवतो जन्म परं जन्म विवस्वतः ।
कथमेतद्विजानीयां त्वमादौ प्रोक्तवानिति ॥४॥

श्री भगवानुवाच
बहूनि मे व्यतीतानि जन्मानि तव चार्जुन ।
तान्यहं वेद सर्वाणि न त्वं वेत्थ परंतप ॥५॥

Slokas 4 - 5
arjuna uvaacha:
aparam bhavato janma
param janma vivasvataha
katham etad vijaaneeyaam
tvam aadau proktavaan iti

sree bhagavaan uvaacha:
bahooni me vyateetaani
janmaani tava chaarjuna
taany aham veda sarvaani
na tvam vettha parantapa

4 - Arjuna said: You were born much later than Vivasvan. How am I to understand that you taught this yoga in the beginning?
5 - Lord Krishna said: You and I have passed through many births Arjuna. I remember them all, but you have forgotten.

None of us are able to remember our previous births because, quite simply, we would become overwhelmed by the past. The Lord, however, remembers everything. The Lord is our innermost nature lying within our pure awareness. This means that deep within ourselves we remember *everything*. Do you ever wonder where your habits and tendencies came from? Childhood? Or even before that? Krishna says we have forgotten.

Today

Remember that all blocks from previous lives can be removed by devotion to the Lord.

अजोऽपि सन्नव्ययात्मा भूतानामीश्वरोऽपि सन् ।
प्रकृतिं स्वामधिष्ठाय संभवाम्यात्ममायया ॥६॥

Sloka 6
ajo 'pi sann avyayaatmaa
bhootaanaam eesvaro 'pi san
prakritim svaam adhishthaaya
sambhavaamy aatma maayayaa

6 - The truth is that I am eternal; I am never born and never die although I am the Lord of all who lives in every creature. By controlling the three elements of nature (the gunas) I appear to take birth through the power of my own illusion (maya).

This verse is very reassuring. Krishna is saying there is a part of Him that is never born and never dies. Think about standing in a great hall of mirrors in which you can see an infinite number of reflections of yourself that seem to go on forever. Each one is a reflection of you but the real reflection - which *is* you - is sitting in the middle.

In the same way, we are seeing on the earth an infinite number of reflections of the Lord. We cannot see the real, eternal Lord but only His reflection. Within every reflection, though He is every other reflection also. So while He is unborn and never dies, His manifestations will appear everywhere.

Today

Remember that all the people that you meet are a reflection of the Lord, as well as a reflection of you also. So treat each person you meet as if they were you. How would you like to be treated? Give love, simply because it's what you would want to receive.

यदा यदा हि धर्मस्य ग्लानिर्भवति भारत ।
अभ्युत्थानमधर्मस्य तदात्मानं सृजाम्यहम् ॥७॥

Sloka 7
yadaa yadaa hi dharmasya
glaanir bhavati bhaarata
abhyutthaanam adharmasya
tadaatmaanam srijaamy aham

7 - Whenever there is a decline in righteousness, O Bharata, and the purpose of life is lost, I appear on earth in a physical form.

Whenever disharmony appears in the world the Lord sends a reflection of Himself to correct that disharmony. But this also happens from moment to moment. Even in yourself, you know when there is disharmony if you choose to stop and look. A little voice tells you. The Lord can reveal Himself in nature. It can be in a flower, a bird song or a coincidence that makes us stop and think, 'should I do this?' And so it is that the Lord manifests from age to age.

Today

Listen to your inner voice and act on it. If inside you know not to have that cream cake - don't! If it says 'yes' - do it!

परित्राणाय साधूनां विनाशाय च दुष्कृताम् ।
धर्मसंस्थापनार्थाय संभवामि युगे युगे ॥८॥

Sloka 8
paritraanaaya saadhoonaam
vinaasaaya cha dushkritaam
dharma samsthaapanaarthaaya
sambhavaami yuge yuge

8 - For the protection of the good and the destruction of the wicked I am born in every age.

Krishna is also saying there are times He will appear physically when there is disharmony in the world. He comes to set an example, as Christ did when he turned over the tables in the temple. Because it is the nature of the mind to shy away from divinity, the Lord has to re-establish the principles of harmony over and over again. If He did not, and we were left to our own devices, we would be in a sorry state.

Today

Be encouraged by the fact that you will never be left alone, even when life appears to be at its very worst. There is always somebody holding your hand.

जन्म कर्म च मे दिव्यमेवं यो वेत्ति तत्त्वतः ।
त्यक्त्वा देहं पुनर्जन्म नैतिमामेति सोऽर्जुन ॥९॥

Sloka 9
janma karma cha me divyam
evam yo vetti tattvataha
tyaktvaa deham punar janma
naiti maam eti so ‘rjuna

9 - He who knows Me, in My true light, as his own divine Self, breaks through the belief that he is the body and is not born again. He becomes united with Me, Arjuna.

One who understands the manifestations of the Lord becomes free rom the need to return here. Once we understand the creation, we ecognise that the illusion (maya) is a reflection of God's energy. Recognising this, we can then disassociate from it because - *it's only a dream.*

Today

Break the fetters of unconscious humanity and rise to the very highest in our being. Choose a moment in the day and during that one moment, ry to be 100 percent awake and aware of everything that's going on. Hold your awareness in that concentration for a minute or two.

वीतरागभयक्रोधा मन्मया मामुपाश्रिताः ।
बहवो ज्ञानतपसा पूता मद्भावमागताः ॥१०॥

Sloka 10
veeta raaga bhaya krodhaa
man mayaa maam upaasritaaha
bahavo jnaana tapasaa
pootaa mad bhaavam aagataaha

10 - Those who have become free from fear, anger and passion, having taken refuge in Me, absorbed in Me, purified by the fire of knowledge and wisdom, enter into My being and become united with Me.

Be assured that you can get there! Thousands have gone before you, which proves it is not impossible. All you have to do is to 'be absorbed in Him.' We cannot really free ourselves - from our desires, anger and the controlling mind - but *we can always love God.* Krishna comes back to this one truth over and over again in the Gita.

Today

Be grateful for everything. Stand proud and affirm: 'I am one of God's children.'

ये यथा मां प्रपद्यन्ते तांस्तथैव भजाम्यहम् ।
मम वर्त्मानुवर्तन्ते मनुष्याः पार्थ सर्वशः ॥११॥

Sloka 11
ye yathaa maam prapadyante
taams tathaiva bhajaamy aham
mama vartmaanuvartante
manushyaah paartha sarvasaha

11 - In whatever way people approach Me, that is how I receive them. All paths lead to Me Arjuna.

Although we don't seek reward, every sacrifice will be rewarded, because every selfless act spirals out into the universe, and returns to us amplified. This is also true for every selfish thought and deed that will come back and create more weight for us.

Today

When someone comes to you, listen to them from their point of view rather than your own. Hear them without any opinions or judgements coming in the way. Listen in such a loving way that your listening creates a healing for them. If you can imagine you are looking through their eyes, it helps bring your senses back to the Self. Through this practice your enemies become your friends, because the only thing that causes separation in us as human beings is that we do not really understand each other.

काङ्क्षन्तः कर्मणां सिद्धिं यजन्त इह देवताः ।
क्षिप्रं हि मानुषे लोके सिद्धिर्भवति कर्मजा ॥१२॥

Sloka 12
kaankshantah karmanaam siddhim
yajanta iha devataaha
kshipram hi maanushe loke
siddhir bhavati karma jaa

12 - Those who desire success in this world pray to the Gods of the Vedas. For those who pray in this way, success in the world comes very quickly.

In praying to the Gods we are addressing the controllers of the forces of nature such as the wind, sky, earth, luck, prosperity and opportunity. These are all inherent within us and in praying to the representatives of these natural forces their power is turned to our material benefit. Krishna assures us then, that results are obtained quickly. In Sanskrit, this is called 'devam.'

Today

Get these forces on your side by paying respect to nature. Be friendly to this world and respect her resources.

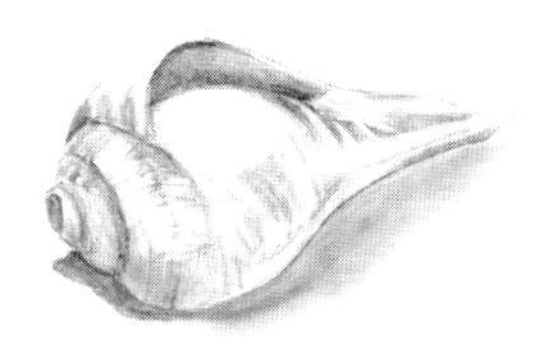

चातुर्वर्ण्यं मया सृष्टं गुणकर्मविभागशः ।
तस्य कर्तारमपि मां विद्ध्यकर्तारमव्ययम् ॥१३॥

Sloka 13
chaatur varnyam mayaa srishtam
guna karma vibhaagasaha
tasya kartaaram api maam
viddhy akartaaram avyayam

13 -The system of four castes (character types) and the three modes of material nature (the gunas) have come from Me. Although I am the creator of this system, understand that I am not the doer and I never change.

The Lord has given us different ways of looking at things. The caste system, or four divisions of human society, actually has its roots in the four emotional types (thinkers, feelers, intuiters and doers) and has arisen *because* of these four kinds of characters.

'Highly born' actually means born of the spirit - a spiritual family. The four divisions of human society, therefore, relate to our fundamental nature. They have come from Krishna and this is the natural way of things and the way they should be. But that is not the Lord's nature, merely the way He has set them up. *His* nature is beyond the gunas.

Today

Try to recognise people for what they are and not what they present to you. You may not like the way somebody does something, but try to see that they are just being the way they are.

न मां कर्माणि लिम्पन्ति न मे कर्मफले स्पृहा ।
इति मां योऽभिजानाति कर्मभिर्न स बध्यते ॥१४॥

एवं ज्ञात्वा कृतं कर्म पूर्वैरपि मुमुक्षुभिः ।
कुरु कर्मैव तस्मात्त्वं पूर्वैः पूर्वतरं कृतम् ॥१५॥

Slokas 14 - 15
na maam karmaani limpanti
na me karma phale sprihaa
iti maam yo 'bhijaanaati
karmabhir na sa badhyate

evam jnaatvaa kritam karma
poorvair api mumukshubhihi
kuru karmaiva tasmaat tvam
poorvaih poorvataram kritam

14 - Actions do not affect Me because I have no desire for their fruits. He who understands this quality in Me is also free from the binding nature of action.
15 - The ancients who knew and understood this freedom within action also engaged in action. Like those great sages, you too should continue to act.

God is beyond the gunas and the different types of character. One who understands the nature of God and his own God-nature is also not entangled by them. He is, therefore, detached from the fruits of all actions. All liberated beings of the past understood this, and therefore we should follow their example.

Today

Stop and realise that everything is absolutely fine. Say to yourself out loud, 'All is well!'

किं कर्म किमकर्मेति कवयोऽप्यत्र मोहिताः ।
तत्ते कर्म प्रवक्ष्यामि यज्ज्ञात्वा मोक्ष्यसेऽशुभात् ॥१६॥

कर्मणो ह्यपि बोद्धव्यं बोद्धव्यं च विकर्मणः ।
अकर्मणश्च बोद्धव्यं गहना कर्मणो गतिः ॥१७॥

कर्मण्यकर्म यः पश्येदकर्मणि च कर्म यः ।
स बुद्धिमान्मनुष्येषु स युक्तः कृत्स्नकर्मकृत् ॥१८॥

Slokas 16 - 18
kim karma kim akarmeti
kavayo 'pyatra mohitaaha
tat te karma pravakshyaami
yaj jnaatvaa mokshyase 'subhaat

karmano hyapi boddhavyam
boddhavyam cha vikarmanaha
akarmanas cha boddhavyam
gahanaa karmano gatihi

karmany akarma yah pasyed
akarmani cha karma yaha
sa buddhimaan manushyeshu
sa yuktah kritsna karma krit

16 - What is action? What is inaction? This question has confused even the greatest sages. I will now explain the secret of action to you so that you can become free from bondage.
17 - You need to know what action is, and also the nature of inaction. The intricacies of action are very hard to understand.

18 - Those who see inaction in action and action in inaction live in wisdom. He or she is a yogi and can accomplish anything.

The secret of action is one of the most important statements that Krishna makes. We all have to act - and everyone does - but not everyone becomes liberated through those actions. Action and inaction need to be seen from a *divine* perspective. When we can act with an attitude of devotion, offering our actions to the Lord, we create a sense of detachment within us that enables us to become the observer of our actions and not the doer.

It is like driving a car. We say that *we* drive it, but in fact we just sit behind the wheel and observe the whole phenomenon. We each have to learn the art of *non-doing*, for when we *know* we do nothing, everything gets done. On the other hand, a person may appear inactive, like a writer or a composer, but may in fact be intensely active within themselves in their moments of creativity.

Today

Stop every hour and affirm: 'I have done all these things, but I am not really the doer, merely the observer.'

यस्य सर्वे समारम्भाः कामसंकल्पवर्जिताः ।
ज्ञानाग्निदग्धकर्माणं तमाहुः पण्डितं बुधाः ॥१९॥

Sloka 19
yasya sarve samaarambhaaha
kaama sankalpa varjitaaha
jnaanaagni dagdha karmaanam
tam aahuh panditam budhaaha

19 - He who does everything without desire for personal reward or anxiety about results, and has burned up his karma in the fire of knowledge, the wise men call a sage.

Planning, scheming and manipulating events for our own selfish ends actually drains our energy and robs us of our joy. A wise man is selfless nd unattached to results, simply because he knows he is not the doer. If ou are able to be the observer, then you are not bound by the senses.

Krishna is saying that one of the results of having attained knowledge s mastery over sense desires. There is, in fact, a point inside us where he sensations of the senses simply do not register. We will not be ouched by pleasure or pain, heat or cold.

Today

When tempted by desires, try to see yourself as the watcher; the being nside yourself - and notice how the desire evaporates.

त्यक्त्वा कर्मफलासङ्गं नित्यतृप्तो निराश्रयः ।
कर्मण्यभिप्रवृत्तोऽपि नैव किंचित्करोति सः ॥२०॥

निराशीर्यतचित्तात्मा त्यक्तसर्वपरिग्रहः ।
शारीरं केवलं कर्म कुर्वन्नाप्नोति किल्बिषम् ॥२१॥

Slokas 20 - 21
tyakvaa karma phalaasangam
nitya tripto niraasrayaha
karmany abhipravritto 'pi
naiva kinchit karoti saha

niraaseer yata chittaatmaa
tyakta sarva parigrahaha
saareeram kevalam karma
kurvan naapnoti kilbisham

20 - Having let go of all attachment to the fruits of his actions, and having abandoned all external supports he is always content. Though he appears to be doing things, he is, in fact, not the doer.
21 - Because he doesn't want anything for himself, and does not consider possessions as his own, with mind and body firmly controlled by the Self, his actions do not incur bad merit.

We can invest so much energy into our actions and if our expectations are not met, we feel intense pain. If we can recognise that it is the *Self within*, and not us, that acts, we become free inside and therefore, 'always content'. The realised being moves through this world making great waves, but he himself does nothing. He makes sure his actions create stillness, and not karma, either for himself or anyone else.

Today

Whatever job you have to do, stop from time to time and say, 'I am perfectly happy doing this.'

यदृच्छालाभसंतुष्टो द्वन्द्वातीतो विमत्सरः ।
समः सिद्धावसिद्धौ च कृत्वापि न निबध्यते ॥२२॥

Sloka 22
yadrich~chhaa laabha santushto
dvandvaateeto vimatsaraha
samah siddhaav asiddhau cha
kritvaapi na nibadhyate

22 - Content with whatever comes his way, beyond the pairs of opposites such as pleasure, pain, success or failure, he is never entangled, even though he acts.

Anything that comes to us is a gift from the Lord, but it may not always be what we like. When we are grateful for *everything*, both good and bad, it creates an equanimity inside us. For a realised being, gain often happens of its own accord. He doesn't hanker after things and when they come, he offers them back to the Lord.

Today

Receive everything that happens to you as a gift from God, whether pleasant or unpleasant.

गतसङ्गस्य मुक्तस्य ज्ञानावस्थितचेतसः ।
यज्ञायाचरतः कर्म समग्रं प्रविलीयते ॥२३॥

Sloka 23
gata sangasya muktasya
jnaanaavasthita chetasaha
yajnaayaacharatah karma
samagram pravileeyate

23 - Those who work free from attachment find freedom. Their minds are absorbed in knowledge. Performing work freely, in the spirit of sacrifice, all their karma is dissolved away.

When such a person works in the world, their work will carry the energy of God with it. People coming in contact with this work will be inspired, uplifted and often not even know why.

Today

Think about someone who really inspires you, like Gandhi, St. Francis or Mother Teresa. Spend a few moments thinking about how many people have been affected by their actions.

ब्रह्मार्पणं ब्रह्म हविर्ब्रह्माग्नौ ब्रह्मणा हुतम् ।
ब्रह्मैव तेन गन्तव्यं ब्रह्मकर्मसमाधिना ॥२४॥

Sloka 24
brahmaarpanam brahma havir
brahmaagnau brahmanaa hutam
brahmaiva tena gantavyam
brahma karma samaadhinaa

24 - The process of offering is Brahman; what is offered is Brahman. Brahman offers the sacrifice into the fire of Brahman. He who sees Brahman in every action attains Brahman.

We tend to see ourselves as separate from God and therefore different. The truth is that *there is only God.* Our emotional nature is God, our body is God in another form, the world around us is God and the very energy we have to perform action is God. We should, in fact, treat everything in front of us as God.

Even eating becomes an act of worship. The food is God (Brahman), as is the hand that takes it, the mouth that chews it and even the process of eating. When food is treated as God we will know that God is nourishing God.

Today

Chant this verse before you eat. It purifies the food, the eater and the intention behind the eating. As you take each mouthful of food say to yourself, 'This is God and this is God consuming God.'

दैवमेवापरे यज्ञं योगिनः पर्युपासते ।
ब्रह्माग्नावपरे यज्ञं यज्ञेनैवोपजुह्वति ॥२५॥

श्रोत्रादीनीन्द्रियाण्यन्ये संयमाग्निषु जुह्वति ।
शब्दादीन्विषयानन्य इन्द्रियाग्निषु जुह्वति ॥२६॥

सर्वाणीन्द्रियकर्माणि प्राणकर्माणि चापरे ।
आत्मसंयमयोगाग्नौ जुह्वति ज्ञानदीपिते ॥२७॥

द्रव्ययज्ञास्तपोयज्ञा योगयज्ञास्तथापरे ।
स्वाध्यायज्ञानयज्ञाश्च यतयः संशितव्रताः ॥२८॥

अपाने जुह्वति प्राणं प्राणेऽपानं तथापरे ।
प्राणापानगती रुद्ध्वा प्राणायामपरायणाः ॥२९॥

अपरे नियताहाराः प्राणान्प्राणेषु जुह्वति ।
सर्वेऽप्येते यज्ञविदो यज्ञक्षपितकल्मषाः ॥३०॥

यज्ञशिष्टामृतभुजो यान्ति ब्रह्म सनातनम् ।
नायं लोकोऽस्त्ययज्ञस्य कुतोऽन्यः कुरुसत्तम ॥३१॥

Slokas 25 - 31

daivam evaapare yajnam
yoginah paryupaasate
brahmaagnaav apare yajnam
yajnenaivopa~juhvati

srotraadee~neendriyaany anye
samyamaagnishu juhvati
sabdaadeen vishayaan anya
indriyaagnishu juhvati

sarvaaneendriya karmaani
praana karmaani chaapare
aatma samyama yogaagnau
juhvati jnaana deepite

dravya yajnaas tapo yajnaa
yoga yajnaas tathaapare
svaadhyaaya jnaana yajnaas cha
yatayah samsita vrataaha

apaane juhvati praanam
praane 'paanam tathaapare
praanaapaana gatee ruddhvaa
praanaayaama paraayanaaha

apare niyataahaaraaha
praanaan praaneshu juhvati
sarve 'pyete yajna vido
yajna kshapita kalmashaaha

yajna sishtaamrita bhujo
yaanti brahma sanaatanam
naayam loko 'sty ayajnasya
kuto 'nyah kuru sattama

25 - Some yogis perform sacrifices to the Gods. Others offer selfless service as sacrifice in the fire of Brahman.
26 - Some sacrifice the hearing process and the senses in the fire of restraint while others sacrifice the objects of the senses in the fire of the senses.
27 - In their search for realisation others offer the functions of the senses and vital energy in the fire of self-restraint which is kindled by knowledge.
28 - Some offer their material possessions or their suffering. Some take vows and offer knowledge and study of the scriptures as sacrifice.
29 - Some of those who control the life-force by regulating the flow of breath offer the outbreath as a sacrifice to the inbreath, restraining the breath altogether.
30 - Others who restrict their diets offer the outgoing breath into itself as a sacrifice. All these understand the meaning of sacrifice and will be purified of all sins.
31 - This world and the world to come are for those who make sacrifices, but those who do not seek to serve are without a home in this world. How could they be at home in any world to come?

People have their own ways of sacrificing and each type of sacrifice wil benefit that person in its own special way. Krishna is telling us that without sacrifice, you cannot be happy in this life or the next. Everything can become an offering, even our breath. We don't even have the right to say, 'this breath is mine' because it is a gift.

Today

Spend some time working for the benefit of somebody else. An old person, local hospice or charity, or simply comforting a friend. Do it with love.

एवं बहुविधा यज्ञा वितता ब्रह्मणो मुखे ।
कर्मजान्विद्धि तान्सर्वानेवं ज्ञात्वा विमोक्ष्यसे ॥३२॥

Sloka 32
evam bahu vidhaa yajnaa
vitataa brahmano mukhe
karma jaan viddhi taan sarvaan
evam jnaatvaa vimokshyase

32 - All these different types of sacrifices are born of action and each guides nan along a path to Brahman. Understanding this, you will attain iberation.

The ancients recognised these forms of sacrifice and even gave ways of now to perform them effectively, and there are as many ways of acrificing as there are people. Giving of your love, time and energy for God's purpose is true sacrifice.

Today

See what opportunities are presented to you to give something to omebody else. They are opportunities to love. And when you recognise hem, please give unconditionally.

श्रेयान्द्रव्यमयाद्यज्ञाज्ज्ञानयज्ञः परंतप ।
सर्वं कर्माखिलं पार्थ ज्ञाने परिसमाप्यते ॥३३॥

Sloka 33
sreyaan dravya mayaad yajnaaj
jnaana yajnah parantapa
sarvam karmaakhilam paartha
jnaane parisamaapyate

33 - The offering of wisdom is better than any material offering, Arjuna, for he goal of all seekers is spiritual wisdom.

Sacrifice of knowledge means we are sacrificing ourselves, our time, energy, love and will.

Today

Find an inspiring quote and meditate on it for a few moments. Then do a good deed for someone you don't particularly like, so that the action arises out of wisdom.

तद्विद्धि प्रणिपातेन परिप्रश्नेन सेवया ।
उपदेक्ष्यन्ति ते ज्ञानं ज्ञानिनस्तत्त्वदर्शिनः ॥३४॥

यज्ज्ञात्वा न पुनर्मोहमेवं यास्यसि पाण्डव ।
येन भूतान्यशेषेण द्रक्ष्यस्यात्मन्यथो मयि ॥३५॥

Slokas 34 - 35
tad viddhi pranipaatena
pariprasnena sevayaa
upadekshyanti te jnaanam
jnaaninas tattva darsinaha

yaj jnaatvaa na punar moham
evam yaasyasi paandava
yena bhootaany aseshena
drakshyasy aatmany atho mayi

34 - You must try to learn the truth by approaching a spiritual master. Through humble submission and enquiry, the knowing ones will be led to teach you knowledge.
35 - When you realise this truth, Arjuna, you will never be confused again. You will clearly see that all things in creation are part of you and part of Me.

The quickest way to receive wisdom is to enquire from someone who has already received it. Krishna invites us to find beings who have the qualifications Krishna has spoken of and to learn from them. Without reverence, however, knowledge is never revealed.

Today

Realise that teachers are all around us. The universe, our friends and enemies - they all teach us and we should have an attitude of acceptance and enquiry. 'How can I learn more?'

अपि चेदसि पापेभ्यः सर्वेभ्यः पापकृत्तमः ।
सर्वं ज्ञानप्लवेनैव वृजिनं संतरिष्यसि ॥३६॥

Sloka 36
api ched asi paapebhyaha
sarvebhyah paapa krit tamaha
sarvam jnaana plavenaiva
vrijinam santarishyasi

6 - Even if you have been the worst sinner you would cross over all ickedness on the raft of spiritual wisdom.

[ave tremendous reassurance that with 'direct knowledge of the Self' doesn't matter what you have done, you can be free. If you turn to ›ve God you can be freed from anything.

ōday

e reassured. There is only love.

यथैधांसि समिद्धोऽग्निर्भस्मसात्कुरुतेऽर्जुन ।
ज्ञानाग्निः सर्वकर्माणि भस्मसात्कुरुते तथा ॥३७॥

न हि ज्ञानेन सदृशं पवित्रमिह विद्यते ।
तत्स्वयं योगसंसिद्धः कालेनात्मनि विन्दति ॥३८॥

Slokas 37 - 38
yathaidhaamsi samiddho 'gnir
bhasma saat kurute 'rjuna
jnaanaagnih sarva karmaani
bhasma saat kurute tathaa

na hi jnaanena sadrisam
pavitram iha vidyate
tat svayam yoga samsiddhaha
kaalenaatmani vindati

7 - As the heat of fire reduces firewood to ashes, Arjuna, so the fire of nowledge reduces all your karma to ashes.

38 - Nothing in this world purifies like the awakening of true knowing. In time, one who is perfected in yoga finds that knowledge in the Self.

The fire of knowledge - knowing the nature of God - burns away all attachments to the gunas and takes us beyond them to a place where we recognise the dream nature of the world. There is no knowledge as good as this and be assured that with practice, this knowledge will surely come to us.

Here's a powerful thought to contemplate upon: If we focus on God and ask Him to answer our prayers, He will, and that is a way of connecting with the Divine. But what He really wants us to do is to answer *His* prayers, to be His instrument and to be open to do His will.

Today

Send a fervent prayer to God asking nothing for yourself but only to be His servant. 'How may I serve you today?'

श्रद्धावाँल्लभते ज्ञानं तत्परः संयतेन्द्रियः ।
ज्ञानं लब्ध्वा परां शान्तिमचिरेणाधिगच्छति ॥३९॥

अज्ञश्चाश्रद्दधानश्च संशयात्मा विनश्यति ।
नायं लोकोऽस्ति न परो न सुखं संशयात्मनः ॥४०॥

Slokas 39 - 40
sraddhaavaan labhate jnaanam
tat parah samyatendriyaha
jnaanam labdhvaa paraam saantim
achirenaadhigach~chhati

ajnas chaasraddadhaanas cha
samsayaatmaa vinasyati
naayam loko 'sti na paro
na sukham samsayaatmanaha

39 - Anyone who has sincere belief and devotion, and takes control of the senses, will rise to this wisdom and soon enters into supreme peace.

0 - The ignorant who are sceptical and without faith are ruined. They annot be happy in this world or the next if they doubt.

It is helpful to encourage qualities of faith and dedication. Without **edication** you are easily turned away from your path. Without **faith** here can be no knowledge of the presence of God in your life. Put both ogether and you are sure to succeed.

oday

Never give up. Whatever task you have to do, invite the presence of God nto it and ask for His guidance.

योगसंन्यस्तकर्माणं ज्ञानसंछिन्नसंशयम् ।
आत्मवन्तं न कर्माणि निबध्नन्ति धनंजय ॥४१॥

तस्मादज्ञानसंभूतं हृत्स्थं ज्ञानासिनात्मनः ।
छित्त्वैनं संशयं योगमातिष्ठोत्तिष्ठ भारत ॥४२॥

Slokas 41 - 42
yoga sannyasta karmaanam
jnaana sanchhinna samsayam
aatmavantam na karmaani
nibadhnanti dhananjaya

tasmaad ajnaana sambhootam
hrit stham jnaanaasinaatmanaha
chhittvainam samsayam yogam
aatishthottishtha bhaarata

41 - Those who have renounced the fruits of their actions, O Dhananjaya, and cut through doubt with spiritual wisdom, act in freedom and remain poised in the Self.
42 - Cut through this doubt in your mind, born of ignorance, O Bharata, with the sword of knowledge. Stand up, Arjuna, and resort to yoga!

One who practises this yoga, sits at the very heart of themselves, untouched by the material world, not bound to anything.

Today

Take courage in this and cut away any doubts you have had - and always remember: never give up!

Om tat sat iti
sreemad bhagavad geetaa su
upanishad su
brahmavidyaayaam
yoga shastre
sree krishna arjuna samvaade

jnaana karma sannyaasa yogo naama
chaturtho 'dhyaayaha

Thus in the
glorious Bhagavad Gita,
the cream of the Upanishads,
the science of the Eternal,
the scripture of Yoga,
the dialogue between Sri Krishna and Arjuna,

ends the fourth discourse entitled:
The Yoga of Wisdom

गीतोपनिषद्

Chapter Five

The Yoga of Renunciation of Action

अर्जुन उवाच
संन्यासं कर्मणां कृष्ण पुनर्योगं च शंससि ।
यच्छ्रेय एतयोरेकं तन्मे ब्रूहि सुनिश्चितम् ॥१॥

श्री भगवानुवाच
संन्यासः कर्मयोगश्च निःश्रेयसकरावुभौ ।
तयोस्तु कर्मसंन्यासात्कर्मयोगो विशिष्यते ॥२॥

Slokas 1 - 2
arjuna uvaacha:
sannyaasam karmanaam krishna
punar yogam cha samsasi
yach chhreya etayor ekam
tan me broohi su nischitam

sree bhagavaan uvaacha
sannyaasah karma yogas cha
nihsreyasa karaav ubhau
tayos tu karma sannyaasaat
karma yogo visishyate

1 - Arjuna said: O Krishna, you seem to be advising both the path of selfless action and the renunciation of action. Please tell me definitely which one is better.
2 - Lord Sri Krishna said: The renunciation of action and selfless action will both lead to the supreme goal, but the path of selfless action is better.

Arjuna is obviously still confused even though Krishna has gone to some lengths to explain the answer to this question. This confusion arises in our hearts even when we have been given spiritual truths, for the simple reason that we are attached to the material world. A spiritual truth only has meaning for us when we *realise* it. To realise it we have to have a vision of something greater than ourselves.

Krishna has already given Arjuna advice on what to do and told him that this knowledge will bring him realisation. But so far, Arjuna has only *thought* about it. He hasn't *done* it yet, so although he is aware that something remarkable is happening, he hasn't yet seen the truth of it. Consequently he is still confused!

Krishna is offering him an aerial view, but Arjuna is still grounded, his eet planted firmly on the earth, and has not as yet been able to perceive he heavens. Krishna is weaving a pattern around Arjuna who is still only ın observer of this process. As he starts to change, he will gradually ›ecome part of the pattern.

It is the same with our lives. The Creator is weaving a beautifully ntricate pattern around us which we can choose to observe or ›articipate in. Either way, through the process of evolution, we will ›ecome a part of the tapestry of life. It is only a matter of time.

Krishna says definitively that skilful action is best!

Today

Start to work in skilful action. Plan your day in accordance with a higher ›urpose. Make a list of goals and realistic objectives that will really make a lifference - and try to achieve them.

ज्ञेयः स नित्यसंन्यासी यो न द्वेष्टि न काङ्क्षति ।
निर्द्वन्द्वो हि महाबाहो सुखं बन्धात्प्रमुच्यते ॥३॥

Sloka 3
jneyah sa nitya sannyaasee
yo na dveshti na kaankshati
nirdvando hi mahaa baaho
sukham bandhaat pramuchyate

3 - A perfect renunciate is one who neither hates nor desires anything. Freedom from such dualities of the mind brings liberation, O mighty-armed Arjuna.

The meaning of freedom is more than just having choice over our *actions.* It is being able to have choice over our *desires* and *feelings.* We can choose to be happy or unhappy, although unhappiness is often an unconscious choice due to our attachment to preferences - the things we do and do not like.

The one who is free (a sannyasin) has no preferences and easily accepts the results of whatever happens. He or she will have total dispassion for results but a *passion* for the action.

Today

To overcome preferences, do something you normally avoid, but in a very positive way. Smile when you do it! Deliberately approach someone you find difficult and say, 'Good morning!' with enthusiasm.

सांख्ययोगौ पृथग्बालाः प्रवदन्ति न पण्डिताः ।
एकमप्यास्थितः सम्यगुभयोर्विन्दते फलम् ॥४॥

यत्सांख्यैः प्राप्यते स्थानं तद्योगैरपि गम्यते ।
एकं सांख्यं च योगं च यः पश्यति स पश्यति ॥५

संन्यासस्तु महाबाहो दुःखमाप्तुमयोगतः ।
योगयुक्तो मुनिर्ब्रह्म नचिरेणाधिगच्छति ॥६॥

Slokas 4 - 6
saankhya yogau prithag baalaaha
pravadanti na panditaaha
ekam apy aasthitah samyag
ubhayor vindate phalam

yat saankhyaih praapyate sthaanam
tad yogair api gamyate
ekam saankhyam cha yogam cha
yah pasyati sa pasyati

sannyaasas tu mahaa baaho
duhkham aaptum ayogataha
yoga yukto munir brahma
na chirenaadhigach~chhati

4 - It is the childish, not the wise, who say that knowledge and action are different. The wise know that whoever applies himself well to one will achieve the rewards of both.

- Both followers of knowledge and action reach the same goal. They see learly who understand that knowledge and selfless action are the same.
- Perfect renunciation is difficult to attain without being engaged in ction. But the wise who follow the path of action can quickly achieve the upreme.

Krishna is saying that only the ignorant see the path of action and nowledge as different, because they only appear to be so. The truth is hat one leads to the other.

Today

Carry a stone in your pocket and call it your 'God stone'. Every time you eel it there remind yourself that God is with you. It will help you to see God in all things.

योगयुक्तो विशुद्धात्मा विजितात्मा जितेन्द्रियः ।
सर्वभूतात्मभूतात्मा कुर्वन्नपि न लिप्यते ॥७॥

Sloka 7
yoga yukto visuddhaatmaa
vijitaatmaa jitendriyaha
sarva bhootaatma bhootaatmaa
kurvann api na lipyate

7 - He who is devoted to the path of yoga, a purified soul, who controls his nind and senses, who recognises his Self as the Self in all beings, is intouched by any action he may perform.

You can tell when somebody is pure, devoted and in control of their mind and senses because everyone is attracted to them. If you achieve knowledge, know that you will become a magnet for people.

Today

Give something to someone. It could be a cup of tea, a card or just a simple message, but give it with such love that they almost feel the weight of your love. Remember to expect nothing in return.

नैव किंचित्करोमीति युक्तो मन्येत तत्त्ववित् ।
पश्यञ्शृण्वन्स्पृशञ्जिघ्रन्नश्नन्गच्छन्स्वपञ्श्वसन् ॥८॥

प्रलपन्विसृजन्गृह्णन्नुन्मिषन्निमिषन्नपि ।
इन्द्रियाणीन्द्रियार्थेषु वर्तन्त इति धारयन् ॥९॥

Slokas 8 - 9
naiva kinchit karomeeti
yukto manyeta tattva vit
pasyan srinvan sprisan jighrann
asnan gach~chhan svapan svasan

pralapan visrijan grihnann
unmishan nimishann api
indriyaa~neendriyaar~theshu
vartanta iti dhaarayan

8 & 9 - By identifying with your innermost Self you will clearly see that it is not you but the senses that move among the sense objects, whether seeing, hearing, touching, smelling, eating, walking, sleeping, breathing, talking or eliminating. You should think, 'I do nothing at all.'

One who has this vision has such a clarity about the illusory nature of the world that he is never entangled by it. The spiritual eyes are turned inwards and therefore the physical eyes are detached. He is therefore aloof from all the organs of sense and action.

Today

Go outside and take nourishment from the sky, the trees, the wind and sun. Be one with them and become strengthened by them in your heart and spirit. Find a tree and make it your special friend. Use your breath to still the mind and go to a deeper place inside yourself. If you go deep enough, you will be able to connect to the being that resides within the tree and then the strength of that tree will become your strength. The result will be that you will find that things that normally attract you will have less power over you today.

ब्रह्मण्याधाय कर्माणि सङ्गं त्यक्त्वा करोति यः ।
लिप्यते न स पापेन पद्मपत्रमिवाम्भसा ॥१०॥

Sloka 10
brahmany aadhaaya karmaani
sangam tyaktvaa karoti yaha
lipyate na sa paapena
padma patram ivaambhasaa

10 - Those who let go of attachment to the fruits of their actions are not affected by sin just as a lotus leaf is untouched by water.

If you have this awareness and serenity, you will be able to recognise when people around you are behaving in a way that would normally draw you into something that degrades you. You can see the illusory nature of it so clearly that its effects will roll off you like water off a duck's back - or a lotus leaf!

Today

If you go shopping, walk through the store with a sense of freedom, saying to yourself, 'Whatever I buy is because I need it and not because I want it.' Shops can be very oppressive places as they are actually a vast watering hole for people's emotions where negativity is exchanged for desired objects. When you only buy what you need, there will never be an exchange of negative energy. Notice how light you feel when you leave the shop.

कायेन मनसा बुद्ध्या केवलैरिन्द्रियैरपि ।
योगिनः कर्म कुर्वन्ति सङ्गं त्यक्त्वात्मशुद्धये ॥११॥

Sloka 11
kaayena manasaa buddhyaa
kevalair indriyair api
yoginah karma kurvanti
sangam tyaktvaatma suddhaye

11 - Yogis, having abandoned attachment, work with the body, mind, intellect and senses for the purpose of self-purification.

One who has this knowledge knows what to do to keep the mind, body and spirit free and so does everything to ensure that this freedom stays: yoga to keep the body clear, mental exercises to clear the mind and breathing exercises to purify the heart. They know and understand that purification is an ongoing process.

Today

Make sure you spend at least five to ten minutes practising breathing exercises.

युक्तः कर्मफलं त्यक्त्वा शान्तिमाप्नोति नैष्ठिकीम् ।
अयुक्तः कामकारेण फले सक्तो निबध्यते ॥१२॥

Sloka 12
yuktah karma phalam tyaktvaa
saantim aapnoti naishthikeem
ayuktah kaama kaarena
phale sakto nibadhyate

12 - At one with yourself, with no attachment to the results of actions, you attain eternal peace; but those who are fragmented, motivated by selfish desire and attached to the results of their work, become entangled.

A person who is in union sees everything as a gift from God and offers all gifts straight back to God. All their actions, made as offerings to the Lord, bring them great peace. A person who is not at peace however, who is attached to preferences, will become more entangled.

Today

If you really want something, try a little experiment first. Pick up a piece of fruit, hold it in your hand and look at it. Keep looking at it from every side, turning it round and think to yourself, 'This apple is here to nourish my spirit and not my desires.' Then eat it, savouring every mouthful. Feel the difference in the intensity of the experience.

सर्वकर्माणि मनसा संन्यस्यास्ते सुखं वशी ।
नवद्वारे पुरे देही नैव कुर्वन्न कारयन् ॥१३॥

Sloka 13
sarva karmaani manasaa
sannyasyaaste sukham vasee
nava dvaare pure dehee
naiva kurvan na kaarayan

13 - Mentally renouncing the fruits of all actions, the self-controlled live happily in the city of nine gates, neither acting nor causing others to act.

The body is often referred to as the City of Nine Gates. The ancients used to chant special prayers every morning whilst offering water to purify the entrances and exits of the body.

Today

When you wake up, focus on the eyes, nostrils, ears, mouth, anus and genital openings and affirm, 'May these nine gateways be closed to negative influences and open to allow the light of the spirit to emerge.'

न कर्तृत्वं न कर्माणि लोकस्य सृजति प्रभुः ।
न कर्मफलसंयोगं स्वभावस्तु प्रवर्तते ॥१४॥

Sloka 14
na kartritvam na karmaani
lokasya srijati prabhuhu
na karma phala samyogam
svabhaavas tu pravartate

14 - The indwelling Lord does not directly create activities in this world, nor actions, nor the fruits of actions. All this is enacted by the modes of nature.

The three modes of nature (gunas) are responsible for all actions, according to our own tendency, and can be tamasic, rajasic or sattvic. Once again Krishna is saying that we have nothing to do with it. Like an actor on a stage, we say our lines and perform our actions, but we are only *acting.*

Today

Whatever you have to do, act with real sincerity, *knowing that the action arises out of nature. Be generous today and generosity will come tomorrow.*

नादत्ते कस्यचित्पापं न चैव सुकृतं विभुः ।
अज्ञानेनावृतं ज्ञानं तेन मुह्यन्ति जन्तवः ॥१५॥

Sloka 15
naadatte kasyachit paapam
na chaiva sukritam vibhuhu
ajnaanenaavritam jnaanam
tena muhyanti jantavaha

15 - The Lord does not measure anyone's good or evil deeds. When knowledge is obscured by ignorance, people are misled and judgement is clouded.

In the eyes of God, all actions are equal no matter which guna they spring from. A person will be attached to actions when there is confusion about what is 'good' or 'bad.' It is important to know, however, that the consequence of tamasic or rajasic actions will always be painful.

Today

Be aware that what you do today affects what happens to you tomorrow.

ज्ञानेन तु तदज्ञानं येषां नाशितमात्मनः ।
तेषामादित्यवज्ज्ञानं प्रकाशयति तत्परम् ॥१६॥

Sloka 16
jnaanena tu tad ajnaanam
yeshaam naasitam aatmanaha
teshaam aaditya vaj jnaanam
prakaasayati tat param

16 - When knowledge of the Self arises, ignorance disappears, just as night vanishes with the rising sun.

Know that one thing, knowing which all things become known. Once known, the illusory nature of everything is seen straight away. Knowledge of the Self is the only thing that is not illusory.

Today

As you look around you, realise that nothing is real except your Self.

तद्बुद्धयस्तदात्मानस्तन्निष्ठास्तत्परायणाः ।
गच्छन्त्यपुनरावृत्तिं ज्ञाननिर्धूतकल्मषाः ॥१७॥

Sloka 17
tad buddhayas tad aatmaanas
tan nishthaas tat paraayanaaha
gach~chhanty apunar aavrittim
jnaana nirdhoota kalmashaaha

17 - Those whose minds are absorbed in the Supreme, whose intellect and faith are always fixed in the Supreme, with that as their single goal and only refuge, cast off all bad deeds and are never born again.

One of the beautiful things about being on the spiritual path is that the fear and misgivings that may exist when you started just melt away at some point. You realise you were right. The Lord actually gives tremendous inner comfort that, 'Yes, I have made the right choice.'

Today

Be grateful that you are taking the time to study your Self - because it is a very rare thing in this world.

विद्याविनयसंपन्ने ब्राह्मणे गवि हस्तिनि ।
शुनि चैव श्वपाके च पण्डिताः समदर्शिनः ॥१८॥

Sloka 18
vidyaa vinaya sampanne
braahmane gavi hastini
suni chaiva sva paake cha
panditaah sama darsinaha

18 - The wise see with equal vision the same Self in a gentle Brahmin endowed with wisdom, in a cow, an elephant, a dog and an outcast.

The one who is truly wise sees people according to their nature and accepts them as they are. They recognise people are different but see all beings as equal.

Today

If you have a disagreement with someone ask yourself, 'Am I able to see this situation from their point of view?' Put yourself in their shoes.

इहैव तैर्जितः सर्गो येषां साम्ये स्थितं मनः ।
निर्दोषं हि समं ब्रह्म तस्माद्ब्रह्मणि ते स्थिताः ॥१९॥

Sloka 19
ihaiva tair jitah sargo
yeshaam saamye sthitam manaha
nirdosham hi samam brahma
tasmaad brahmani te sthitaaha

19 - In this life such people, whose minds are established in equanimity, conquer rebirth. They are spotless like Brahman and reflect the unity and perfection of Brahman.

Because of the continuity of our awareness we think time is a continuous flow. When we are aware that every moment that passes constitutes a birth and a death, we realise our awareness exists even before our birth and beyond our own death. This sets us free from birth and death.

Today

Take some time to watch the coming and going of your breath and notice how the thoughts gently subside, leaving a wonderful sense of peace. Hold on to that peace for as long as you can. This is your real nature.

न प्रहृष्येत्प्रियं प्राप्य नोद्विजेत्प्राप्य चाप्रियम्।
स्थिरबुद्धिरसंमूढो ब्रह्मविद्ब्रह्मणि स्थितः ॥२०॥

बाह्यस्पर्शेष्वसक्तात्मा विन्दत्यात्मनि यत्सुखम्।
स ब्रह्मयोगयुक्तात्मा सुखमक्षयमश्नुते ॥२१॥

Slokas 20 - 21
na prahrishyet priyam praapya
nodvijet praapya chaapriyam
sthira buddhir asammoodho
brahma vid brahmani sthitaha

baahya sparseshv asaktaatmaa
vindaty aatmani yat sukham
sa brahma yoga yuktaatmaa
sukham akshayam asnute

20 - They are not elated by good fortune, or depressed by bad. With a firm intellect and an undeluded mind established in Brahman, they are free from delusion.
21 - Not dependent upon any external support they delight in the bliss of the Self. With the Self engaged in meditation on Brahman they live in abiding joy.

A person who has such equanimity, who has embraced the source within, achieved pratyahara (sense withdrawal) and is clear in his vision, is already seated in the heart of God. They don't have to look anywhere for God because they have already found Him.

Today

When you find that moment of peace and calm, extend it just a bit further and realise this: you are face to face with God.

ये हि संस्पर्शजा भोगा दुःखयोनय एव ते ।
आद्यन्तवन्तः कौन्तेय न तेषु रमते बुधः ॥२२॥

Sloka 22
ye hi samsparsa jaa bhogaa
duhkha yonaya eva te
aady antavantah kaunteya
na teshu ramate budhaha

22 - Pleasures born out of contact with the senses are sources of pain and distress because they come and go, O son of Kunti. The wise do not look for happiness in them.

With this awareness we awaken to our real nature. The more we embrace this space, the more we learn that nothing in the material world can ever last and that there is no point in searching for anything except this one realisation. After a while we stop looking outwards and instead turn our eyes inwards to see the face of God.

Today

Realise that the only happiness you can ever give to people is your own innate peace. There is no point in trying to give anything else, so stop trying and just start to love.

शक्नोतीहैव यः सोढुं प्राक्शरीरविमोक्षणात् ।
कामक्रोधोद्भवं वेगं स युक्तः स सुखी नरः ॥२३॥

योऽन्तःसुखोऽन्तरारामस्तथान्तर्ज्योतिरेव यः ।
स योगी ब्रह्मनिर्वाणं ब्रह्मभूतोऽधिगच्छति ॥२४॥

Slokas 23 - 24
saknoteehaiva yah sodhum
praak sareera vimokshanaat
kaama krodhodbhavam vegam
sa yuktah sa sukhee naraha

yo 'ntah sukho 'ntar aaraamas
tathaantar jyotir eva yaha
sa yogee brahma nirvaanam
brahma bhooto 'dhigach~chhati

23 - One who is able to overcome the impulse of lust and anger before giving up the body, is a disciplined and happy man.
24 - He who finds his happiness within, his light and delight within, that yogi attains absolute freedom and becomes united with the Divine.

When you manage to achieve that kind of peace you are freed while living. We call such a being a *jivanmukta.* They are always happy whatever is going on in their life, in touch with the one true source within.

Today

Recognise the preciousness of each moment. Begin with the moment you are in now...and now...and now... It is precious. Each moment has its own unique opportunity. Smile inwardly and enjoy this beautiful inner peace.

लभन्ते ब्रह्मनिर्वाणमृषयः क्षीणकल्मषाः ।
छिन्नद्वैधा यतात्मानः सर्वभूतहिते रताः ॥२५॥

कामक्रोधवियुक्तानां यतीनां यतचेतसाम् ।
अभितो ब्रह्मनिर्वाणं वर्तते विदितात्मनाम् ॥२६॥

Slokas 25 - 26
labhante brahma nirvaanam
rishayah ksheena kalmashaaha
chhinna dvaidhaa yataatmaanaha
sarva bhoota hite rataaha

kaama krodha viyuktaanaam
yateenaam yata chetasaam
abhito brahma nirvaanam
vartate viditaatmanaam

25 - Those sages whose happiness is within and who are free from inner conflict and beyond duality are always busy working for the welfare of all living beings and attain the bliss of Brahman.
26 - Those who are free from desire and anger and who have controlled their thoughts through constant effort are knowers of the Self and for them the bliss of Brahman exists everywhere.

When we doubt something in life or our ability to cope, we are admitting to our own sense of inadequacy in life and are constantly thrown to the extreme ends of joy and pain. Because of this, doubt can only bring us unhappiness. One whose mind is engaged within doesn't exist on this level and is liberated and free from doubt.

How do we achieve freedom from doubt? By satisfying three conditions, the most important of which is:

1. **Faith in an unseen power which upholds all creation.**

This arises out of

2. **Controlling anger** and
3. **Directing your thoughts** towards sattva guna (purity).

Faith in God brings real clarity about yourself. The only clarity you *can* have, in fact, is about yourself. Who you are, where you are and when. Me, here, now!

Today

When you get up in the morning recognise that you are here on this earth to make a difference and today resolutely decide to help someone whose need is greater than your own. Be assured that peace is just round the corner.

स्पर्शान्कृत्वा बहिर्बाह्यांश्चक्षुश्चैवान्तरे भ्रुवोः ।
प्राणापानौ समौ कृत्वा नासाभ्यन्तरचारिणौ ॥२७॥

यतेन्द्रियमनोबुद्धिर्मुनिर्मोक्षपरायणः ।
विगतेच्छाभयक्रोधो यः सदा मुक्त एव सः ॥२८॥

Slokas 27 - 28
sparsaan kritvaa bahir baahyaams
chakshus chaivaantare bhruvoho
praanaapaanau samau kritvaa
naasaabhyantara chaarinau

yatendriya mano buddhir
munir moksha paraayanaha
vigatech~chhaa bhaya krodho
yah sadaa mukta eva saha

27 & 28 - Shutting out all external sense objects, focusing the attention between the two eyebrows, equalising the inbreath and the outbreath, thus controlling the mind, senses and intellect, the sage whose highest aim is freedom and from whom desire and anger have departed, is forever free.

Krishna begins to draw Arjuna towards the way to achieve a quiet mind. 'If you want to be quiet,' He says, 'Practise focusing the senses.'

The mind moves like the wind, and the wind inside us is stilled when the breath is stilled. Just like the space that exists between the heaven and earth, in the stillness that exists between the inbreath and the outbreath, there is spaciousness. In this space, anger and fear can no longer exist.

Today

*If you are troubled by anything, do not hold the breath, but naturally pause and watch how the mind becomes quiet.**

भोक्तारं यज्ञतपसां सर्वलोकमहेश्वरम् ।
सुहृदं सर्वभूतानां ज्ञात्वा मां शान्तिमृच्छति ॥२९॥

Sloka 29
bhoktaaram yajna tapasaam
sarva loka mahesvaram
suhridam sarva bhootaanaam
jnaatvaa maam saantim rich~chhati

29 - He who knows Me, the enjoyer of sacrifices and austerities, to be the mighty Lord of all the world and the friend of all creatures, attains eternal peace.

God wants you to know and feel His peace. He is beyond all experiences, being the force behind the movement of the worlds. He is in the depths of the oceans, the farthest recesses of space and is the bringer of peace.

Today

Make sure you find space to be in His peacefulness. Even a little of this peace can bring great benefit.

**see The Bhagavad Gita Workbook for specific techniques*

Om tat sat iti
sreemad bhagavad geetaa su
upanishad su
brahmavidyaayaam
yoga shastre
sree krishna arjuna samvaade

sannyaasa yogo naama
panchamo 'dhyaayaha

Thus in the
glorious Bhagavad Gita,
the cream of the Upanishads,
the science of the Eternal,
the scripture of Yoga,
the dialogue between Sri Krishna and Arjuna,

ends the fifth discourse entitled:
The Yoga of Renunciation of Action

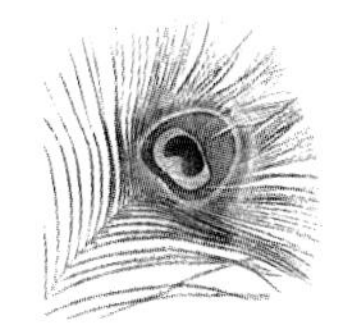

Chapter Six

The Yoga of Meditation

श्री भगवानुवाच
अनाश्रितः कर्मफलं कार्यं कर्म करोति यः ।
स संन्यासी च योगी च न निरग्निर्न चाक्रियः ॥१॥

यं संन्यासमिति प्राहुर्योगं तं विद्धि पाण्डव ।
न ह्यसंन्यस्तसंकल्पो योगी भवति कश्चन ॥२॥

Slokas 1 - 2
sree bhagavaan uvaacha
anaasritah karma phalam
kaaryam karma karoti yaha
sa sannyaasee cha yogee cha
na niragnir na chaakriyaha

yam sannyaasam iti praahur
yogam tam viddhi paandava
na hyasannyasta sankalpo
yogee bhavati kaschana

1 - Lord Krishna said: One who is unattached to the fruits of his work is a sannyasin and a yogi, but not he who lacks energy and enthusiasm for work.
2 - Therefore yoga and renunciation are the same. No one becomes a true yogi until he renounces personal desire.

Krishna once again emphasises that a renunciate is one who renounces the fruits of his actions and *not the actions* themselves. He is preparing Arjuna for the fact that true Karma Yoga must be performed from a point of meditation; acting in stillness and not for self-satisfaction in results.

Enjoyment comes from the pure pleasure of working selflessly for God, which puts us in touch with our real selves and the source of all true pleasure. Krishna is emphatic that yoga itself is renunciation. In fact, anyone who acts and renounces the fruits is a true yogi, but not someone who gives up work because it might 'entangle' them. The key here is that there exists an intimate link between action, knowledge and love - the three aspects of yoga. And there is a place for each one.

Today

By now you will be aware of what it is that makes you reactive - what things push your own personal buttons. Today make a resolution to act only from a point of love. So when someone throws anger at you - please respond only with selfless love. If you can do this, you are becoming a yogi.

आरुरुक्षोर्मुनेर्योगं कर्म कारणमुच्यते ।
योगारूढस्य तस्यैव शमः कारणमुच्यते ॥३॥

यदा हि नेन्द्रियार्थेषु न कर्मस्वनुषज्जते ।
सर्वसंकल्पसंन्यासी योगारूढस्तदोच्यते ॥४॥

Slokas 3 - 4
aarurukshor muner yogam
karma kaaranam uchyate
yogaaroodhasya tasyaiva
samah kaaranam uchyate

yadaa hi nendriyaartheshu
na karmasv anushajjate
sarva sankalpa sannyaasee
yogaaroodhas tadochyate

3 - For one who is just starting on the Eight-Fold System of yoga, the path of selfless action is said to be the means. But for one who has attained to unity with God, the path is one of stillness and tranquillity.
4 - When you are free from attachment, the results of work, and the sense desires, you are said to have attained yoga.

For one who is right at the base of the spiritual mountain and just starting to climb, *action* is the way. Once realisation is reached then *total harmony* is the way; being free from material activities as described in Chapter Four, verse eighteen. This means that action can take place within inaction and inaction within action. The sign of an elevated person is that they simply *don't need anything* and every act they perform exemplifies this. Krishna is telling us that if we want to reach the peak of the spiritual mountain, we must follow the Eight-Fold System according to Patanjali, as practised by the sages of old.

These are:

1. Yamas - things we should avoid
2. Niyamas - things we should do
3. Asana - practice of yoga postures
4. Pranayama - control of the breath
5. Pratyahara - withdrawal of the senses
6. Dharana - concentration
7. Dhyana - meditation
8. Samadhi - liberation

As we climb the mountain, through the practice of *asana* we can rise above the lower levels of self-restraint and climb upwards through *pranayama.* This will take us up to the cliff of *pratyahara* to reach the plateau of *dharana.* The peak of the mountain is *dhyana* and beyond that the path disappears altogether and we reach the ultimate state - *samadhi.*

Today

The ten yamas and niyamas have often been described as ten points for liberation. They are: truthfulness, non-violence, self-control, not stealing, not coveting, purity of body, contentment, austerity, self-study, and dedication to God. Choose one of these ten values and dedicate the day to that value. For the next few days, choose a different value for each day.

उद्धरेदात्मनात्मानं नात्मानमवसादयेत् ।
आत्मैव ह्यात्मनो बन्धुरात्मैव रिपुरात्मनः ॥५॥

बन्धुरात्मात्मनस्तस्य येनात्मैवात्मना जितः ।
अनात्मनस्तु शत्रुत्वे वर्तेतात्मैव शत्रुवत् ॥६॥

Slokas 5 - 6
uddhared aatmanaatmaanam
naatmaanam avasaadayet
aatmaiva hyaatmano bandhur
aatmaiva ripur aatmanaha

bandhur aatmaatmanas tasya
yenaatmaivaatmanaa jitaha
anaatmanas tu satrutve
vartetaatmaiva satru vat

5 -You should lift yourself up by the power of your self and never allow self-will to degrade you. The self can be a friend to the Self,* but it can also be an enemy.*
6 - As you gain control of your self with the help of the Higher Self, it becomes an ally, but the uncontrolled mind behaves like an enemy.

In the East there is a lovely tradition of lighting camphor as part of a spiritual ceremony. As soon as it is lighted, it quickly turns from a solid into a gaseous state, becoming smaller and smaller until nothing is left. This is symbolic of the burning up of the mind and in the same way, it is said that when we apply the light of knowledge by turning our awareness inside, the mind will burn up like camphor, until there is nothing left. When the processes of the mind are engaged in this way, it becomes your greatest friend. When, however, we allow the mind free rein it becomes a vitriolic tyrant.

Today

The mind will only become your friend if you make friends with it and to do this you have to set the ground rules. Like any naughty child, it has to know how far it can go, otherwise it will go too far. If you are still, and practising meditation, tell your mind that this is your meditation time and to ***please be quiet.***

**see glossary*

जितात्मनः प्रशान्तस्य परमात्मा समाहितः ।
शीतोष्णसुखदुःखेषु तथा मानापमानयोः ॥७॥

Sloka 7
jitaatmanah prasaantasya
paramaatmaa samaahitaha
seetoshna sukha duhkheshu
tathaa maanaapamaanayoho

7 - The one who has controlled the self is peaceful and serene, identifying with the Higher Self. To such a man happiness and distress, heat and cold, honour and dishonour are all the same.

The mind is like a mirror which, when still, can reflect the face of God. We find it very hard, however, to see divinity reflected in our mind, because of all the turmoil and turbulence it creates. In order to connect with the deepest levels of the mind, our awareness must not be distracted by its agitated movements. In other words, *the mind must become still.* When it does, our awareness will automatically slip into a higher, finer and more acute state, where nothing can touch us any more. This inner stillness is the most natural place for us to be - a place of pure joy.

Today

At some time, stop and allow your senses to expand outwards. Sense what is going on around you. Be aware of the attraction and smile inwardly knowing that even though there is so much to enjoy, there is so much more enjoyment in inner peace.

ज्ञानविज्ञानतृप्तात्मा कूटस्थो विजितेन्द्रियः ।
युक्त इत्युच्यते योगी समलोष्टाश्मकाञ्चनः ॥८॥

Sloka 8
jnaana vijnaana triptaatmaa
koota stho vijitendriyaha
yukta ity uchyate yogee
sama loshtaasma kaanchanaha

8 - They are completely fulfilled by the knowledge and wisdom of the Self, having controlled and calmed the senses and achieved the very highest. They see everything as the same, whether it be a clod of dirt, a stone or gold.

When knowledge and realisation is all that you want, you are called a yogi. There is nothing else you could want, for you become equally happy in each of the gunas (see also Chapter Two, verse 45).

Today

Spend time today just being happy with yourself - as you are, where you are, doing whatever you are doing. Me, here, now.

सुहृन्मित्रार्युदासीनमध्यस्थद्वेष्यबन्धुषु ।
साधुष्वपि च पापेषु समबुद्धिर्विशिष्यते ॥९॥

Sloka 9
suhrin mitraary udaaseena
madhyastha dveshya bandhushu
saadhushv api cha paapeshu
sama buddhir visishyate

9 - They are equally friendly towards friends, companions, enemies, someone indifferent, hateful people, saints and sinners.

The wise being sees everyone as equal and not as individuals. He will see beyond the intentions of a person to the being behind and what is really going on. A yogi who has mastered *brahmacharya* sees human beings as mere vessels containing a divine spark. All of us come from God, exist in God and return to God and when we can see this divinity in everyone, we have made it! Imagine how peaceful you would feel if you could treat anger and love as the same.

Today

Make a list of six people's names. Three close friends and three people you do not get on with so well. Go through your list one by one and say to each person: 'I enshrine you in my heart today with all the loving kindness I can give to you. Thank you for being in my life.'

योगी युञ्जीत सततमात्मानं रहसि स्थितः ।
एकाकी यतचित्तात्मा निराशीरपरिग्रहः ॥१०॥

Sloka 10
yogee yunjeeta satatam
aatmaanam rahasi sthitaha
ekaakee yata chittaatmaa
niraaseer aparigrahaha

10 - The yogi should make time to be alone, concentrating constantly on the Self, free from desires and possessiveness, with the mind and body controlled.

A practitioner should always engage body, mind and spirit with God, otherwise laziness and distraction will destroy his steadiness. Krishna advocates we live alone and away from people, but in our modern day life we can interpret this as always making time for ourselves.

Today

Give yourself a daily appointment with yourself. *Here is a simple preliminary technique to help you:*
Sit comfortably on a firm chair or in a yogic sitting posture.
Relax your body systematically from head to toe using the inbreath to focus on one part of the body and relax that part on the exhalation.
Allow yourself simply to be still in the relaxation.
To finish, slowly exteriorise yourself, bringing the awareness to the arms, legs and then the whole body. Smile before you open your eyes.

शुचौ देशे प्रतिष्ठाप्य स्थिरमासनमात्मनः ।
नात्युच्छ्रितं नातिनीचं चैलाजिनकुशोत्तरम् ॥११॥

तत्रैकाग्रं मनः कृत्वा यतचित्तेन्द्रियक्रियः ।
उपविश्यासने युञ्ज्याद्योगमात्मविशुद्धये ॥१२॥

Slokas 11 - 12
suchau dese pratishthaapya
sthiram aasanam aatmanaha
naaty uch~chhritam naati neecham
chailaajina kusottaram

tatraikaagram manah kritvaa
yata chittendriya kriyaha
upavisyaasane yunjyaad
yogam aatma visuddhaye

11 - To practice meditation you need to establish a firm seat for yourself in a clean and secluded place, not too high or too low, covered with a cloth, a deer skin and kusha grass.
12 - Then, having made the mind one-pointed and focused, with the mind and senses under control, practice meditation to purify yourself.

As you become more established in yoga, you will find a sense of peace wherever you are, but for a beginner, it is important to create an environment that helps you to find that peace. Krishna tells us to find a place where we will not be disturbed, to have a special seat and be free from distractions or aspirations. In ancient times animal skins were used because they contained the animal's energy. For example, a deer skin will contain peaceful energy and a tiger skin contains a *different* kind of energy! Krishna says that if the environment is correct, when we sit firmly, our senses will become still, because we have established the habit of being still. If we can create an environment that is conducive to concentration, it becomes much easier.

Today

Create your own very special place to meditate and make it sacred. Wear special clothes. Create a central focus, like a shrine or altar, and place on it the four elements of earth, air (bell or incense), fire and water. (Practise the preliminary practice technique opposite.)

समं कायशिरोग्रीवं धारयन्नचलं स्थिरः ।
संप्रेक्ष्य नासिकाग्रं स्वं दिशश्चानवलोकयन् ॥१३॥

प्रशान्तात्मा विगतभीर्ब्रह्मचारिव्रते स्थितः ।
मनः संयम्य मच्चित्तो युक्त आसीत मत्परः ॥१४॥

युञ्जन्नेवं सदात्मानं योगी नियतमानसः ।
शान्तिं निर्वाणपरमां मत्संस्थामधिगच्छति ॥१५॥

Slokas 13 - 15
samam kaaya siro greevam
dhaarayann achalam sthiraha
samprekshya naasikaagram svam
disas chaanavalokayan

prasaantaatmaa vigata bheer
brahmachaari vrate sthitaha
manah samyamya mach chitto
yukta aaseeta mat paraha

yunjann evam sadaatmaanam
yogee niyata maanasaha
saantim nirvaana paramaam
mat samsthaam adhigach~chhati

13 - Keep the body, head and neck erect and motionless, gazing at the tip of your nose.
14 - When the mind has ceased to wander and becomes quiet, serene and fearless, you should sit, firm in the vow of bramacharya, concentrating on Me, having Me as your supreme goal.
15 - By continually disciplining oneself in this way the yogi gains control over the mind and realises the supreme peace that is My nature.

The flow of life force that runs up and down the spine is inhibited by bad posture. In order to be full of life energy and awareness, the spine must be straight, with the head held erect. It is important to relax the limbs and face. The eyes should also be relaxed but focused because it is said that when the eyes are focused the mind becomes still. Krishna advocates fixing the eyes at the tip of the nose without straining. Then, like the limbs of the tortoise, our senses and awareness start to withdraw and we move into the place where the Lord resides. Now we can meditate on His presence within us.

Today

Practise gazing at a candle flame for five minutes without staring or straining. This practice strengthens the eyes as well as the pituitary gland. Sit in front of a lit candle, 1½ arm's lengths away at eye level. Gaze at the tip of the candle flame until your eyes begin to water. Close your eyes and take the image of the candle point between your eyebrows and hold it in your mind's eye for as long as you can. Open your eyes and repeat three times.

नात्यश्नतस्तु योगोऽस्ति न चैकान्तमनश्नतः ।
न चाति स्वप्नशीलस्य जाग्रतो नैव चार्जुन ॥१६॥

Sloka 16
naaty asnatas tu yogo 'sti
na chaikaantam anasnataha
na chaati svapna seelasya
jaagrato naiva chaarjuna

16 - You will not succeed in the practice of meditation, O Arjuna, if you eat too much or too little, or sleep too much or too little.

Krishna offers more practical advice. The truth is that over-indulgence in anything (including lack of sleep or food) will always create problems for us, because we never learn to transend the modes of nature and recognise our true nature.

Today

It is a good idea to practise a simple fast once a week to help the mind to clear and give the body a chance to rest. Try eating only fruit or just one main meal.

युक्ताहारविहारस्य युक्तचेष्टस्य कर्मसु ।
युक्तस्वप्नावबोधस्य योगो भवति दुःखहा ॥१७॥

Sloka 17
yuktaahaara vihaarasya
yukta cheshtasya karmasu
yukta svapnaavabodhasya
yogo bhavati duhkha haa

17 - Practising moderation in sleeping, eating, working and recreation, and avoiding extremes in everything you do, you will see that yoga eliminates all your pain and suffering.

When we have an intelligent contact with the senses and are in control of our eating and sleeping patterns, we will find ourselves untroubled by most of the problems that beset other people. Practising meditation *as well,* Krishna assures us, means we can become completely free.

Today

Eat only what your body needs. Exercise your body and walk in nature. Go to bed early enough - but not too early, so that you get enough sleep. Be balanced in all things - moderation is the key.

यदा विनियतं चित्तमात्मन्येवावतिष्ठते ।
निःस्पृहः सर्वकामेभ्यो युक्त इत्युच्यते तदा ॥१८॥

यथा दीपो निवातस्थो नेङ्गते सोपमा स्मृता ।
योगिनो यतचित्तस्य युञ्जतो योगमात्मनः ॥१९॥

Slokas 18 - 19
yadaa viniyatam chittam
aatmany evaavatishthate
nisprihah sarva kaamebhyo
yukta ity uchyate tadaa

yathaa deepo nivaata stho
nengate sopamaa smritaa
yogino yata chittasya
yunjato yogam aatmanaha

18 - When the perfectly controlled mind rests in the Self alone, free from wanting anything, then you have found union with God.
19 - Just as a lamp in a sheltered place does not flicker, the controlled mind, absorbed in meditation, remains ever steady.

A firm test of how established a person is in yoga is indicated by the lack of any unnecessary needs or wants in them. In any situation their attitude and mind remains unwavering, unaffected by anger or happiness. They rest in a beautiful state of bliss.

Today

As you sit quietly for meditation, notice how the mind/awareness flows. Ask yourself a question. Is your awareness steady or is it wavering from one thought to another? If the stream of awareness wavers then you know that you have to establish the principles of meditation more firmly in your heart.

यत्रोपरमते चित्तं निरुद्धं योगसेवया ।
यत्र चैवात्मनात्मानं पश्यन्नात्मनि तुष्यति ॥२०॥

सुखमात्यन्तिकं यत्तद्बुद्धिग्राह्यमतीन्द्रियम् ।
वेत्ति यत्र न चैवायं स्थितश्चलति तत्त्वतः ॥२१॥

यं लब्ध्वा चापरं लाभं मन्यते नाधिकं ततः ।
यस्मिन्स्थितो न दुःखेन गुरुणापि विचाल्यते ॥२२॥

तं विद्याद्दुःखसंयोगवियोगं योगसंज्ञितम् ।
स निश्चयेन योक्तव्यो योगोऽनिर्विण्णचेतसा ॥२३॥

Slokas 20 - 23
yatroparamate chittam
niruddham yoga sevayaa
yatra chaivaatman~aatmaanam
pasyann aatmani tushyati

sukham aatyantikam yat tad
buddhi graahyam ateendriyam
vetti yatra na chaivaayam
sthitas chalati tattvataha

yam labdhvaa chaaparam laabham
manyate naadhikam tataha
yasmin sthito na duhkhena
gurunaapi vichaalyate

tam vidyaad duhkha samyoga
viyogam yoga samjnitam
sa nischayena yoktavyo
yogo 'nirvinna chetasaa

20 - Disciplined by yoga, the mind becomes calm and still and then the Self reveals itself. Once seen, a man becomes completely fulfilled and satisfied in the Self.
21 - He knows the abiding joy beyond the senses which, once known, there is absolutely nothing else to achieve. Never again does he slip from this truth.

22 - Once established in this truth he wants for nothing else and is never shaken again, not even by the greatest sorrow.
23 - This disconnection from union with pain is known as yoga, which should be practised with firm determination and a mind that is never despondent.

The practice of yoga culminates in the total absorption of the awareness in the Self. Having experienced the Self, there is nothing you could want more than this. There is no higher aim or greater responsibility than this and those who have achieved this state are called 'awake'. The Sanskrit word for awake is 'Buddhi' and the one who is awake, 'Buddha'. A person who is awake is never removed from that wakefulness and nothing can shake them from it.

Today

Wake up! Contemplate upon this poem:

Men of the Earth, brothers in eternity, shake your souls awake.
The hour so long waited for,
the promised hour, has come.
Over the dark firmament of suffering humanity
is rising the moving star,
heralding the day when you will understand
man's most sacred duty to be man.
That is, to manifest life, intelligence, truth and love.
And you who realise this will break the fetters of ignorance and fear
that bind unconscious humanity.
And know yourself to be eternal manifestations
of the unmanifest,
Witnesses of the Absolute,
Sons of the great All whom we call - God.

poem inspired by Vedantic truth - author unknown

संकल्पप्रभवान्कामांस्त्यक्त्वा सर्वानशेषतः ।
मनसैवेन्द्रियग्रामं विनियम्य समन्ततः ॥२४॥

Sloka 24
sankalpa prabhavaan kaamaams
tyaktvaa sarvaan aseshataha
manasaivendriya graamam
viniyamya samantataha

24 - Completely letting go of all selfish desires and expectations use your mind to withdraw from the senses' constant demands for attention.

Never give up. Three very important words! The nature of the mind is such that it is very unpredictable in the way it acts from one day to the next. If you have a good meditation today, there is no guarantee that you will tomorrow. We are creating the environment for the mind to be still and it depends on many factors. Because we acquire many energies and emotions throughout the day, we should not worry if our meditation is not quite what we would like it to be. It is often said that expectation is our greatest enemy and should be eradicated firmly.

Today

*At the end of your meditation practice hold your hands together as if you are holding a beautiful white dove of peace. Raise up your hands and as you do so, see the dove flying up into the sky carrying the fruits of your meditation to the world.**

शनैः शनैरुपरमेद्बुद्ध्या धृतिगृहीतया ।
आत्मसंस्थं मनः कृत्वा न किंचिदपि चिन्तयेत् ॥२५॥

Sloka 25
sanaih sanair uparamed
buddhyaa dhriti griheetayaa
aatma samstham manah kritvaa
na kinchid api chintayet

**see The Bhagavad Gita Workbook for a pratyahara technique.*

25 - Little by little, through patience and continuous effort, with the intellect firmly held, the mind should be focused on the Self, not thinking of anything else.

It is important to recognise that there is a process taking place in meditation. Without this understanding one might think that the results will happen to you overnight. Some people practise meditation for many years before achieving inner harmony and peace.

Before beginning your meditation*, ask the Lord to allow you to connect with His presence. Focusing your awareness inside and with the attention fixed on the breath, immerse yourself in the silence until you feel the presence of God by your side. Now you can face anything in life.

Today

As you get up, make a promise to spend some time in the garden. Look at the earth and the sky, or a flower - and contemplate on the beauty of it. God is in all things.

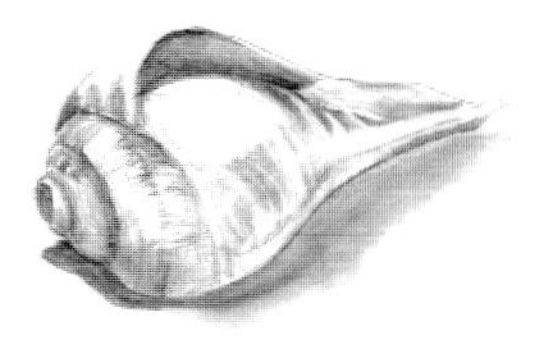

यतो यतो निश्चरति मनश्चञ्चलमस्थिरम् ।
ततस्ततो नियम्यैतदात्मन्येव वशं नयेत् ॥२६॥

Sloka 26
yato yato nischarati
manas chanchalam asthiram
tatas tato niyamyaitad
aatmany eva vasam nayet

26 - Whenever the unsteady mind wanders, continue to draw it back again to rest in the Self.

**see The Bhagavad Gita Workbook for a Vipassanna meditation*

Very often in meditation the mind behaves like a slippery eel or a flapping octopus with tentacles going everywhere! Sometimes we feel as though we have accomplished very little, as we keep trying to bring the mind back to this moment. But even this practice is better than allowing the mind to wander and twenty minutes spent bringing the mind back to the present is time well spent. (Practise the technique on page 288.)

Today

Take a coin in your hand and toss it. If heads are up, this is to be a day of generosity. If tails are up, a day of empowering and complimenting people.

प्रशान्तमनसं ह्येनं योगिनं सुखमुत्तमम् ।
उपैति शान्तरजसं ब्रह्मभूतमकल्मषम् ॥२७॥

युञ्जन्नेवं सदात्मानं योगी विगतकल्मषः ।
सुखेन ब्रह्मसंस्पर्शमत्यन्तं सुखमश्नुते ॥२८॥

Slokas 27 - 28
prasaanta manasam hyenam
yoginam sukham uttamam
upaiti saanta rajasam
brahma bhootam akalmasham

yunjann evam sadaatmaanam
yogee vigata kalmashaha
sukhena brahma samsparsam
atyantam sukham asnute

27 - The yogi whose mind is peaceful and who has learned to quell his passions experiences supreme joy, and is freed from all sins, having become one with God.
28 - Continually directing his mind in this way the yogi, freed from all sins, achieves the very highest state of happiness.

If, in meditation, our focus merges with the presence of God within, He bestows the highest, most perfect state of consciousness and frees us from all past karma.

Today

To aid the process of releasing past karmas, dedicate an action which has created problems for you to God and affirm: 'I place this action in your hands. I know that you are the knower of all things and will manage this much better than I can. May your love redress any imbalance I have created.'

सर्वभूतस्थमात्मानं सर्वभूतानि चात्मनि ।
ईक्षते योगयुक्तात्मा सर्वत्र समदर्शनः ॥२९॥

Sloka 29
sarva bhoota stham aatmaanam
sarva bhootaani chaatmani
eekshate yoga yuktaatmaa
sarvatra sama darsanaha

29 - As the mind becomes harmonised through the practice of yoga, one begins to see the Self in every creature and all beings as part of the Self. The same Self is seen everywhere, in everything.

As your practice progresses you start to see and feel the unity of all things. You are able to perceive the inner tides of nature and to recognise people for who they are and not how they appear to be. Eventually you begin to realise that all beings and things are nothing more than the manifestation of God, the same God that resides in your own heart and who exists in the light of the sun and stars.

Today

If you have a watch with an alarm, set it to go off every hour and when it does, look around you and say, 'He/She is God, that is God and God is in my own heart.'

यो मां पश्यति सर्वत्र सर्वं च मयि पश्यति ।
तस्याहं न प्रणश्यामि स च मे न प्रणश्यति ॥३०॥

सर्वभूतस्थितं यो मां भजत्येकत्वमास्थितः ।
सर्वथा वर्तमानोऽपि स योगी मयि वर्तते ॥३१॥

Slokas 30 - 31
yo maam pasyati sarvatra
sarvam cha mayi pasyati
tasyaaham na pranasyaami
sa cha me na pranasyati

sarva bhoota sthitam yo maam
bhajaty ekatvam aasthitaha
sarvathaa vartamaano 'pi
sa yogee mayi vartate

30 - Those who see Me everywhere and everything in Me, never become separated from Me, nor do I become separated from them.
31 - They live in Me who worship Me in every creature and all their actions proceed from Me.

If we are able to perceive God in everything, then we will always be reminded of Him. In focusing on God, He is aware of us as well. Similarly, when we forget God, His awareness is taken away from us. In other words, we *create* separation, although God always wants to get close to us. Consequently, if we always try to see Him in everything, we are naturally brought closer to the true nature of God.

Today

God is just around the corner. If you walk round the corner, will you see Him? He is outside the door - can you sense His presence? If you think like this, surely He will be there.

आत्मौपम्येन सर्वत्र समं पश्यति योऽर्जुन ।
सुखं वा यदि वा दुःखं स योगी परमो मतः ॥३२॥

Sloka 32
aatmaupamyena sarvatra
samam pasyati yo 'rjuna
sukham vaa yadi vaa duhkham
sa yogee paramo mataha

32 - He who responds to the joys and sorrows of others as if they were his own, is a perfect yogi.

If you are beyond the three gunas and see God in all things, you cannot help but see the true nature of all beings. When you see someone being sad or happy you can say to yourself, 'That is God manifesting sadness or happiness.' In actual fact, you will see it all as God.

Today

When we are generous we should be equally generous to all beings and not just to some. It is easy to recognise someone in need, like a beggar in the street, but sometimes we neglect the greatest needs which are lying right under our noses, in the heart of our friends and family.
Our generosity should be such that we are aware that all beings need to be loved unconditionally, just as a flower radiates its scent indiscriminately to all.

अर्जुन उवाच
योऽयं योगस्त्वया प्रोक्तः साम्येन मधुसूदन ।
एतस्याहं न पश्यामि चञ्चलत्वात्स्थितिं स्थिराम् ॥३३॥

चञ्चलं हि मनः कृष्ण प्रमाथि बलवद्दृढम् ।
तस्याहं निग्रहं मन्ये वायोरिव सुदुष्करम् ॥३४॥

श्री भगवानुवाच
असंशयं महाबाहो मनो दुर्निग्रहं चलम् ।
अभ्यासेन तु कौन्तेय वैराग्येण च गृह्यते ॥३५॥

असंयतात्मना योगो दुष्प्राप इति मे मतिः ।
वश्यात्मना तु यतता शक्योऽवाप्तुमुपायतः ॥३६॥

Slokas 33-36
arjuna uvaacha:
yo 'yam yogas tvayaa proktaha
saamyena madhusoodana
etasyaaham na pasyaami
chanchalatvaat sthitim sthiraam

chanchalam hi manah krishna
pramaathi balavad dridham
tasyaaham nigraham manye
vaayor iva su dushkaram

sree bhagavaan uvaacha:
asamsayam mahaa baaho
mano durnigraham chalam
abhyaasena tu kaunteya
vairaagyena cha grihyate

asamyataatmanaa yogo
dushpraapa iti me matihi
vasyaatmanaa tu yatataa
sakyo 'vaaptum upaayataha

33 - Arjuna said: O Madhusudana, this union you describe is impractical to me because of the restlessness of the mind.
34 - Not only is the mind restless, O Krishna, but trying to control it is like trying to control the wind.
35 - Lord Krishna said: Without doubt, O mighty-armed Arjuna, the mind is unsteady and difficult to control. But it can be controlled by steady practice (abhyasa) and detachment (vairagya).
36 - If you cannot control your mind, Self-realisation is hard work. But if you persist and earnestly strive to control your mind using the right methods, you will certainly succeed.

We can all appreciate this because when confronted with the task of making the mind still, it is the last thing it wants to do. Arjuna recognises this and questions Krishna's instructions. He clearly hasn't been really listening because Krishna has been very precise in saying that stillness of mind will arise when the right environment and conditions have been created.

A good General makes use of the weaknesses of his enemy. When you are practising yoga you should not only accept and be concerned about the restlessness of the mind, you also need to realise its limitations. It is only finite after all, as opposed to the infinite and boundless depths of the soul. Sri Krishna empowers Arjuna's mightiness by addressing him as 'mighty-armed one,' acknowledging how difficult it is to curb a restless mind. *But it is possible* - through constant practice and detachment!

Today

When you begin to meditate, it soon becomes clear how great a task it is to still the mind. Arjuna's doubts are all of ours when confronted with this problem. It takes Krishna to answer, 'Yes, it is possible, but only by regular practice and determination.' So today make sure that your practice is determined and strong.

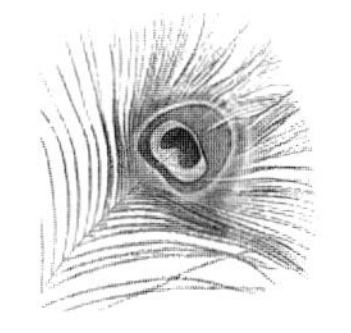

अर्जुन उवाच
अयतिः श्रद्धयोपेतो योगाच्चलितमानसः ।
अप्राप्य योगसंसिद्धिं कां गतिं कृष्ण गच्छति ॥३७॥

कच्चिन्नोभयविभ्रष्टश्छिन्नाभ्रमिव नश्यति ।
अप्रतिष्ठो महाबाहो विमूढो ब्रह्मणः पथि ॥३८॥

एतन्मे संशयं कृष्ण छेत्तुमर्हस्यशेषतः ।
त्वदन्यः संशयस्यास्य छेत्ता न ह्युपपद्यते ॥३९॥

Slokas 37 - 39
arjuna uvaacha:
ayatih sraddhayopeto
yogaach chalita maanasaha
apraapya yoga samsiddhim
kaam gatim krishna gach~chhati

kach~chin nobhaya vibhrashtas
chhinnaabhram iva nasyati
apratishtho mahaa baaho
vimoodho brahmanah pathi

etan me samsayam krishna
chhettum arhasy aseshataha
tvad anyah samsayasyaasya
chhettaa na hy upapadyate

37 - Arjuna said: O Krishna, what happens to someone who has sincere faith, but cannot quite control the mind and wanders away from the path, losing sight of his goal?
38 - Does he perish like a cloud dispersed by the wind? Deluded on his path, has he fallen both from this world and the next? Does he find himself without support or position anywhere?
39 - O Krishna, you are the only one who is able to dispel this doubt of mine, because you are the dispeller of all doubts.

Arjuna is seriously doubting his ability to succeed and seeks reassurance from Krishna begging him to free him from this doubt. He says a beautiful thing, 'because you are the dispeller of all doubts.'

Today

Consider your own practice and ask yourself, 'Where are my own doubts? What do I doubt?'
Do you have no doubts? Would you brave the fire and challenge fate to lift the sword from the stone as Arthur did? Spend time today at the end of your meditation asking God to take your doubts away and dispel them like the clouds in the sky. He can remove them all.

श्री भगवानुवाच
पार्थ नैवेह नामुत्र विनाशस्तस्य विद्यते ।
न हि कल्याणकृत्कश्चिद्दुर्गतिं तात गच्छति ॥४०॥

प्राप्य पुण्यकृतां लोकानुषित्वा शाश्वतीः समाः ।
शुचीनां श्रीमतां गेहे योगभ्रष्टोऽभिजायते ॥४१॥

Slokas 40 - 41
sree bhagavaan uvaacha:
paartha naiveha naamutra
vinaasas tasya vidyate
na hi kalyaana krit kaschid
durgatim taata gach~chhati

praapya punya kritaam lokaan
ushitvaa saasvateeh samaaha
sucheenaam sreemataam gehe
yoga bhrashto 'bhijaayate

40 - Lord Krishna said: Do not worry, O Partha, for there is no destruction on earth or in heaven for anyone who does good.
41 - One who falls from the path dwells many years in the land of the righteous and is born again into a home which is pure and prosperous.

Krishna gives reassurance that whatever good we have done, it is never forgotten and will always lead us on. Those who are unsuccessful move into a state of enjoyment where they receive their just rewards for all the good they have done. Your efforts will always come back to you, and in the end you will be put into a position where you can continue your yoga. You will be born into a family that is conducive to your growth and the greater your accumulated good deeds, the greater your growth.

Today

Moment to moment, the good times you enjoy, Krishna says, are carried by the good things you have done previously. This comfort zone can be very deceiving however, because you do not grow in the comfort zone. Simplify a little and then a little more, so you are always balancing comfort against growth.

अथवा योगिनामेव कुले भवति धीमताम् ।
एतद्धि दुर्लभतरं लोके जन्म यदीदृशम् ॥४२॥

तत्र तं बुद्धिसंयोगं लभते पौर्वदेहिकम् ।
यतते च ततो भूयः संसिद्धौ कुरुनन्दन ॥४३॥

पूर्वाभ्यासेन तेनैव ह्रियते ह्यवशोऽपि सः ।
जिज्ञासुरपि योगस्य शब्दब्रह्मातिवर्तते ॥४४॥

Slokas 42 - 44
atha vaa yoginaam eva
kule bhavati dheemataam
etad dhi durlabhataram
loke janma yad eedrisam

tatra tam buddhi samyogam
labhate paurva dehikam
yatate cha tato bhooyaha
samsiddhau kuru nandana

poorvaabhyaasena tenaiva
hriyate hyavaso 'pi saha
jijnaasur api yogasya
sabda brahmaativartate

42 - Or he is born into a family of wise yogis. Such a birth is very rare in this world.
43 - There the wisdom he acquired in previous lives will be re-awakened and he will try again even harder to reach perfection.
44 - His previous practice will carry him forward in spite of himself. Even one who simply wants to know how to practice yoga will rise above those who merely go through the motions of religious life.

For those who really deserve it, they are born in the presence of wisdom and this wisdom awakens inside them whatever they have forgotten. It is very rare for someone in life to go beyond the point where they finished off previously, but one who is really deserving, can be brought to that point very quickly by being in the presence of great knowledge. This is a very great gift and one of the highest gifts you can give to an embodying soul.

Because such a being is already immersed in yoga, it is easy to remember the yogic way of life.

Today

Affirm your willpower to grow. Rebirth happens from moment to moment and the opportunity can be given to you by practising the precepts Krishna has outlined. They can be given to you now if you have earned it.

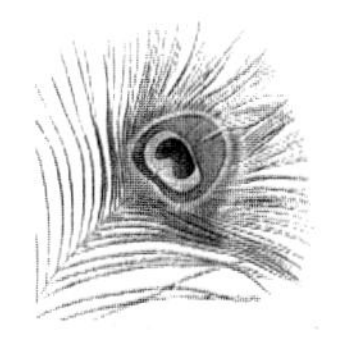

प्रयत्नाद्यतमानस्तु योगी संशुद्धकिल्बिषः ।
अनेकजन्मसंसिद्धस्ततो याति परां गतिम् ॥४५॥

Sloka 45
prayatnaad yatamaanas tu
yogee samsuddha kilbishaha
aneka janma samsiddhas
tato yaati paraam gatim

45 - Through constant effort and gradual purification over many lifetimes he will eventually attain the supreme goal.

Recognising there is such a process of growth over lifetimes, then gradually we achieve the highest. The highest is *knowledge of Him.* We all have had 'many births' but there can be many births even in our own lifetime; many changes and transformations and things we have to do which help us to grow. We are taken through some unconsciously and others our teacher or guru will take us through. It is possible to complete the journey in one lifetime!

Today

Be prepared for what this day will bring. It may be happiness, distress or healing - or perhaps others to be healed. Be prepared to change to meet the needs of the day.

तपस्विभ्योऽधिको योगी ज्ञानिभ्योऽपि मतोऽधिकः।
कर्मिभ्यश्चाधिको योगी तस्माद्योगी भवार्जुन ॥४६॥

Sloka 46
tapasvibhyo 'dhiko yogee
jnaanibhyo 'pi mato 'dhikaha
karmibhyas chaadhiko yogee
tasmaad yogee bhavaarjuna

46 - The yogi is superior to the ascetics and the knowledgeable and even those who do great selfless works. Therefore, O Arjuna, in all circumstances, be a yogi!

Greater than all spiritual paths is the path of yoga. When we say 'greater' we don't mean the aim is any different, because all spiritual paths lead to God. But yoga is the greatest path because it is the quickest.

Today

Choose one of the niyamas from Patanjali's Eight-Fold Path (see page 283) and hold that one quality in your heart today. It could be something like truthfulness or non-violence. According to Patanjali the yamas and niyamas are very important to master.

योगिनामपि सर्वेषां मद्गतेनान्तरात्मना ।
श्रद्धावान् भजते यो मां स मे युक्ततमो मतः ॥४७॥

Sloka 47
yoginaam api sarveshaam
mad gatenaantar aatmanaa
sraddhaavaan bhajate yo maam
sa me yuktatamo mataha

47 - Of all yogis, the one who has become completely absorbed in Me and worships Me with complete faith is the highest of all.

If you practise yoga according to Krishna's precepts, with faith that God is always with you, then that beautiful union between you and God is assured and Krishna says you are most dear to Him.

Today

Whatever problems come your way, take them to God first. He is your closest friend, your most intimate companion and the one you should always go to first. He is the one who resides inside your heart.

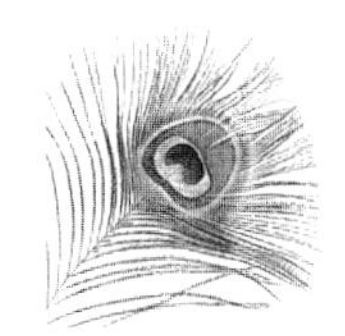

Om tat sat iti
sreemad bhagavad geetaa su
upanishad su
brahmavidyaayaam
yoga shastre
sree krishna arjuna samvaade

dhyaana yogo naama
shashtho 'dhyaayaha

Thus in the
glorious Bhagavad Gita,
the cream of the Upanishads,
the science of the Eternal,
the scripture of Yoga,
the dialogue between Sri Krishna and Arjuna,

ends the sixth discourse entitled

The Yoga of Meditation

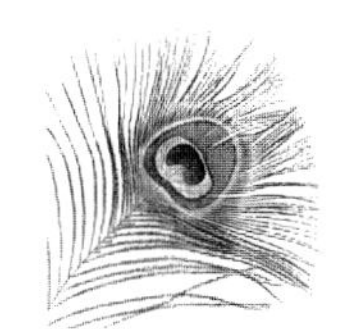

How to work with the Bhagavad Gita

These are the methods that have helped us the most over the years. We offer you these simple guidelines for your own personal study. If you can follow them every day, you will soon find that the Gita will soon begin to reveal its secrets to you.

How many verses should I study each day?
Start off by reading one a day and gradually build up to three or four.

What is the best time to read the Gita?
Any time is a good time, but if you can fit your Gita reading into your morning practice, it will set you up for the day.

Where is the best place to read the Gita?
We always recommend that the Gita is read outside in nature as much as possible. The best place is under a tree, otherwise it should be read in solitude during your morning meditation time.

What is the best way to read the Gita?
Approach the Gita with reverence.

1. Start off by holding the Gita in your hands. Close your eyes and imagine that you are holding a beautiful flower. Open it carefully and with a feeling that it contains something very precious. It does!

2. Chant the introduction to the chapter as explained on page 316.

3. Chant the Sanskrit verse twice with the appropriate tune.

4. Now read the English twice:
 The first time, read it through *without trying* to understand what it is saying.
 The second time, read it *slowly* so that you can form a relationship with the verse. How does it touch you? What does it signify to you?

What do I do after reading the verse?

Study the daily application. You could write it on a card with the verse and carry it with you during the day as a reminder.

Are there specific verses to help with different situations?

We have chosen a few verses from chapters 1- 6, but for more detailed advice on how to work with specific issues please see our *Bhagavad Gita Workbook.*

Chapter 1 - verse 1	- creating distance from a situation
Chapter 2 - verse 7	- to help resolve conflict
Chapter 3 - verse 17	- to ease worry
- verse 43	- to help with overcoming a difficult desire
Chapter 4 - verses 7 & 8	- developing hope and faith in times of despair
- verse 24	- to alter your consciousness before eating
Chapter 5 - verse 11	- empowering renunciation and selflessness
Chapter 6 - verse 23	- overcoming pain
- verse 30	- overcoming loneliness
- verse 31	- overcoming anger

Sanskrit Pronunciation Guide

In order to make the verses easier to read we have simplified the symbols normally used to write phonetic Sanskrit.

a is short - halfway between *but* and *bat*
aa is long as in *aaaargh*
u is short as in *put*
oo is long as in *moo*
i is short as in *me*
ri as in *ring*
ee is long as in *wheeee*
e is long as in *made*
ai as in *might*
o is long as in *foam*
au as in *sound*

The following are pronounced as in English.

k as in *cat*
g as in *go*
n as in *now*
ch as in *church*
j as in *joy*
t as in *tip*
d as in *dear*
p as in *palace*
b as in *bell*
m as in *mother*
l as in *love*
r as in *room*
v as in *vet*
h as in *hope*
s as in *sun*
sh as in *shine*
y as in *yet*

Beware the following

th as in ligh**th**ouse
kh as in wal**k h**ome
ph as in ski**p h**op
chh as in chur**ch h**ouse
gh as in bi**g h**eart
jh as in he**dge**hog
dh as in re**d h**ouse
bh as in jo**b h**unt
jn as in sin**g y**ellow

Where lines are broken up into separate words with a final **y**, again this is simply to make the Sanskrit easier to read, (the **y** is really a final **i.**) Y is always pronounced as in *yet.*
e.g. Chapter 4, Verse 35, last line: drakshyasy aatmany atho mayi

What tune should I use?

We chant the verses to the melodies shown below. Try to keep the rhythm free and sing in a very flowing way. Most verses are sung to the melody given for Chapter 1 verse 1, however there are several lines that are sung to the melody in the second example for Chapter 2 verse 5. * You will notice these ones have their 2nd and 4th lines indented.

Before we start chanting, it is traditional to begin the chapter by singing an introductory line to the tune indicated below.

For example: for Chapter 1 verse 1 we chant:

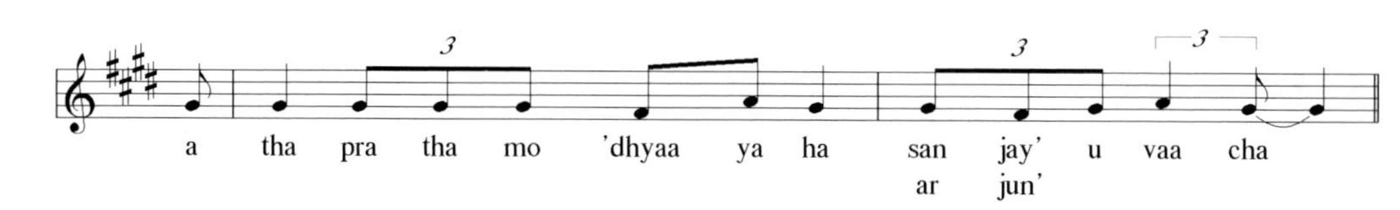

Atha prathamo 'dhyaayaha.

Chapter introductions

Chapter 1 - atha prathamo 'dhyaayaha

Chapter 2 - atha dviteeyo 'dhyaayaha

Chapter 3 - atha triteeyo 'dhyaayaha

Chapter 4 - atha chaturtho 'dhyaayaha

Chapter 5 - atha panchamo 'dhyaayaha

Chapter 6 - atha shashtho 'dhyaaayaha

For examples shown please use G# and D#.

N.B. *Using a drone instrument such as a tampura, will enhance your clarity and help you to keep time.*

धृतराष्ट्र उवाच
धर्मक्षेत्रे कुरुक्षेत्रे समवेता युयुत्सवः ।
मामकाः पाण्डवाश्चैव किमकुर्वत संजय ॥१॥

chapter 1 verse 1

dhritaraashtra uvaacha:
dharma kshetre kuru kshetre
samavetaa yuyutsavaha
maamakaah paandavaas chaiva
kim akurvata sanjaya

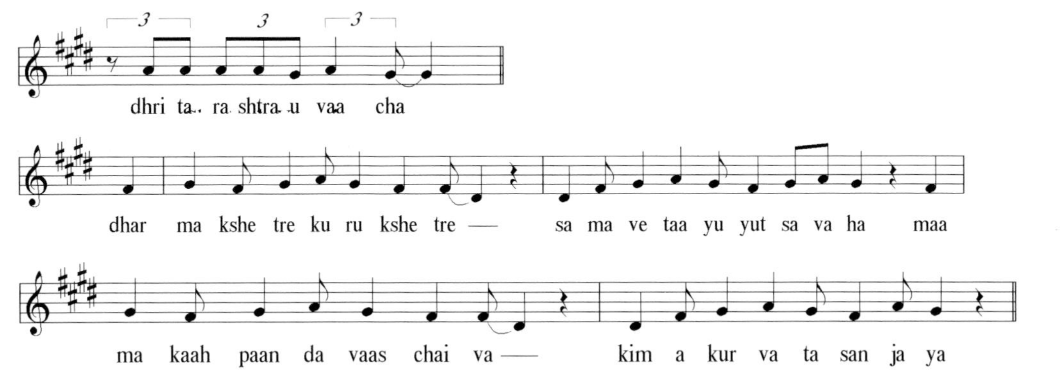

गुरूनहत्वा हि महानुभावान्
श्रेयो भोक्तुं भैक्ष्यमपीह लोके ।
हत्वार्थकामांस्तु गुरूनिहैव
भुञ्जीय भोगान्रुधिरप्रदिग्धान् ॥५॥

* **_chapter 2 verse 5_**

guroon ahatvaa hi mahaanubhaavaan
sreyo bhoktum bhaikshyam apeeha loke
hatvaartha kaamaams tu guroon ihaiva
bhunjeeya bhogaan rudhira pradigdhaan

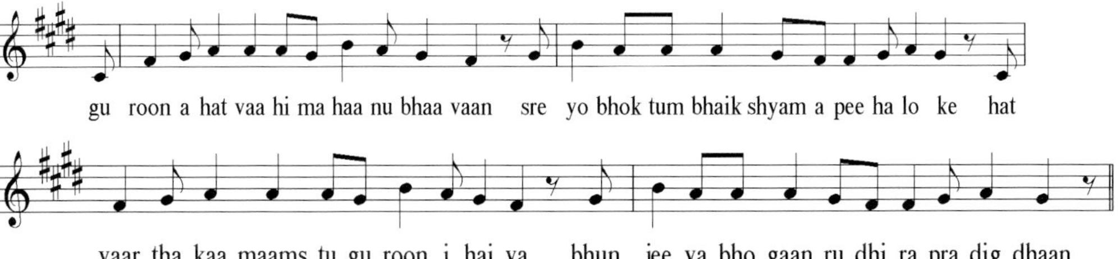

Glossary

A

Abhyasa - constant and regular practice.
Advaita - not one.
Ahamkar - ego sense of 'I'.
Ahimsa - non-violence.
Arjun - an affectionate abbreviation of Arjuna.
Arjuna - the third Pandava known for his great courage and ability as a warrior.
Asana - yogic posture.
Ashwatta - the tree of life - the sacred fig tree.
Atman - the divine soul in every living creature - the Supreme Self.
Aum - the primordial sound from which the universe was born and the essence of all mantra. The sound which represents the Absolute Truth.
Aviveka - lack of discrimination.
Avatar - an incarnation of God who comes down to earth for a specific purpose.
Avyaya - the eternal, changeless reality.

B

Bhagavad Gita - the great song of God.
Bhagavan - the Supreme Lord.
Bhakti - devotion.
Bharata - an ancient king from whom the Pandavas are descended.
Bhima - the second Pandava son known for his great strength and joviality.
Bhishma - the noble and immortal general known as the grandfather of the Kuru dynasty.
Brahma - the Creator.
Brahmacharya - one who has control of his or her senses. Usually understood to be celibacy, but not necessarily so.
Brahman - the imperishable eternal consciousness that pervades the whole of creation.
Brahmin - a member of the most intelligent and learned caste in the Hindu system.
Buddha - the one who is awake.
Buddhi - intelligence and understanding.

C

Chakora - a bird that is said to live on moonbeams.
Chakra - wheel - refers to the main power centres in the spine which are said to turn like wheels.
Conch - a scared shell that creates the sound of a horn when blown.

D

Deva - literally 'shining one' or 'controller'. A being who looks after one of the natural forces in the world or ourselves e.g. Indra - controls the rains.
Devaki - Krishna's mother.
Devi - a goddess.
Dharana - concentration.
Dharma - one's duty or natural occupation - purpose.
Dhritarashtra - the blind Kaurava king.
Dhyana - meditation.
Draupada - King of Panchala and an ally of the Pandavas.
Draupadi - one of Draupada's two children and the wife of the five Pandavas.
Dukha - pain and sorrow.
Dronacharya - the Pandavas' and the Kauravas' teacher.
Dvaitam - the philosophy of dualism whereby you are seen to be separate in nature from the creator as opposed to monism which holds to the principle that 'There is only God'.

G

Gandhari - Mother of the Kauravas.
Gandiva - Arjuna's bow.
Gita - song.
Gunas - the three qualities of nature; tamas - dissolution, rajas - energy or passion, and sattva - purity, stillness in action.
Guru - spiritual master.

H

Hanuman - the monkey-god, Lord of the wind.
Hari - the Supreme Lord. He who removes all the suffering of his devotees.
Hrishikesha - the form of the Lord that assures victory.

J

Jiva - the individual soul.
Jnana - wisdom, knowledge.

K

Kama - selfish desire.
Karma - actions that determine our future.
Karma yoga - the path of action.
Kaunteya - son of Kunti. Krishna addresses Arjuna as Kaunteya to remind him of his noble birth.
Kauravas - the sons of Dhritarasthra.
Keshava - the name of the Lord that means 'destroyer of the demon of illusion'.
Krishna - the name of the Lord that means 'the all attractive one who captures everybody's hearts'.
Kshatriya - a warrior, or prince, who belongs to the ruling class in Hindu society.
Kshetra - field or sacred place.
Kuru - the ancient king and ancestor of Pandu and Dhritarasthra.
Kurukshetra - the field of the Kurus.
Kusha grass - sacred grass regarded as very auspicious to sit on for meditation.

M

Madhusudhana - killer of the demon Madhu. Arjuna addresses Krishna in this way because he wants him to kill the demon of misunderstanding in his mind.
Mahabharata - the great epic poem that portrays the war between the Pandavas and the Kauravas, composed by Veda Vyasa some five thousand years ago.
Mahatma - great soul - a title of great respect.
Manas - the mind.
Mantra -a sacred word or syllable; a Vedic hymn.
Manu - the father of the human race.
Maya - the goddess of illusion.

N

Nakula - one of the heavenly twins and youngest Pandava son who epitomises the quality of beauty.
Niyamas - observances, or practices that cultivate the right internal environment for realisation.

O

Om - see Aum.

P

Partha - son of Pritha, Kunti - sister to Krishna's father. When Krishna addresses Arjuna in this way, he is reminding him of his great heritage.
Pandavas - the sons of Pandu, Dhritarashtra's brother who died at an early age.
Parantapa - 'scorcher of foes.' Krishna addresses Arjuna in this way to encourage him to fight.
Patanjali - the father of yoga who composed the unmatched system of yoga, the Eight-Fold Path.
Prajapati - a name for the Creator.
Prakriti - energy or nature.
Prema - pure devotional love for God.
Preya - the joy that is fleeting and is soon gone.
Purusha - the divine nature of man - the enjoyer.

R

Rajas - the quality of passion and energy, one of the three gunas.

S

Sadhana - a personal spiritual practice.

Sahadev - one of the heavenly twins, the youngest Pandava, who epitomises the quality of wisdom.
Samsara - a pre-conditioned tendency, or personality trait.
Sanjaya - the narrator of the Bhagavad Gita who has been gifted with divine sight.
Sannyasa - the renounced order of life.
Sannyasi - one who has renounced the pleasures of the world.
Sankhya - direct knowledge of the Self.
Sat - truth.
Sattva, sattvic - the highest guna, the quality of goodness and purity.
self - the conscious awareness of your being - mind, ego, intellect (manas, ahamkar and buddhi).
Self - sometimes called the Higher Self, the awareness of your being as part of Brahman - i.e. merging into oneness with all beings.
Shanti - peace.
Shraddha - faith.
Shreya - real, lasting joy.
Sri - a respectful form of address that indicates holiness.
Sukha - pleasure.
Swadharma - your own personal dharma which is appropriate to you.

T

Tabor - a small drum.
Tamas - inertia, decay; the first and lowest of the three gunas.
Tat - Brahman, the impersonal godhead.

U

Upanishads - ancient mystical texts that form the final parts of the Vedas.
Uvaacha - said.

V

Vairagya - discrimination.
Vasudeva - Krishna's father.
Vaasudeva - Krishna, the son of Vasudeva.
Vedas - holy scriptures which form the basis of the Hindu religion.
Veda Vyasa - compiler of the Vedas, Puranas, Mahabharata, Vedanta sutras and the Bhagavad Gita.
Vivasvan - the sun-god.
Vyaasa - scribe.

Y

Yaadavas - descendents of King Yadu.
Yajna - offering or sacrifice as an act of worship.
Yama - the God of Death.
Yamas - restraints, or practices that develop inner strength.
Yoga - union, from the Sanskrit 'yuj', which means 'to unite'.
Yoga maya - Krishna's web of illusion, often depicted as a goddess - Maya.
Yogi - one who follows a life of spiritual discipline.
Yudhishthira - eldest of the Pandavas, known for the quality of honesty and truth.

Acknowledgements

We are very grateful for all the time, energy and love that has been offered towards making this book possible. Our heartfelt thanks to:

Chris Barrington
Sally Langford
Barbara Wood
Jane Clapham
Barbara Worrall
Regina Doerstel
Jane Patel
Craig Robertson
Jessica and John Scard
Anne and Colin Douglas
Gwyneth Clapham
Ruth Boaler
Walter Devine

What great thinkers say about the Bhagavad Gita

I owed a magnificent day to the Bhagavad-Gita. It was the first of books; it was as if an empire spoke to us, nothing small or unworthy, but large, serene, consistent, the voice of an old intelligence which in another age and climate had pondered and thus disposed of the same questions which exercise us.

Ralph Waldo Emerson

The Gita is the universal mother. She turns away nobody. Her door is wide open to anyone who knocks. A true votary of the Gita does not know what disappointment is. He ever dwells in perennial joy and peace that passeth understanding. But that peace and joy comes not to the sceptic or to him who is proud of his intellect or learning. It is reserved only for the humble in spirit who brings to her worship a fullness of faith and an undivided singleness of mind. There never was a man who worshipped her in that spirit and went back disappointed.

Mahatma Gandhi

The Bhagavad Gita is perhaps the most systematic scriptural statement of the Perennial Philosophy. To a world at war, a world that, because it lacks the intellectual and spiritual prerequisites to peace, can only hope to patch up some kind of precarious armed truce, it stands pointing, clearly and unmistakably, to the only road of escape from the self-imposed necessity of self-destruction.

Aldous Huxley

The Gita is a bouquet composed of the beautiful flowers of spiritual truths collected from the Upanishads.

Swami Vivekananda

In the morning I bathe my intellect in the stupendous and cosmogonal philosophy of the Bhagavad Gita, in comparison with which our modern world and its literature seem puny and trivial.

Henry David Thoreau

The Bhagavad Gita gives utterance to the aspirations of the pilgrims of all sects who seek to tread the inner way to the city of God. We touch reality most deeply, where men struggle, fail and triumph. Millions of Hindus, for centuries, have found comfort in this great book.

S. Radhakrishnan

Among the priceless teachings that may be found in the great Hindu poem of the Mahabharata, there is none so rare and precious as 'The Lord's Song'. Since it fell from the divine lips of Sri Krishna on the field of battle, and stilled the surging emotions of the disciple and friend, how many troubled hearts has it quietened and strengthened, how many weary souls has it led to Him!

Dr Annie Besant

In the Bhagavad Gita, there is a wonderful intensification of the narrative, so that if nothing else were to touch the soul of one studying this sublime Gita, he still could not help being impressed with its marvellous composition.

Rudolf Steiner

The Gita's influence is not merely philosophic or academic but immediate and living, an influence both for thought and action, and its ideas are actually at work as a powerful shaping factor in the revival and renewal of a nation and a culture. It has even been said recently by a great voice that all we need of spiritual truth for the spiritual life is to be found in the Gita.

Aurobindo Ghose

The Bhagavad Gita is a message addressed to each and every human individual to help him or her to solve the vexing problem of overcoming the present and progressing towards a bright future. This holy scripture is not just an 'old scripture', nor is it just a book of 'religious teachings', or even a Hindu holy book. It transcends the bounds of any particular religion or race.

Swami Chidananda

Also by the authors...

The Inside Story
Come with Me
The Dance Between Joy & Pain
Face to Face with Life
Crisis and the Miracle of Love
Mastering the Laws of Relationships
The Bhagavad Gita Workbook

For a list of related titles please write to Life Foundation Publications
Maristowe House,
Dover Street,
Bilston
West Midlands
WV14 6AL

Tel: 01902 409164
Fax: 01902 497362
Email: lfst@ukemail.com
http://www.nwi.co.uk/life

Printed on Fineblade smooth paper, which is made from virgin wood fibre from sawmill residues, forest thinnings and sustainable forests and is elemental chlorine free.